PK

*A report
on the power of
Psycho**K**inesis,
Mental Energy
that moves
matter*

Michael H. Brown

Illustrated

STEINERBOOKS
*affiliate of
Multimedia Publishing Corp.
Blauvelt, N.Y. 10913, U.S.A.*

About the Author

Michael H. Brown, 24, was born in Niagara Falls, N.Y.
He attended Fordham University in New York
City where he majored in journalism and briefly interned
at Long Island's *Newsday*. For the last three years, while
earning a living as a newspaper reporter much of the
time, he has tracked through haunted houses and extensively interviewed psychics and scientists in what
became a full-time journalistic investigation into parapsychology. Mr. Brown is now a freelance writer.

Copyright © 1976 by Multimedia Publishing Corp.

All rights in this book are reserved. No part of this book
may be reproduced in any form without written per-
mission from the publishers except for brief quotations
embodied in critical articles for reviews. For information,
address STEINERBOOKS, 100 South Western Highway,
Blauvelt, New York 10913, U.S.A.

Library of Congress Catalogue Card Number: 76 — 21121

ISBN#: 0-8334-0716-3 (Cloth Edition)
          0-8334-1776-2 (Quality Paperback)

Printed in the United States of America

First Edition

The publication of this book has been made possible, in part,
through the assistance of the *Steiner Institute for Spiritual
Research,* Blauvelt, New York, 10913.

"For me the world is weird because it is stupendous, awesome, mysterious, unfathomable; my interest has been to convince you that you must assume responsibility for being here, in this marvelous world, in this marvelous desert, in this marvelous time. I wanted to convince you that you must learn to make every act count, since you are going to be here for only a short while; in fact, too short for witnessing all the marvels of it."

— *Castaneda's Juan Matus*

To: Rose and Harold, and also to Natalie, Dominic and Evelyn.

Acknowledgements

I am indebted in varying degrees to the following people, all of whom helped this book into being with their scientific knowledge, their investigative assistance or simply their moral support, even though, in certain cases, they may not have known they were doing so:

Donald Kennedy, Kenneth J. Batcheldor, Colin Brookes-Smith, Dr. and Mrs. A.R.G. Owen, Dr. Wilbur Franklin, Dr. Sheridan Speeth, Rose Engle, Dr. Justa Smith, Jeanne Rindge, Jehile Kirkhuff, Sylvia Saxby, Phil Jordan, Dr. Gary Truce, Dr. J. B. Rhine, Hidy Ochiai, Herb Seiler, Margaret McVinnie, Dr. William Roll, Rev. Mae York, Jose Silva, Gary Anderson, Paul Cozad, David Martin, Douglas and Betty Thurmond, Patricia Jeffers, Barbara Lerned, Terrie Benvenuti, Grant Marshall, Leta Berecek, Elaine Fortson, Henry Peterson, Robert Manning. Luigi and Mary Ricciuto, Jamie Stricoff, Jack Maloy, David Tinney, David Stockton, Suzanne Dalton, Michael Doll, Richard Dennis, Uri Geller, Peter Gardner, Bernard Garber; also, members of the Toronto Society for Psychical Research, the British Society for Psychical Research and the Physics Department at Kent State University, contributors to the *New Horizons* Journal, Charles Panati, and Lynn Schroeder.

This book would not have been possible but for the pioneering work of:

Dr. Andrija Puharich, Drs. J.B. and Louisa Rhine, Dr. Thelma Moss, Dr. John G. Taylor, Dr. Hal Puthoff and Russell Targ, Edgar Mitchell, Sheila Ostrander and Lynn Schroeder, the staffs of *Psychic* magazine and the Journal of the (London) Society for Psychical Research, Frank Edwards, Semyon Kirlian, William Crookes, Vincent Gaddis and Carlos Castaneda.

For logistical help during the research, I thank:

Michael and Maureen Cacace, Kathy, Chris, Steve, Pat and Jeannine Brown, William Turner and Dorothy Hatsell.

Contents

Author's Note

It was Goethe who once remarked that when the mind is at sea, a new word provides a raft. And so it is with the steady stream of neologisms flowing from the uncharted world of psychic (or "psi") phenomena. In fact, so numerous are new terms used in this book that a brief review of the key words is in order.

Throughout, the prefix "para" is employed to mean above, beyond, or beside the current meaning of the word it is coupled with. The most glaring example is the word "parapsychology," which stands for the areas like ESP and PK and implies phenomena that skim above normal psychological and physical functionings. Partial synonyms are words like "paraphysics," the "occult," the "super-normal," and the "paranormal." Likewise, the term "psi," which arrives from the Greek alphabet, is a rather general term encompassing that which goes on beyond our normal senses and limbs. Perhaps the most frequently used word is "psychic." It is used to describe phenomena that appear quasi-spiritual in nature, and those persons who possess ESP, PK, or both. A person who is a "psychic" can be viewed as different than a "medium," the latter attributing his mysterious abilities to "spirits" while the former usually feels his psychic talents come from his own existence. (The reader will note the term "spirit" oft-times will appear in quotes to emphasize the murkiness of the term, and its general unacceptability.) The term PK (psychokinesis) is a more modern version of "telekinesis" and "parakinesis" and hardly needs defining since it's the main topic of the book. Many other terms are likewise self-explanatory. And while they may seem a bit confusing and insufficient, we must hold on to them: they are our rafts.

Prologue

Historians studying parapsychology will probably one day think of the period roughly spanning 1920 to the present as the Age of ESP. The increasing number of scientists who have infiltrated the territory of the occult in this period have mainly focused their attention on extra-sensory perception, their goal being statistical proof for and a theoretical understanding of elusive phenomena like mind reading, thought sending, clairvoyance and precognition. Indeed, parapsychological research has been so exclusively devoted to this kind of study that the term "parapsychology" has almost come to mean "the study of ESP."

Though this era of ESP investigation is nowhere near over, there is now a new scent in the winds of psychic research. Parapsychology, which could also be called "cryptophysics" or "paraphysics" ("hidden" or "beside or beyond" physics), seems lately to be digging a channel to another reservoir of the unknown, a strange area where objects move through no physical means, furniture inexplicably levitates, and spoons bend through what could be a power of the human psyche. Perhaps we are about to enter the Age of Psychokinesis (PK for short). *Psyche* means "mind" or "soul" in Greek, *kinesis* means "motion"; by joining the two we have coined a term that, vague as it may be, heralds a new category in the realm of science, a branch of parapsychology that will certainly be providing rich material for decades of future study.

This is not to say, of course, that PK is new, just that previously it was referred to even more ambiguously as "mind-over-matter" or, when it took to exotic manifestations, as "magic" or "spirit signs." For brief periods during the nineteenth century, this kind of psychic phenomena was even studied by some serious scientists, and in the 1930s and 1940s was proven to exist by Duke University's J.B. Rhine, the ESP researcher who crossed the PK frontier and showed statistically that human thought could affect the roll of dice.

It has only been in the last decade, however, that there has been scientific interest in PK on a large scale, and this for two major reasons. Firstly, parapsychology in general has gained a new respectability, thus encouraging more and more reputable scientists to investigate bizarre phenomena such as those produced through PK; and secondly, there has recently been a startling number of authentic-sounding PK events.

Actually, the stage for this new era of research was set in 1969, when the American Association for the Advancement of Science finally admitted parapsychology as a legitimate subject of study. That constituted respectability, and researchers were attracted to the field accordingly. Shortly after, accounts started to flow in from Russia of the documenting of PK phenomena by prominent scientists; a Soviet woman was filmed making small objects placed on a table move paranormally, and there were numerous reports of levitation. That Russian science was dabbling in PK was enough to make many an American scientist sniff the air.

In the wake of a growing public interest in PK in this country came a significant development: the arrival here from Israel of Uri Geller, the psychic metal-bender, or *alleged* psychic metal-bender, whose fame spread overnight. Whereas "ESP" had previously been almost the only household word parapsychology could supply, now, quite suddenly, "PK" became its rival.

Uri Geller had a stunning effect on many Americans and caused a certain amount of éclat in Europe as well.

What he was doing was taking spoons, forks or keys, gently rubbing them with his thumb and one of his fingers, and watching as excitedly as everyone else as they started to bend, eventually twisting totally out of shape. Representatives from many of the most responsible research organizations in Britain and America wanted to have a look for themselves, and Geller ended up spending time at places like the Max Planck Institute for Plasma Physics, King's College, Kent State University and Stanford Research Institute, and even submitted to experiments conducted by researchers from the U.S. Naval Surface Weapons Center. None of the scientists involved could offer a logical explanation for what he was doing, and even investigators for the Society of American Magicians could spot no fraud.

Away from labs, Geller was even more impressive, often causing spoons and forks to twist completely around and bending their shafts to 180-degree angles, just through that slight rubbing motion.

As a newspaper journalist and newly weaned, investigative free-lancer, I became interested in the whole Geller stir. In light of all the tales ancient and modern I'd heard and read about occult powers, sorcerers, ghosts, magicians and medicine men, I figured there very well might be something to it all. But though I had tracked through scores of "haunted" houses and for some two years spent most of my spare time talking with Spiritualists, seance mediums and psychics, I had never been witness to anything like the phenomena Geller was said to produce and as a result strongly doubted that he was "for real." A magician with a clever stunt — that was how I thought of him.

My attitude changed dramatically in 1975. It was that year that I watched, in shock, as a man who called himself a psychic caused a heavy wood card table to rise off a living room floor by means of what I could only describe as PK energy. He did it by lightly touching the table's surface. The more often I saw him repeat this feat the more excited I became. Here was a phenomenon, levitation, that had somehow not been taken into account in the recent upsurge in PK studies, and yet it was a phenomenon that lent support to the claims of Geller and certain scientists interested in PK.

After having scores of others watch the psi table-lifting and then writing a newspaper story on it for a local tabloid and a wire service, I was besieged with other accounts of table levitation. They came from all over: England, Canada, many areas of the United States. Naturally I'll never know just how many were genuine, but subsequent personal investigation convinced me that at least some of those I'd heard about were the real thing. For the next sixteen months I launched into a full-time investigation of PK, leafing through all the obscure literature on the subject that I could find and once in a while getting a rare opportunity to watch tables rise or observe a metal-bender. It seemed to me that, in these rather fleeting cases, an energy as yet undiscovered by the scientific establishment was at work and that all available data, no matter how fragmentary, should be recorded as a first step in understanding its ways. In the first section of this book, this is the task I've set myself.

It's not an easy task to substantiate an unfamiliar psychic phenomenon, particularly when that phenomenon appears to be disobeying scientific laws. It has, for example, taken decades and thousands of diverse experiments for psi researchers to persuade mainstream scientists of just the *possibility* of ESP, and even now it's a subject that is only beginning to filter into science classrooms. The same is likely to be true of PK. With that realization in mind, I have set out not to try and prove that PK exists but to persuade potential researchers that *something* is out there waiting and that plans should be drawn up now on ways of approaching it and eventually proving its existence. My role, then, is that of a reporter in the field, anxious to show, by means of evidence, that PK deserves to be intensively documented and tested. As the reader will quickly see, I chose to start with table levitation and establish as many facts regarding that phenomenon as possible before branching off into a general discussion of PK.

Though this may sound like a humble task, there are complicated problems involved in trying to show the subject is worthy of journalistic, let alone scientific, attention. Most of them are practical: they have to do with the personalities involved in the research and with money. In my investigation I found both kinds of problems plaguing me at every turn.

The personality issue is complex. The fact that, at least at present, researchers have to rely on *people* for experimentation tends to inhibit progress. I found it hard, in many cases, to convince some of my subjects of the need to practice and try to perfect their PK demonstrations. Most of them weren't interested in spending hours of their spare time learning to levitate tables under controlled conditions; many were plain bored with the idea. One of the most spectacular groups I watched disbanded shortly after I first observed them totally levitating a dining room table and I was not able to gather anywhere near as much data as I would have liked. This happened time and again. To make matters worse, there were many individuals who feared publicity, and for good reason. Though Americans and Europeans have become increasingly responsive to psi phenomena, there are still those who either think the whole business is evil or mock it as childish. In the cases in which I was involved, reputations were often at stake, and there were many levitators depressed by the knowledge that no matter what they did there were skeptics who would not believe them.

I encountered perhaps the most closed-minded person in my whole inquiry while seeking the opinions of professional magicians on some of the phenomena I had seen and heard about. That was New Jersey's James (the Amazing) Randi, a boisterous Canadian who was then feverishly and vainly trying to discredit Uri Geller, despite diminishing support from some of his colleagues. So ardent a critic was Randi that, soon after I had co-authored a newspaper feature on a psychic table-lifter with Donald Kennedy, a university instructor in literature, we received a letter from him in which he decried our belief that our subject had real psi ability. Though Randi had never met or even heard of this particular psychic, he went so far as to proclaim him a "fraud" in his own handwriting. Kennedy and I laughed as we imagined the courtroom headline: Professional Magician versus Psychic.

I had already heard a professional magician say one of our subjects was using no known stage trick in his table levitations, and I wanted to see if Randi could intelligently argue otherwise. I figured the ideal situation would be for Randi to don a disguise and bring his own table to a psychic's home so that he wouldn't upset the latter's psychological equilibrium, an absolutely vital factor in PK manifestations, as the reader will later see. After he saw the table rise, I wanted the magician to explain the feat and then attempt to duplicate it under identical circumstances. Randi was not interested in my proposal, however — he wanted to set up his own "controls," whether to guard against fraud or to harass the psychic I couldn't be sure — and when I pressed him on how levitators in fact raised tables, he said simply, "They cheat."

Here was an attitude, and a brand of personality, that

those in the PK field have had to live with.

The problem of money came into play when I tried to have scientists look at some of the table-lifters I had found who were at the time willing to cooperate briefly with research. J.B. Rhine was very interested in testing some in his labs, but I couldn't immediately raise the funds that would have been necessary. I was able to get a small sum of expense money from Ohio's Kent State University so a physicist there, Wilbur Franklin, could watch two psychics perform at tables for a few days, but research funding for a complete experimental process just was not to be found. And without the benefit of a full-fledged, recorded investigation with which to back themselves up, the scientists I dealt with tended to hedge their opinions in on-the-record interviews. Though in private most admitted to a belief that tables were being lifted by some form of mental or spiritual energy, they were cautious about softening their skeptical public stands until many more concrete data were available. I certainly could not blame them for their prudence.

Hopefully, more concrete data *are* on the way, but until then we must make do with what we have. And the data *I* have? — well, I think the reader will find them fascinating. Again, this work makes no claim to completeness. I have set out to illustrate a few specific manifestations of PK, to touch on some of the area's major developments and historical precedents, and to present information that best underscores its infinite implications. I adopted this approach with a view to constructing a paradigm of this still mysterious field. Perhaps my book will inspire some ordinary people to look further into PK, and some scientists, particularly those in parapsychology, to consider it a subject that's as worthy of serious study as ESP.

July 1976   Michael H. Brown

Section One: The Case of the Rising Tables

Phil Jordan raising a table with no one else accompanying him. His hands, barely touching in this shot, seem to produce an unknown energy that alters the table's weight, (Photo by David Tinney)

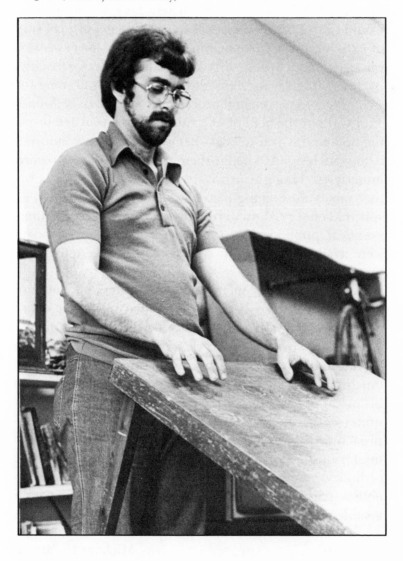

A Man Named Jordan

"If you wish to upset the laws that all crows are black, you must not seek to show that no crows are: it is enough if you prove a single crow to be white."

— *William James*

The white wood-frame house was set unobtrusively on a back road of Spencer, New York, behind it a barn housing not sows but a Pontiac, around it a lawn film-coated with remnants of a January snow that had nudged the neighbors into their isolated homesteads where they kicked on gas burners or threw wood onto afternoon fires. Certainly it was not a scenario to evoke visions of wily gremlins peeking from the porch, nor was the quaint countryside quite the stage for Lewis Carroll's White King sitting sulkily among the ashes. But still the modest two-family home presented the other side of the real, and it was from this subtle side that a young teacher named Philip Jordan peered.

"Two hundred years ago someone like me would've been burnt at the stake," said Jordan, turning a frown to the two reporters. "You know, even now people get terrified of things they don't understand."

He was standing in the middle of the living room, slowly unfolding a heavy, old-fashioned card table. Though home with the specific purpose of taking a break from his statewide demonstrations of what the world of 1975 was vaguely calling "psychic phenomena," the twenty-five-year-old medium was only too glad to go through all his wild stories for the chain-smoking journalists, who for a lark had decided to pay a quick visit to the guy in the farmlands who was supposed to have ESP.

"You can what?" interrupted one of them suddenly.

"Levitate," said the psychic. "Make things like this table go in the air."

He looked sincere enough when he said it. His neat mustache, long, well-styled hair surrounding an almost innocent face, and rather syrupy voice didn't fit their conceptions of a fly-by-night fraud. Despite that, they sat cynically awaiting a display of some shoddy sleight-of-hand, never imagining that what they were to see would eventually reverberate throughout the state.

It started with a series of rappings, sharp taps that seemed to come from within the wood, moving clockwise from Jordan and passing under the sitters' hands. Minutes before, the three men had taken seats at the table, merely resting their hands lightly on its surface, and now suddenly there were inexplicable noises, as though someone was lightly drumming a pen underneath it. The reporters cocked their heads, one of them putting an ear close to the table as loud creaks and long scratching sounds erupted from it. They took their hands off for a moment and shook the table to see if it had a loose leg or maybe a creaky corner. But they couldn't reproduce the sounds. When they put their hands back on top the rappings immediately returned, moving from the center to the sides in a widening spiral.

Jordan sat motionless. His shirt sleeves were tucked around his elbows, his hands just barely touching the wood. When he took a deep breath it seemed the raps sped up, then grew louder as he exhaled, even though his chest was nearly a foot from the table. "Well, come on table," he kept repeating. "Up."

The taps turned into loud knocks, then into longer creaks and groans. And suddenly it happened: a table leg opposite Jordan rose about an inch off the rug, as if on a cushion of air that had abruptly blown up from the floorboards. Seconds later Jordan's side rose about a foot, quickly, smoothly bouncing upward though the psychic had not moved even slightly. Oddly, the two legs still resting on the floor didn't seem to be taking on any additional stress. Instead it felt as if the table had actually lost weight on the highest side, as if there was an invisible wedge underneath it.

The two reporters started to chuckle, then to laugh. When a third leg levitated the hilarity almost turned hysterical. The sudden shift in force tipped the table at an utterly impossible angle, forcing the sitters to spring up in order to keep up with it. One of the newsmen, Don Kennedy, reached over to try and shove down the uplifted side, but the table gave way only slightly to the pressure. Then, as if resting on tightly-packed foam rubber, it bounded back up to an even higher position, the highest side's legs rising about three feet from the floor. "God, I'm the only one who could be holding it up in this position," said the shocked reporter. "And I'm certainly not!"

Jordan grinned as he moved with the dipping table. "I showed this to a magician once," he said, looking directly into the eyes of his guests. "After he saw it he was so shocked that he said from then on he was going legit."

The reporters could see why. There was no perceptible

way Jordan could be doing it physically. His knees weren't anywhere near the table; his hands were touching its surface very softly, the fingers and palms in no position to create a suction; his hips were leaned away. When the reporters felt his arms the muscles were soft, unflexed, and there was absolutely no sign of strain in his wrists.

The journalists had trouble finding words. As if in defiance of every law Newton ever wrote, the table had cocked over so far one of its corners was only inches from the floor. It didn't seem to be firmly balanced. Indeed it tossed and turned in a way that reminded them of astronauts tumbling about in a capsule, out in the reaches of space. For minutes at a time a cool, breezelike sensation whisked across their hands, usually followed by another series of raps and knocks. Then the table would suddenly shift, rising first on one side, then the other. Though it wouldn't leave the floor completely, the two grounded legs seemed to be barely touching the rug.

Jordan turned to the men. "Last time this happened, some guy claimed I had magnets in my fingernails. So here — try this."

The psychic took his hands off the table, raising them slowly so as not to disrupt its motions. When the two reporters each removed one of their own hands, the result was incredible: the table never flinched from its weird position.

But if that was dramatic, the next occurrence was amazing. The table started to hop around on just one leg for minutes at a time, spinning, weaving, edging its way completely across the room; then it eerily floated down, ending its nearly thirty minutes of antics as it rumbled onto the floor.

Hurrying out to get to work on time that afternoon, the reporters felt like taking a bullhorn so they could shout down the slushy streets: "Objects — solid objects — can be made to float! Tables can up and walk! They can rise through the air!" However they kept their heads about what they'd seen and wasted no time seeking possible explanations.

Was such a phenomenon known to the world of the occult? Were there precedents? Was it caused by some totally unknown energy? These young men didn't know. The excited voice of parapsychologist and behavioral scientist Paul Cozad was soon cutting through the static of a long-distance phone call. "Geez, I don't know what that could be," said the Buffalo scientist. "It's something you hear about once in a great while. But not quite like you described. I'd appreciate coming down and being given a shot at experiencing it right away. I've just never heard of a table getting like that."

Less than a week later he was at the Jordan table with reporter Kennedy, having dropped all his business to hurry down. A man who had turned himself into an amateur magician in order to check supposed parapsychological happenings for fraud, Cozad calmly felt the table for the basic gimmicks, then checked Jordan's arms and looked under the rug. "No offense," said the parapsychologist, his tall, lean body settling into a chair, "but I've run into more than my share of frauds."

As before, Jordan rolled up his sleeves and placed his palms lightly on the tabletop. Cozad and Kennedy rested their hands on the table, too, and another reporter stood guard with a camera, watching Jordan's every move. In no more than two minutes the rappings began, sounding this time as if something was stretching the molecules in the wood. A cool breeze sprang up, yet perspiration exuded from the men's palms. Then Jordan's side lifted just an inch from the floor and settled back down. As loud creaks and groans came from the wood, each leg took its turn rising, then stubbornly settling back down. For minutes the table remained still, vibrating slightly.

Then it suddenly exploded. Violent slamming motions rocked its sides, and these alternated with one end quickly rising and banging down, followed by the other end. It galloped in place, bucked at the center. Even as Cozad held Jordan's arms the incredible force persisted, thrusting so hard it sounded as though the floor would break.

When the commotion had finally halted, the raps returned, the table soon levitating smoothly up on one leg. It rotated; it hopped on one leg. As everyone shifted around the table to make sure they weren't unconsciously holding it up, the table maintained a rigid position with one side nearly three feet off the floor. Then it started to bang wildly again, raging on for about fifteen minutes. "I must say," said Cozad, "I must say I've never seen anything quite like this."

Jordan sure had. A year before, similar phenomena had occurred in Potsdam, New York, where he demonstrated table levitation for a mentalist-magician named Fred G. Hartmann, once president of local radio station WPDM. Jordan had walked briskly into Hartmann's kitchen when the mentalist asked for some proof of what he could do, then placed his hands on a kitchen table as three strangers did the same. Within minutes it had leaped into the air and moved into the living room so quickly and violently that the sitters had been forced to break contact with it. "I don't go for any explanations of spirits and all that malarkey," said Hartmann afterward, "but I do think Phil has some unknown mental power. It's the most incredible thing I've ever seen."

By the time he headed back for his car that day, Cozad could hardly disagree.

Jordan discovered his strange ability to levitate objects back when he was a senior in high school. A year before he had had his first inkling of paranormal power through a shocking dream that had come true — in every vivid detail. In his nighttime vision he saw his uncle on a hospital bed, clutching his chest, definitely dying, yet by the end of the dream he had somehow pulled through.

The next day his uncle was struck by a series of ravaging coronaries that tremored through his system most of the day. That night the physician's verdict was terse and emphatic. Five hours, said the doctor, was the longest he could survive. But suddenly the heart attacks came to a halt, and the sick man miraculously survived.

Curious that something like that could happen, young Jordan grabbed every book at the local library that had anything to do with the occult. Taking time out every day to practice his sixth sense, he soon developed to the point of being able to foresee family events, "read" others' thoughts and see the human aura — the luminous band of energy clairvoyants claim to see around the body. These are the basic "psychic" skills. In addition he went the next step and developed his "mediumship," the supposed ability to see spirits and, in trance, become a channel for messages from so-called higher planes. All this led him to study various cults and quasi-religions that had anything at all to do with ESP or spirit communication.

In a book on Spiritualism he found a section describing how a few mediums were rumored to be able to make objects, mainly furniture, mysteriously rise off the ground by merely touching them. "Along with a friend, I decided to try it," says the medium. "I didn't really believe it could happen, couldn't see how it would work. The first time we got nothing, not even raps. But we tried it again on a card table, and suddenly it went up. And we heard the raps.

We could tell by each other's expression that neither of us had done it."

The preternatural kept coming on. At Brockport State College, where he received a teaching degree in high school Spanish, he was the talk of the campus with his ability to foresee the experiences of classmates and make small wood tables float. So intrigued were his dormitory friends that they would often wander in while he was asleep and, placing the hand of the slumbering psychic on a nearby end table, bet disbelievers that it would rise. More often than not they collected handsome wagers.

Meanwhile the psychic started picking up spending money by giving private "readings" and appearing in small nightspots to demonstrate aura viewing and telepathy. In later years his abilities were to become so developed that he was repeatedly able to astound reporters across the country with feats such as finding objects that had been hidden and then made the focus of others' concentration. Once he took a mere seventeen seconds to find a ring hidden in a tea container that might have been anywhere in a large apartment. Another time it took him only fifteen minutes to locate psychically a staple remover that could have been anywhere in a small town. On yet another occasion he spent just fifty seconds locating a needle that had been hidden in a stick of butter by a skeptical magician. His most sensational display came in August 1975 when he found a four-year-old boy who had been lost for sixteen hours in some woods. Though more than 120 searchers had been unable to find a trace of the youngster, it took Jordan only a few minutes to draw a map from which the sheriff's deputies were able to locate him exactly. When word of his abilities spread to famed researcher J.B. Rhine, the man who coined the very term "extrasensory perception," Jordan was invited down to Duke University's parapsychology department, where he was tested for his ability to pick up thoughts telepathically, describe objects placed out of view in another room, and foretell future events.

Then things turned bad, largely due to his strange talent.

First came another morbid vision, this time without a happy ending. It was about his mother: she was going to die, according to a dream he had, sometime around the end of October, his senior year of college. Back in the waking world he watched the gruesome day approach, watched as she went down with an illness he knew would be fatal.

When she died — the last week of October — the psychic moved back home to look after his father, planning to finish off his degree requirements by teaching at Spencer-Van Etten High School. Innocently, perhaps naively, he started talking about his psychic abilities to the students, often giving them demonstrations in telepathy. The kids would hide an object like a ring while he was in another room, and he'd come in to find it, often succeeding in a matter of seconds. The students loved it; their elders did not.

It was Salem, twentieth century style. Fundamentalists held the religious reins in the town, and to them the matter was pure and simple: Jordan was evil, his "supernatural" abilities a gift from Mephistopheles. "I got the threatening calls at night, the whole satanist spiel," he says. "Got me so scared I finally called the police." The vituperations, the charges that his nature was dark, were not just a case of closed-mindedness but more the symptoms of sheer irrationality. Just months before these attacks, Jordan had been licensed as a lay priest for a local Episcopal church, a strong enough indication of his faith in Christianity.

But hostile phone calls weren't enough for many of the townsfolk. Virtually blackballed from town, Jordan took to the road and tried to make a living the only way he knew how: by lecturing on and demonstrating his strange abilities at colleges, small clubs and private parties. During the day he'd "read" the thoughts of callers ringing into various radio talk shows; at night he'd get together groups of all ages for demonstrations of ESP — and table levitation.

The next year, despite the previous ruckus, he was invited back to school to give workshops on parapsychology, which the more progressive educators were viewing as a valid area of investigation. They should have known better; Jordan was even less popular with the townsfolk than he'd been before.

Upon entering the high school one morning, the medium noticed a long line of cars along the usually empty street. When he opened the school's front door, still staring back at all the cars, he was quickly intercepted by an administrator who warned him that the auditorium had filled with parents opposed to his displays, some of them so mad the official was worried Jordan would be physically attacked. "But I went in," says Jordan, "I figured, hell, if I was going to meet a Waterloo, it might as well be in the auditorium of Spencer-Van Etten High School." When he entered, fear in the audience was as thick as the maple syrup many of them were tapping from their trees. Apparently, two men scrambled out the back door when they saw the psychic walking in. On the stage were four church ministers, waving their Bibles and girded for exorcism.

Townwide meetings followed, two of them drawing more than a hundred people each. Finally authorities bowed to the pressure and relieved Jordan of his duties, a decision viewed by one liberal priest as a reverse replay of the Scopes Monkey Trial. "The scene," he said, "was like something from the play 'Inherit the Wind.' "

*   *   *   *

Parapsychologist Cozad didn't buy the "demonic" claims, of course, nor did he think Jordan was insane, another accusation that had often been the subject of town gossip. Instead he suggested what he had seen had probably been a display of PK, the rare paranormal ability through which mind moves matter by some unknown means. Though he wished the table had totally levitated, leaving absolutely no doubts, Cozad said it was his opinion that the tiltings and bangings had been an authentic demonstration of psychic power. "I have no idea what, exactly, it is," he said, "but it's something that seems to occur with some mediums. Something we're finding through things like this is that the normal laws governing the universe are just going to have to be reexamined."

When the expert's opinion, along with photographs, was presented to editors at Gannett Newspapers in Binghamton, New York, the news center for three surrounding counties, the cigar chomping, stern-faced managing editor looked directly into the other men's eyes, hardly hiding his disbelief. Nervously tapping off a long cigar ash, he bluntly asked them, "Do you mean to tell me this is something I could *see?*"

The reporters could only nod their heads.

On 12 March a contingent of nine witnesses, mainly newsmen from the local papers, were sent to meet Jordan in a Binghamton apartment. Accompanying them was

Richard Dennis, a tall, modish professional magician who had taken a break from preparations for a national tour he called "The Houdini Revival Show" to demonstrate to the reporters that they'd been had. A sleight-of-hand artist, illusionist and escape daredevil (he held the world's record for staying encased in ice), Dennis had himself performed "levitations" on gimmicked stages and couldn't imagine how levitation could be anything but a clever trick. "I hate to bust a fellow magician," he said, "but if you want me to I'll do it."

Dennis arrived that afternoon with his assistant, an apprentice magician, and his own card table, a light metal model he could be sure wasn't rigged. Along with two others who had never met the psychic before, the magician quickly sat down at the table while his assistant took a position where he could watch everything that went on under the table. After preliminary checks, Jordan and three participants placed their hands very softly on the table.

It was obvious that, though he was making jokes, the psychic was nervous. First there was the skepticism he sensed around him: negative emotions, he felt, hindered his "forces." Then there was the metal table. For some reason he felt wood reacted better, that metal "sapped" his strength. For the first ten minutes, nothing happened; Jordan shifted edgily in his chair, the two magicians watching his every move.

Then one of the sitters, a desk editor for the city's evening newspaper, said her hands felt cold. Suddenly the magician pressed his head close to the table's surface: the rappings had started up, making clicking sounds that seemed to come from within the metal. Hands got colder; the rappings grew louder. "Look!" yelled a reporter watching from the side, "the damn leg is going up!"

As several witnesses watched from kneeling positions on the floor, the leg on Jordan's side rose several inches, then softly fell back to the floor. Suddenly a whole side of the table rose, so that two legs were more than a foot off the floor. As he grabbed for Jordan's arm, it was obvious the magician was stunned. How the table could rise so forcefully without the psychic using a hook or lever was beyond his comprehension. Jolted by the magician's reactions, the others started to laugh nervously, some of them shouting as the table bounded up higher, tipping up and down, clattering back and forth on each leg, levitating up on just one leg. Then they sprang off their seats to keep up with the table as it abruptly keeled over on its remaining leg until a corner of its top nearly touched the floor.

When the table settled back down, Jordan suggested he run out to his car to get his own table, which he had brought along in case metal wouldn't work. Perhaps, he said, they could try to get a total levitation. Although it was rare, the psychic had several times gotten tables all the way off the floor before several witnesses, a feat he had come close to duplicating with a large log, which he had gotten partially to rise. He had found, in fact, that a wood table reacted so well it would sometimes move around on the floor and then tilt up even when no one was touching it.

After Dennis checked the table for any hidden devices, Jordan again took a seat at the table, this time with three new sitters who included the apprentice magician. Dennis watched from the side. In less than three minutes one side was high off the floor, then the whole table began to dash around the room while the participants, laughing wildly, chased after it. A photographer scrambled for some shots. The table would suddenly move a few feet, spinning swiftly on one leg, then dart the full length of the room, leaving not a single mark on the apartment's shag rug.

Even that last leg seemed to have come off the floor, though only by a hair. At one point, the table tilted way over on one leg and Jordan took his hands off it, apparently keeping it in that incredible position by sheer will. Sports columnist Joseph Salimando pressed down hard on the highest end to push the table back to the floor while everyone else's hands were barely touching it. "Is it a who?" he asked. "Or is it a what?"

Soon Dennis was asking the same question. For the next few weeks his search for an answer, for a *logical* answer, grew to be an obsession. He called on both old-timers and currently popular magicians. He thumbed through every magic book he could find. He sat for hours at the same table Jordan used, trying to duplicate at least part of the feat. But it was all fruitless.

The majority of magicians, most notably Harry Houdini, had developed elementary explanations for fraudulent table phenomena, but Dennis couldn't see where they applied here. Houdini, who spent the better part of three decades chasing fake mediums, said the strange rappings were caused by fingernails dragging across the table's surface, a knee or shoe tapping against a leg, or by a battery-run clicker concealed in the medium's shoe. None of that explained how Jordan could function while the magician was constantly watching his hands, feet and legs, why the taps came from the center of the table, or how the sounds, which varied in a way those of a clicking device wouldn't, could rotate all around the table, getting far louder as the table lifted. Houdini had also said the raps could be produced by a pistonlike tube going from the floor to the table and attached to the medium's knee by a string. Certainly, in the broad daylight in which Jordan performed, such a device, described as three feet long, would have been easily detected. The great magician's explanations may have been fine for nineteenth century seance rooms where lights were off and a curtain was draped over the table, but in the absence of such aids to deception his answers were beside the point.

Dennis felt that if he could explain how Jordan got the table to lift initially, perhaps he could file away the rest of the motions as a very polished balancing act performed with the help of confederates. But even then there would be loopholes large enough to drive through with the magician's circus van. Jordan had, after all, taken his hands off beforehand, and had never met the participants before. As for any elaborate devices that could have been hidden in the apartment, a major problem popped up there too: Jordan had never previously stepped into the apartment. It was chosen with the express purpose of seeing him perform on a "neutral court."

For an explanation of how the table could have risen, Dennis again turned to Houdini. The great performer had written that tiltings were caused by a medium raising an end of the table with a hair knotted around his fingers, lifting its legs with his shoes, or, if the medium was a woman, by slipping the hem of a dress under a leg and pulling. None of that fit the present case.

Dennis had himself seen scores of spectacular stage stunts where objects had risen up from the floor. He himself knew how to "levitate" a person and then pass a hoop around his floating subject. But the Jordan thing was a quantum leap into the unknown.

When reporters played back tapes recorded at the Jordan sessions, Dennis learned that a strange sound — something like a swift, hushed wind — had come across on the recorder. An electronics expert has concluded it must have been caused by some kind of magnetic field, but he couldn't reproduce it. Yet another problem, another inexplicable phenomenon, was added to the heap. While withholding comment until he had exhausted every possible explanation, Dennis finally, a month after the display, drew up a carefully worded statement and signed his name to it.

"I am now, for the first time ever, searching not only to find a trick, but more accurately to find if, indeed, it was a trick," he wrote. "I will continue to look for an answer, not stopping until I'm sure, beyond a shadow of doubt, that what occurred was anything but a display of some force we know nothing about."

He had to be careful. The magicians' union was spearheading a drive to discredit psychic phenomena across the country, fearful for some reason that it would hurt professional magic. But in personal interviews, Dennis was more candid. "I just didn't believe in these things before — but now it's a tough thing to deny," he told reporters who had come to his home to see if he could duplicate what they had seen. "I know he didn't use magic — there were no gimmicks. I don't know. The whole thing is nearly scary."

Everyone else was convinced something supernormal, something as strange as ESP, had happened, and they submitted written testaments to that effect. Not a single explanation was ventured. After several tries at recreating the levitations through muscle force, a method used in the dark seance rooms of the past, the reporters were satisfied that wasn't the answer. Even when they were allowed blatantly to use their arm muscles, they couldn't get the table up in the strange positions they'd witnessed before. And when the table was tipped under conscious muscular control, it had a completely different movement to it — a jerky one. In addition, when someone pressed at the high end of a muscularly tipped table, it would immediately thump to the floor. That *resistance* was just not there. As for how Jordan got the table up in the first place, no one even tried passing that off as muscle force on account of the *way* he got it up. Magnets in his hands? Suction cups on his fingertips? That brand of speculation was soon exhausted.

There seemed only one possible explanation left: telepathic hypnosis. Could Jordan, a master at ESP, have entranced everyone present, sending them images of the table floating when it had actually remained flat on the floor? If so, he had also hypnotized the camera: the pictures showed exactly what they had seen.

But the idea that the psychic used some kind of entrancing effect, maybe in some way hypnotized the sitters into unconsciously balancing the table, was still intriguing enough for the reporters to want to check it out. A meeting was quickly arranged with Gary Truce, a parapsychology instructor with the State University of New York and respected hypnotist known not only throughout the East but across the Midwest as well.

Using his wood table, Jordan was immediately able to get it into the tilted position though Dr. Truce was the only other participant. Jordan was surprised at how fast it rose, wondering if it had anything to do with the thunderstorm that had been brewing all day. In minutes it was tilted way over on one leg, then began to lurch around the room at roughly jogging speed. The hypnotist was astonished; though he had extensively studied psychic occurrences for the last several years, he had never heard or seen anything like it. He was convinced, too, that this was no case of hypnotism or of some mentalistic trick. "To feel it, to experience the force behind it, the way it moved, was absolutely amazing," says Truce. "It's very hard to believe something like that actually happens. It's plainly obvious what's going on is above any trick."

After the levitation demonstration, the hypnotist put Jordan in a deep trance to see if any insights could be gained while the psychic was performing in an altered state of consciousness. He commanded Jordan to the table. The psychic had turned tense, concentrating hard on getting it up, this time alone. It was just the opposite of the way he usually worked. Most of the time he found a relaxed attitude on his part made the table rise faster, which is why he often told jokes to the sitters before the proceedings started. Finally, after Jordan had put himself to nearly fifteen minutes of considerable mental strain, the table rose into the air, though with much less power than before, and remained there for several minutes, rocking gently. The hypnosis served to underscore the connection between psychological attitude and levitational power. The relatively weak performance Jordan was now putting on showed how important to levitational success was the cheerfully expectant, almost nonchalant attitude he normally displayed. Truce next tried to get him to do a total levitation, but it was as though Jordan's subconscious was hesitant, doubtful that the table *could* be levitated; it also seemed to desire the help of other participants. (Months later, Jordan found he could easily levitate the table by himself, could do so with the fingertips of only one hand lightly touching its surface, and could even levitate his end of the table while his hands were softly resting on the table's center.)

Next the hypnotist directed Jordan over to a bowl of water set up to test other possible manifestations of PK. Floating in it were three paper clips, each attached to a slip of cardboard. As soon as the water was completely motionless, Truce commanded that he visualize the clips floating toward him. Slowly but surely they started to drift across the water, stopping in front of the medium. Several more tries brought the same result. Truce's deduction was simple yet firm: Jordan, he told reporters, was exerting some kind of paranormal force.

On 7 April, satisfied that its reporters had probed every conceivable rational explanation for the Jordan phenomenon, the morning newspaper in Binghamton decided to go with the story. Spread out over two full pages and promoted on the front page, it was perhaps the longest single story in the tabloid's 153-year history. The editors, realizing they could hardly do otherwise, went with a bold lead. "A teacher from Tioga County has demonstrated an ability to make tables rise off floors in a manner that apparently defies known physical laws," it said. "His feats have baffled scientists, magicians, reporters, photographers and the others who have witnessed Philip Jordan of Spencer levitate ordinary household furniture with a force or method no one has been able to logically explain."

In Albany, Jack Maloy, state editor for United Press International, picked up the odd story and moved it across the newswire.

"Nobody Could Believe Us"

"All the wonders of magic are performed by Will, Imagination, and Faith."

— *Paracelsus*

While Philip Jordan was grabbing headlines, drawing scores of people to table demonstrations held in halls and ballrooms, and appearing on numerous local radio and TV talk shows, in the very same state a virtually unknown group was quietly gathering from several counties to produce the same phenomena, though with two major differences. First, the group wasn't working with card tables but with a sixty-five pound dining room table; and second, its displays included not just tiltings of the table but the paraphysical home-run: total levitation. In its own reticent, unassuming way the group, composed mainly of middle-aged professional types, was for a while accomplishing some of the more spectacular psi demonstrations on recent record.

The levitations went back to November 1973, when they started at the home of Douglas and Betty Thurmond, two youngish grandparents comfortably ensconced in a new home in central New York near the Pennsylvania border, where the beautiful scenery includes the smooth-flowing Susquehanna River as it cuts through the Allegheny Plateau. The Thurmonds' interest in psychic phenomena had been kindling for years, mostly because of the weird experiences Betty had always had. A short, heavy-set woman, warm and spiritually inclined, Mrs. Thurmond had lived since she could remember with a strange ability that had been considered anything but a gift. As a child she often heard fleeting "voices" in her head and saw mental images that sometimes forecast future events, facts that caused some apprehension in those around her. "When I was young I just didn't realize what it was," she says. "I was afraid of it — didn't think it was for real — and I guess I kind of tried to turn it off. I was having experiences my friends weren't, and I guess I was scared there might be something wrong with me."

Despite those initial efforts at shutting it out (whatever "it" was), the experiences cropped up time and again in later life, especially after she and her husband moved from their native Massachusetts. In their new home objects sometimes moved when no one was around, rappings occasionally seemed to circulate within their walls, the piano seemed to play by itself.

Thirsting for knowledge about such things, the Thurmonds devoured literature on subjects like ESP and often made their own informal psi experiments, which were uncannily successful more times than not. When Doug, an engineer for International Business Machines (IBM), read of levitation in a book on the history of the occult, it caught his fancy. Could he and his wife use the paranormal powers they apparently possessed to work a levitation? Was this something they too could learn to do? They tossed the questions around one night when two friends dropped over, and before they knew it were standing at their heavy wood table, half-seriously rubbing its surface and coaxing it up.

Incredibly, it worked. Within minutes, one end mysteriously rose, then slammed down, followed by similar motions at the other end despite relatively light hand contact with the tabletop. The table banged around for a while, turned nearly halfway around on the rug, and then, to the utter astonishment of those present, suddenly leaped up — right off the floor — and hung in midair, gently rocking back and forth under their massaging hands. "Who knew it was going to do that?" asks Betty. "We were just fooling around when it went up! It's something we never figured could happen so fast."

Though their reputation as honest, rational neighbors was impeccable, this was something they had trouble telling their friends. "Nobody could believe us," says Mr. Thurmond, "and, well, who could blame them?"

Indeed, the only people really interested in listening was a group they had met a few months before when they took a course called Silva Mind Control, which gives training in self-improvement and extrasensory aptitude through meditation, self-hypnosis and a slowing down of brain wave patterns. Because the course had touched on areas like ESP, dream control, positive thinking and PK, and because they had themselves experienced strange occurrences while in altered states of consciousness, the Silva graduates had open minds on what to most people might have sounded like the ridiculous contrivances of an overactive imagination. Soon a group of about eight adults were meeting regularly at the Thurmonds' home in order to try and levitate the bulky table.

Nearly every time they got together, the same thing would happen. For several minutes they would "warm up" the table, rubbing its every corner as if to send energy into it. "Come on, table, good table; you're going high tonight, table," they would monotonously repeat, hoping to pool their mental powers.

Normally that would provoke a subtle vibration through the tabletop that was often accompanied by a tingling sensation in the sitters' hands. Then, usually within ten minutes, the table would start creaking oddly and eventually each of its ends would start lifting off the floor and somewhat violently banging down again in a strangely *rhythmical pattern*. Constantly rubbing the legs, the group would urge it to calm down, an exhortation frequently followed by a more fluid motion of the table and even by its ascending off all its legs, many times going so high as to threaten a chandelier hanging above. Like the others in the group, Jean Koprivnikar of nearby Broome County was at a loss to account for what was going on. Said Mrs. Koprivnikar: "I tried to believe it before, but I couldn't. Not that Betty and Doug would lie, but come on! And then you stand there, watching it go up, unable to logically explain it at all. It was awesome."

Once in the air, the table often turned completely around and then flipped over while suspended, bucking from side to side the while. Sometimes it landed upside down on the floor, a position it would rumble around in before rising back up a few feet from the rug. Landing back on its legs it would frequently start spinning so fast the participants had trouble keeping up with it. Other times it would "walk" across the room, swaying back and forth on its legs, then tilt way up on one side before subsiding to the floor. While at times normal muscle pressure was used to get the table going, and at other times hands briefly rubbed its underside, there was not, in the words of one former skeptic, "any way anyone was applying enough pressure to tilt the table, let alone get it to smoothly tip over and then completely rise."

It didn't matter how many were at the table; there had been as few as three, as many as twelve. As long as those present had a strongly positive attitude, the table would levitate. It even performed spectacularly in front of a home movie camera set up by a member of the group one night. Only seconds into the shooting session the table was up off the floor, hovering about a foot off the ground as eight people massaged its top, legs and, occasionally, underside. It then went down, tilted at an angle of seventy-five degrees, and shot back up, moving like a big Ping-pong ball dancing slowly on a stream of psychic air.

The night the short home movie was taken the group was especially hot. At one point, with five people keeping their hands on its surface, the table floated so high one participant, alone on one of the sides, was unable to reach high enough to maintain contact. It rose to within inches of the ceiling, then slowly tipped on its side as though pulled by invisible strings. Arms looked relaxed; hands showed no strain. As the table tipped around in the air the group, shocked at its eerie movements, laughed loudly as they scrambled to keep up with it.

Like those who had been in on the Jordan table-tiltings, the Thurmond group sensed a strong pressure coming up from underneath the table, a pressure that moderate arm force applied from above could not resist. It built up slowly, steadily and as though it was coming not from the specific energy of the group but from some energy they were *directing* with their minds. When one of the sitters pushed the raised end of the table down, it bounced back up like a beach ball that someone is trying to keep under water. "One night our daughter tried it," says Fran

Koprivnikar, an industrial engineer who was in on several of the levitations. "She didn't believe in it and wanted it to stop. Geez, she got mad. No matter how hard she tried it wouldn't go down. That she couldn't figure out. We all had our hands on the surface."

On occasion, so powerful was the force, the table remained in tilted position even while group members took turns sitting on top of it, one time spinning and effortlessly moving across a rug despite the weight of a 223-pound man. Bucking under such weights as this, it often moved up and down so fast it kicked off the rider. The legs still in contact with the floor sometimes appeared to be barely touching the rug despite the human load. When this kind of energy was going through the group's psychic circuits, other equally spectacular phenomena were said to occur. According to eyewitnesses, one such evening Mr. Thurmond and two others were able to cause a small wood end table to tilt without so much as touching it.

Members of the group never got too solemn about what they were doing but looked on it as a sort of game, a pastime that filled in entertainment slots reserved in most middle-class circles for more mundane amusements like rounds of poker and gin. Never did the group consider what they were doing to be of any earth-shattering importance, and because it had come so easy to them they figured it couldn't be particularly rare. They valued levitation mainly as something they could stun friends with, as an hour's worth of laughs. When acquaintances who had never seen it before came over — as long as the newcomers were familiar to the group and had open minds — the Thurmonds would casually take the fruit basket off the table, place their hands on its top, and wait for the first slight movements that always seemed to preface its rise. They were successful nearly every time in at least getting the table to tilt and slide effortlessly across the rug. Even when just a few people had their hands on the table, and even if those participants were children, the table moved and spun so fast they could hardly keep up. When they tried to duplicate these movements through normal and obvious muscle pressure, their efforts failed. In most of the movements, muscle action was definitely not the cause.

The table sessions were held, off and on, until around the fall of 1975, when the group disbanded for many reasons, two being that the majority of its members were growing tired of spending so much time with table PK and wanted to learn about other aspects of psi. Unfortunately, there was no scientific documentation of the group's activities. Proving the phenomenon to others was not the group's concern, and even when they were presented with an opportunity to do just that they showed little interest in devoting to such an enterprise the endless hours it required. Had they consented it might not have made any difference: the "opportunity" was rather hollow since there was in fact almost no research money available for the elaborate equipment that would have been needed. "Let's face it," said Mrs. Thurmond with a sigh, "we'd have to go door-to-door with it. We've proven it to ourselves, and that's the important thing. There's so much else to do."

Total strangers were rarely present at the sessions. Like so many others who have dabbled in the paranormal, the Thurmonds found that the presence of outsiders, even if they were fairly open-minded, hampered or prevented powerful psi manifestations. While personal friends of the group were often welcome, the group was apprehensive about opening up to too many people and feared local publicity. Some members had already been challenged by acquaintances who suggested they were playing with demonic forces or even questioned their sanity.

The Thurmonds did, however, demonstrate for a local journalist during the summer of 1975 after being assured that what they showed him would not hit the local papers. The journalist, accompanied by a photographer, soon found just how disrupting an outsider could be, especially when the intruders were constantly pointing a camera the group's way. For the first thirty minutes nothing happened. Despite constant rubbing of the wood table and endless pleas that it levitate, all that was achieved was a slight rumbling and a few creaks.

After taking a break from this unsuccessful try and sipping some punch, however, the group loosened up a bit. They sang to the table; they chanted to it. Only minutes after they reassembled, one side suddenly lifted two feet off the floor and slammed down; then the whole table started rocking violently from end to end. Hands were only pressing lightly on the surface, and many times the group positioned themselves all at one end of the table. Earlier the newsmen had figured the bangings could be caused by members pressing down at one end, causing the opposite side to rise. But much of the time nearly all the hands were at the end that was rising, seeming to eliminate muscle pressure as the cause.

About ten minutes later the table suddenly lunged over on one end, standing erect at a ninety-degree angle. It shifted restlessly for a while, every now and then jerking over so far that only one corner of its top was still in touch with the floor. Then, quite suddenly, it lifted completely off the rug, dangled for a few seconds and floated back down in an upside-down position. As the newsmen watched in disbelief, the participants changed positions;

one person began rubbing the leg, while seven others massaged the underside. With that the table started to vibrate, at the same time shifting around on the rug, and then completely rose off the floor for an instant even though, as far as observers could see, there were no hands holding it from underneath. Although with so many people involved, muscle tension, however subtle, could have been what boosted the table up, the investigators were actually able to feel the pressure coming up from underneath and noticed that the table seemed to have lost most of its weight. There was a bouncy feeling to it as it went up and down. Obviously, most conventional explanations didn't apply. There were no levers, no strings. And when the observers tried to move the table through normal hand pressure, it didn't move the same way at all; this physical exertion was now obvious, where minutes before, during the moments of paranormality, it was not.

That a relaxed atmosphere was essential for strong PK displays was apparent. During the several other visits made by the journalist, the most meager results were gotten when a camera was trained on the group, while the best results, including total levitations that lasted much longer than the first time, were achieved when the reporter had become known to the group and was not accompanied by a skeptical lensman. Though the Thurmonds' sessions ended soon after the journalist first observed the group, he had seen enough to conclude that, like Phil Jordan, they were having some psychoenergetic effect on their table, an awesome one when the group was in top form.

What or who sparked the table movements on the occasions when they definitely weren't attributable to muscle pressure? And what exactly did this force consist of?

Everyone had their guesses. Because Mrs. Thurmond had chalked up so many psi experiences before, many pointed to her as the main source, as the catalytic medium. If the home was "haunted," perhaps Betty was initiating some kind of spirit activity, figured some. She did have many such encounters outside the group. Objects fell about her in strange ways, she had said, and she claimed that once, in her living room, she had seen the apparition of a beautiful young woman who had supposedly come to drain her (Betty's) energies. Others figured the table was lifted not by spirits but by the PK from their own force fields, and they decided it was perhaps Betty's exceptionally strong force field that energized their own. To them "force field" was similar to if not identical with that aura or spirit body that psychics claim to see extending beyond the physical body.

Maybe it was spirits that moved the table, said Mrs. Thurmond, but she didn't feel she was the only one who activated them. She pointed out that there was one time when her husband got the dining room table jumping around without anyone else's help, and another when relatives from Massachusetts completely levitated a coffee table, all their hands being on top of it and she herself being merely an observer. "I am mediumistic, but in a very minor way," she said. "To tell you the truth, I think anyone can do the table thing, with enough patience and a whole lot of faith that it will work."

Support for that contention is lent by some of the things that another member of the group, Rose Engle, an attractive thirty-four-year-old secretary from Johnson City, New York, had done away from the group. Though nowhere near as consistent or spectacular in her levitations as the regular group, Rose had caused tables to rise while outsiders sat patiently by and even claimed her children had once or twice caused the levitation of small stools, though they failed to do this in front of investigators the only time they tried.

Like the other group members, Mrs. Engle met Betty Thurmond through the Silva Mind Control course. Blonde-haired and always gaily dressed, she had a radiance about her, a warmth that came from her ocean-blue eyes and indeed from the whole of her plump, ruddy, smiling face. The course's brain wave method of control had inspired in the young secretary a deep interest in parapsychology, and mind control, as she put it, "opened the psychic channels, loosened up my mind." She had good reason for believing so. When she conducted telepathy experiments with Mrs. Thurmond, a pastime they regularly indulged in, the results were often startling. Rose would concentrate on randomly chosen objects scattered in her home, which was about twenty miles from Betty's. If it was a pen Rose was concentrating on, Betty might get the impression of something long and pointed, and even that it was used for writing. Their "wavelengths" seemed to match precisely.

Rose was a bit less apprehensive than the rest of the group about trying PK in front of others. In June 1975 she arranged such a demonstration for Gary Truce, the professional hypnotist who had studied Jordan and in fact had brought the table-tilting psychic to the State University at Binghamton for displays in front of large groups. Dr. Truce was only the second psi researcher to take a look at Rose at work. About a year earlier she had trekked to Syracuse to attend a lecture given by Milan Ryzl, the internationally-renowned parapsychologist from Prague, and after the talk had given Dr. Ryzl a brief but intriguing display of her own psychic powers.

Like the others in the group, she didn't really know what exactly caused PK, she told Truce, but she had noticed some revealing consistencies in the group's displays. Of the more than twenty times she claimed to see the Thurmond table totally levitate, the best always seemed to be when everyone was tense yet calm, urging the table up while at the same time forming mental pictures of how it would look when suspended in the air; the participants' attitudes had to be forcefully positive. In some way, she said, the group's collective imagination seemed to project energy outside their bodies, as though cutting a path for outside physical reality to follow. "A table is a bunch of atoms, arranged to act in a certain way," she reasoned, "so why can't they be subtly rearranged in a way that temporarily allows the object to float?"

Borrowing a small wood end table from a neighbor, she hurriedly set it up to show Truce and an accompanying journalist what she meant. At first the table, operated by Rose, Truce and a neighbor, bounded back and forth, once in while oddly perching up on one leg. That went on for nearly thirty minutes. Just before the tilts, strange sounds — rapping, knocking sounds which seemed different than the normal creakings of wood under strain — flowed from the table's center. These sounds were the only interesting thing to occur; the table movements themselves, though often surprisingly quick and rather violent, were impossible to distinguish from those that would have been produced by mere muscle tension.

After a while, however, the table suddenly moved into the adjacent room, the kitchen, gliding swiftly along on just one leg. With three pairs of hands on top, and with Rose constantly urging it up, it started a remarkably fast spinning motion, then tipped over gently, uncannily so, onto one side. "Like cotton," remarked a surprised Dr.

Truce. "It fell as if it had bounced into some cotton."

They coaxed it on for another fifteen minutes or so, watching each other's hands to make sure anything that happened was for real. "Table up," they repeated. "You can do it. Up!"

In a flash it bolted off its side, completely leaving the floor, and rushed a few feet through the air to a nearby wood door, attaching itself there like a metal filing jumping to the end of a bar magnet. With hands still on its upper side, it suddenly straightened to an upright position. It was a weird sight. About a foot off the floor, it seemed an unanswerable challenge to science's book of rules. Although one leg was in bare contact with the door, there was no ledge on which the leg was caught, no way muscle tension could have kept it in its strange position. With all hands on top, it stayed in that position for a few minutes, then suddenly seemed to lose all its "power" and fell to the floor.

When the two men tried to duplicate these movements with their own physical pressure, they were easily able to get the light table rocking and tipping but could in no way reproduce its other activities. Those dashing, floating movements had been extremely odd. At times the table had seemed *polarized,* a characteristic they were unable to simulate. If the cause was invisible strings, they thought, then Mrs. Engle must be a magician of genius. If it was sleight-of-hand, it must have been so subtle as to make Houdini roll over at least twice in his grave from envy.

On other occasions, Rose and a few others were able to cause the tilting of rather heavy tables, along with raps and that cool, breezelike sensation. Still, PK phenomena were always more impressive when Mrs. Thurmond was around.

But even with Betty, there were times when the table

was stubborn, the most memorable such occasion taking place back in 1974. Despite three hours of effort, the dining room remained completely motionless, something that had never happened before. There had been significance even in this failure, however. About halfway into the seemingly fruitless session, Rose had noticed a white, misty form rising from the wood — a ghost-image of the table. She had passed it off as hallucination that night but the next day, still wondering, had mentioned it to Betty. "Now that's strange, really strange," Betty had said, turning on her excited Massachusetts drawl. "I swear I saw the same thing!"

Had the women gotten a glimpse of the PK force? Had a window to another reality been opened for them, if only a crack? "It's so tough to say what's going on," says Rose. "You know how it is; you see it so many times, you feel it. But you don't know what to call it. I say it's energy, an energy we can learn to produce more consistently, an energy everybody could use if they could only get rid of that conditioning that tells them such things don't exist."

Breakthrough In Toronto

Glendower: I can call spirits from the vasty deep.
Hotspur: Why, so can I, or so can any man:
        But will they come when you call for them?
                                — *Shakespeare: Henry IV, Part I*

Can humans manufacture ghostlike effects? Can people train themselves to materialize apparitions? Can anyone learn to be psychic?

The questions had been floating around A.R.G. Owen's head for quite a while, right along with other strange notions that belied his conservative, down-to-earth appearance. For years — when he wasn't in the biology and mathematics classrooms of Trinity College, Cambridge — the stocky, reserved English scientist could be found hunting down Europe's legendary spooks in search of the answers. He roamed the continent to investigate poltergeist manifestations, like those witnessed by England's Matthew Manning or the furniture that mysteriously moved around a "haunted" house in Sauchie, Scotland. But though the trail led him to such faraway places as Barbados, where large tombs supposedly move by themselves, his hunting yielded no concrete evidence of ghosts, nor even a working theory as to their hows and whys.

Now it was 1972, deep into autumn, and the icy winds of Lake Ontario were swishing up Toronto's posh Sherbourne Street, where, on the north end, stood a large old home housing the New Horizons Research Foundation, a new parapsychological group that Dr. Owen and his wife Iris had just been wooed across the Atlantic to direct. Inside, eight volunteers, an accountant, an engineer, an industrial designer, a scientific research assistant and four housewives, listened to Owen's new experiment proposal, an idea that was as exciting as it was bizarre. Though none of the group was psychic, they were going to meet once a week to try and produce the same phenomenon mediums often claim to see. Their goal: to make their own "ghost."

Every week for the first year, ironically around the same time the Thurmonds were levitating heavy tables for the first time, the New Horizons group got together for a few hours on a set day and concentrated on an imaginary being, "Philip," whose "spirit" they tried to materialize in the room through prolonged meditation.

As an aid to their imaginations, "Philip" was given both a detailed physical description and a specific history. The fictive ghost had curly hair and an aristocratic beard and his "portrait" was drawn for the group by a local artist. He was a seventeenth-century Englishman who had conducted an extramarital affair with a ravenhaired gypsy named Margo, an affair that eventually led him to commit suicide from remorse after Margo had been convicted of witchcraft and burnt at the stake. Concentrating on this make-believe entity, the group spent hours trying to make his "spirit" return.

If they succeeded, if the imagined ghost did show, the implications would surely shake the world of the supernatural to its roots. As far as Owen was concerned, the experiment could show that at least in some cases ghosts were a form of collective hallucination, or perhaps of collective psi energy released from the subconscious.

But it didn't work, however hard they tried. Though on some occasions members felt they saw a white mist in the center of the room, it was nothing they witnessed together, nothing that could be corroborated. "Philip" did not want to appear.

A year later they decided to end the practice of meditating before each "Philip" session, choosing instead simply to sit relaxed at a card table under normal lighting and place their hands lightly on its surface in the immemorial manner of mediums. Instead of concentrating deeply, they would behave as though they were having a normal evening get-together, except that once in a while they would call "Philip" to appear at the table.

The first time they tried this method, nothing happened. But that, of course, was no surprise. As they had done while trying to materialize a mist, they persevered. The next week, on the recommendation of several English parapsychologists who had tried similar experiments, the group came prepared with jokes and songs in order to create an even more relaxed atmosphere. Suddenly the table began vibrating: it was as though some kind of subtle force was steadily building up under the sitters' hands. Soon the table was sliding rapidly and randomly around the room, moving easily across a thick rug without leaving a mark. The sitters' first reaction was to accuse one another of pushing, but in no time the table was sliding right from under their hands in a way they couldn't explain.

Speculating on what could cause this extraordinary movement, one of the members asked, "I wonder if, by chance, 'Philip' is doing this?"

Immediately a loud knock came from the wood. The

group interpreted it as yes. "Philip" had finally arrived.

Like seance mediums of yesteryear, the group set up a code to communicate with its "ghost." One rap meant yes, two meant no. Starting each session by merely touching the card table, an ordinary plastic-topped model with foldaway legs, the group would ask, "Hello, Philip, are you there?" And virtually every time would come a loud affirmative rap. When "Philip" was confronted with questions he wasn't sure how to answer there would be a weak, hesitant reply, or sometimes an odd scratching sound. Not only were the raps heard, at times so loudly as to be audible in the adjacent room, but they were also felt, as though the molecules in the table's wood sections were shifting in a specific pattern.

All the while the table would slide quickly across the room as the participants struggled to keep up, at times tilting at awkward angles the group were sure they weren't physically causing. It seemed to have a personality of its own. When a visitor came into the room it would slide over to nudge him or reel over on just one leg.

"At first we thought maybe it was just subliminal muscle movement. But some things just didn't fit that answer," says Iris Owen, who became the leader of the group. "One time we were ready to take a break, and Dorothy [a member of the group] suggested that the table just kick up its legs and land on its top before we went for some lemonade. Well, the table did just that, tilting slowly sideways and then flipping right over, the legs in the air. Nobody's hands were in a position where they could have done that. They were all placed lightly at the middle of the tabletop."

It performed for videotape, for Canadian television crews, for hundreds of curious visitors. Even when shiny paper doilies were placed on top of the table's slippery

plastic surface to reduce the possibility of muscle movement, it moved just as easily. When the group tried physically to push the table, their hands slipped off the doilies.

Other times, however, there appeared to be a certain
amount of muscle movement, or at least there were movements that *could* have been attributed to physical force.
Sometimes when the table tilted there seemed to be some
involuntary muscular force at work, and on rare occasions,
when it was stubborn, the group would deliberately give it
a shove to get it moving.

But, as in the experiences of Philip Jordan and the
Thurmonds, there was a strange upward thrusting force
beneath the table during some of the sessions, one that
manual force was unable to counteract. Once in a while
this force was accompanied by a cool breeze, and on at
least one occasion by a mistlike form that seemed to hover
around the table, though this was not seen by everyone.

When the table had been warmed up for a few hours, it
often swerved in a way that was inconsistent with manual
pressure, while its legs danced round in circles. Nor could
muscle movement explain the fact that on two occasions
the Owen group had also produced total levitation.

The first time this happened the group were using the
card table, "rapping" with "Philip" as the table slid around
the room. Suddenly the Owens' son Robin, who was
crouched on the floor, noticed that all the legs were off
the rug, if only by an inch. Then the whole table moved
about five feet across the room. Though it was a light
table, one that could easily be tipped with finger force, all
hands were just lightly resting on its top, poised in a way
that could not have caused it to lift completely.

The second occurrence was perhaps even more significant. The date was 24 July 1975, and this author had just
arrived to show the movies taken of the Thurmond group

completely levitating a sixty-five pound dining room table. While Dr. Owen and company had figured that such spectacular levitations were a possibility, the actual sight of the heavy table floating in the air amazed them and, more to the point, inspired them to try and do the same. "Now that we've seen it can be done, maybe we can do it," said one excited member. "All we need is the positive thinking, so let's give it a go!"

For the better part of an hour the group prepared, loudly singing to a small wood table that had been specially built for their sessions after other tables succumbed to the knocks taken as they darted about the room. The table started rocking from side to side as the members struck up with tunes like "Lloyd George Knew My Father" and "Onward Christian Soldiers." "Philip, show our guests that we can do it even better than the Yankees. All the way up in the air tonight, Philip," they repeated, as the table frequently tilted over on its side.

Most of the movements, however, seemed insignificant, even looked as though group members were unconsciously causing them. Then, two hours into the session, the table's legs, which branched down from the middle of its round top, started to rotate and swerve away from the participants in a way that didn't suggest any physical cause. But still the table wouldn't rise completely, and still there was no way of telling for sure whether these movements were the result of muscle tension, for the force behind them was nowhere near as strong as that experienced by Phil Jordan.

The group decided to try the method the Thurmond group employed: rubbing every corner of the wood for a while, visualizing how the table would look dangling in the air. For ten minutes hands moved softly over its surface while one of the group lay on the floor, imagining there were foam cushions under the table's legs. Suddenly the table glided swiftly across the room and lifted off the floor like an airplane leaving a runway. It stayed up for a few seconds, then softly touched down. "We finally did it!" shouted the thrilled members. "Philip, we finally did it!"

But their most consistently impressive results continued to be the rapping noises. While the tiltings were somewhat inconclusive and the total levitations extremely rare, the noises could be turned on and off at will. They rapped out when a member was leaving to go home; when one was arriving they reverberated through the wood as if to say hello.

"The actual mechanism by which the raps are created as a physical phenomenon is a complete puzzle. We still have no idea how a shared or telepathic thought of a group of ordinary people can be transformed into a physical event," says Mrs. Owen. "We have discussed this ad infinitum. We do not, ourselves, feel any differently from normal when the raps occur. We are not conscious of directing them all the time, and, in fact, sometimes they surprise us when they happen. We are beginning to recognize within ourselves whether or not we have reached the right psychological state so things can happen, and generally we can, so to speak, turn it on and off."

Using their simple code, the group often solicit answers from the table, or from "Philip," though most of the time they themselves are aware of the correct answers. Phil Jordan and the Thurmond group had likewise elicited coded responses from "the beyond" which came through as rappings. Sometimes they had gotten answers that were not only unknown to them, but also precognitive in nature.

In the fall of 1973, Dr. Owen brought in Joel L. Whitton, a medical doctor who had the equipment to set up an acoustical analysis of the raps. By placing a tape recorder microphone against the underside of the table, Dr. Whitton got several samples of the "Philip" raps, noises that came on command. ("Philip, are you there?" "Good, now another rap.") Through a process known technically as a qualitative time-domain analysis, he compared them to sounds produced when someone rubbed a hand or fingernail across the table's surface, dragged jewelry across it, tapped one of the legs with a knee or the like. These sounds were recorded with the Bell and Howell cassette set that same fall. A microphone was taped to the midpoint of the underside of the table, a card table with a wood top and metal legs and rims, and the paranormal rapping sounds were fed into a strip-chart recorder.

The results of the analysis were dramatic. The "Philip" raps showed an unusual acoustical pattern which indicated the raps were low frequency sounds that very quickly lost their vibrance. While to the human ear the paranormal raps sounded like those created through ordinary physical means, under laboratory scrutiny their patterns showed a short duration in percussion, appearing on the charts as noises that quickly reached a peak, then rapidly faded. The deliberate "control" raps were radically different, behaving like any normal percussive sound and petering out in a more gradual pattern. While the "Philip" raps had durations as short as 160 microseconds (i.e. 0.16 seconds), the control raps typically lasted about three times as long. Indeed, it appeared an unknown force was modifying the elasticity of the table, altering the rate at which vibrations were damped. In March 1976 Whitton took another set of samples, this time of paranormal sounds created in a sheet of metal that was hung over the "Philip" table, and he found the same paranormal (or "paramorphic") patterns. The charts showed high bursts followed by rapid decay. Similar sounds, incidentally, had been tape-recorded seventeen years earlier, by an American group headed by psychic researcher Dr. Margaret Paul, and sent to Dr. Whitton. They, too, had shown the unusual patterns.

When the group requested "Philip" to "send" the noises to other objects in the room, they were astonished to find they could create the same results, even though the objects were a good distance away. Pings came from nearby radiators and sheets of metal at which they directed the "Philip" force, the noises erupting in predictable fashion though no one was physically touching the metal.*

That, however, wasn't the only long-distance work "Philip" could do. One night when the group asked for something different, the lights in the room suddenly flickered on and off.

"Of course this is like the phenomena you often hear about in a haunted home. But we know there's no real ghost doing this, and it's obviously not hallucination," says Dr. Owen. "The imaginary device, 'Philip,' is used to focus energy generating what I believe is not only a legitimate act of psychokinesis, but a repeatable one as well. It's something we feel could be taught to any willing group."

Another member of the group, Sue Sparrow, chairman of prestigious Mensa of Canada, an orgaization of people with extremely high IQs, agrees: "We found that some of the phenomena you hear about as happening in the

---

*The American psi investigator/author Raymond Bayless had found, in tests conducted from 1973 to 1975, that he and co-researchers could cause very slight rapping sounds to come from *wood* without actually touching it. He recorded the sounds with various tape recorders and sometimes heard strange "voices" from the tapes when he played them back.

seances held in dark Spiritualist rooms aren't at all frightening, but probably just a force of mind. I was really surprised when it first started to happen, but you get accustomed to it quickly, and you see it do so many weird things you know it's beyond what scientific laws currently allow."

Sue Sparrow's linking of what occurs in scientifically controlled psychic experiments with what goes on in seances (or, one might add, in "haunted" houses) is apt. Once in the Owens' home, while Iris was setting dinner for some guests, who included two visiting psychics, a serving spoon that had been placed in a bowl of rice suddenly rose from the dish and floated across the room. Iris had been talking with a committee member of the Toronto Society for Psychical Research. "I had asked him a question that I knew would cause a bit of turmoil in his mind, and the levitated spoon seemed to be his unconscious answer," she says.

The most spectacular evidence that the group has learned to produce PK effects occurred at the end of 1974, a time when the world of parapsychology was aflame with news of Israeli psychic Uri Geller, who was astounding scientists with his apparent ability to bend metal mentally.

Wondering if the same energy that moved tables and caused the raps could also distort metal, the group asked "Philip" to bend a medallion set some distance away on an end table in the Owens' living room. They concentrated for quite a while, but to no apparent avail.

Taking a break for a quick Chinese lunch, the group left for a nearby restaurant. When they returned they found the piece of metal wrinkled completely out of shape as if it had been melted despite the fact that no one had been in the house after they left. Before their very eyes it slowly continued to bend, as if "Philip" had caused a delayed reaction.

Next they tried keys and spoons, with similar results. When a reporter from the *National Enquirer* visited the group in February 1975, his apartment key was placed on the "Philip" table, the group exhorting it to bend. Slowly one end bent up, curling over so gradually it may have been still bending while the reporter was flying back to his office in Florida. By the time he got home, anyway, his key was so out of shape he couldn't get into his apartment until the landlord hurried up with another key.

Yet, in contrast to the table raps, the group didn't seem to have much control over the metal-bending, and that led to problems. One of the members, an engineer, finally asked that the group suspend the metal feats lest he lose his job. Every time he walked near certain machinery, thin metallic parts, some of them very expensive, began inexplicably bending out of shape.

"God knows what it is. We just know that we can do it," says a housewife member of the group. "We have no way of explaining it." An identical view was held by several prominent scientists who witnessed the table movements, including Dr. J. Norman Emerson, president of the Canadian Archeological Society.

However, despite their inability to explain the "Philip" phenomenon scientifically, the group's main goal had been realized. Though not as previously planned, Dr. Owen had certainly found his "ghost."

England's Floating Tables

"Scientists — and I am one of them — do believe in 'miracles.' "
— *Arthur Compton, atomic scientist*

If today someone was to build a psychic hall of fame, wax effigies of Edgar Cayce, D.D. Home, J.B. Rhine, Jeane Dixon and Harry Price would be near the entrance.

Nowhere in such a monument, no matter the length of its halls, would one be likely to find effigies of Kenneth J. Batcheldor and Colin Brookes-Smith. Yet it was these two obscure English researchers who, with the help of dedicated assistants and without the knowledge of the news media, were perhaps the first to demonstrate repeatably and quasi-scientifically that ordinary people can, in certain circumstances, acquire the ability to perform large-scale PK,* once considered the monopoly of the psychically gifted.

This rather dramatic discovery was in many ways a product of the venerable London Society for Psychical

---

*Batcheldor and other parapsychologists considered the psi movement of objects larger than dice to be "large-scale."

Research (SPR), an organization that has functioned for nearly a century as the Smithsonian of the psychic world, leading a sophisticated search into areas ranging from ESP to the possibilities of life-after-death. For years Batcheldor, head of the psychology clinic at Exe-Vale Hospital in the Southwest and a close associate of the proud society, had been fascinated by the voluminous SPR accounts of the grand old PK mediums who were all the rage before the turn of the century. A widely experienced psychologist, whose career had included a stint as a physics researcher for General Electric and whose interests ranged from astronomy to cybernetics and brain models, he longed to know whether these spectacular reports could actually have been true and, if so, what the mental mechanics were that supposedly allowed the famous psychics to perform the incredible feats they were said to have accomplished at dark spiritualistic seances. Because it would afford a better glimpse into the physics of PK, he was especially interested in the alleged levitation of tables, which he didn't really believe in though it kept popping up in the literature he browsed through.

The days of the superstar mediums seemed to have passed, however, and by age forty-five Batcheldor hadn't found anyone who could perform on command in a controlled situation. At the time, modern psychics appeared not only less powerful than some of their illustrious predecessors, but also rather moody when requested to perform specific tasks. If he wanted to study PK phenomena firsthand, Batcheldor had no option but to produce some for himself.

On 25 April 1964, the psychologist met with two friends, a nurse and a farm owner, at the home of a fellow SPR member in Exeter. None of the three had ever had any mediumistic experiences, nor had they even seen a levitational display. Not knowing what, if anything, to expect, the small group followed the directions of old-time spiritualists, flicking off the living room lights and placing their hands palms down on a thirty-six pound refectory table made mainly of wood.

To no one's shock, nothing happened.

But the threesome kept their heads high, their optimism to the fore, and by the second meeting it looked as though Batcheldor's longshot just might come in. During the session a loud knock suddenly rumbled from the wood, and the table, this time a fifteen-pound one, started to rock wildly.

Soon, operating mostly under candlelight or by the glow of a coal fire, the group were getting strong tilts and slides from their various tables, the power being so forceful that one member described trying to push down the uplifted sides as like holding an open umbrella against the wind. Because they still suspected that *unconscious* muscle movement might be all that was behind most table-tipping accounts, they were suddenly caught off guard during the eleventh meeting when the fifteen-pound table lifted totally off the floor by at least a full inch, then swayed swiftly back and forth four times, like a pendulum. In one quick stroke the amused skepticism that the group had brought to the session turned to utter amazement.

"The explanation of unconscious muscle action was suddenly no longer applicable, since one can not push a table into the air, either consciously or unconsciously, when the hands are on top of it," wrote an excited Batcheldor. "I had been prepared to witness table-tiltings, as could be caused by unconscious muscular action. I had heard of the supposed total levitation of tables but never believed it. When it happened, it came as quite a shock. It seemed we had stumbled upon a genuine paranormal force, and we determined to continue the meetings and find out all we could."†

Over the next two years the group, occasionally admitting outsiders as additional participants, detailed in 800 pages of written notes and endless hours of tape about 200 table sittings, while Batcheldor himself went on to observe some 300 more. His approach was highly controversial for it was radical in the basic sense of the word. Whereas others, like Duke University's J.B. Rhine, had started their experiments by setting up controls that would screen out anything but the paranormal, Batcheldor was more interested in first developing the phenomena to the point where they could be clearly observed. "Rigid tests always caused the phenomena to dwindle to a size where they might not exist at all, only to flare up again as soon as controls were relaxed," claimed the psychologist. "So I chose to use favorable, even loose conditions deliberately, to get the phenomenon to occur in some obvious and frequent way, hopefully to find out *why* it was elusive and sensitive to controls. In this method [called the 'gambling method'] verification comes *last*, not first. As we all know, psi capacities are uniquely elusive and unlike any new discovery have resisted being pinned down for over a century. Physicists will find their results terribly elusive unless they pay more attention to the psychological factors."

However unorthodox a scientific approach that may seem, for Batcheldor it paid handsome dividends. Using tables that ranged in weight from six to sixty pounds and eventually progressing to an extremely heavy piano, his

† Kenneth Batcheldor, "A Case of Table Levitation and Associated Phenomena," *Journal of the Society for Psychical Research*, vol. 43, no. 729, p. 340.

group was so successful in producing levitation under semi-controlled conditions that he concluded PK is much more widespread in the population than has been thought, and that maybe it's the conditions, rather than the subjects, that are the most important factor in PK manifestations. Said Batcheldor, "We carried out systematic experiments to show no one person was the medium." This suggested, he went on, that perhaps "anyone can do it." Though he never guaranteed that PK could be learned quite like other psychological skills, he did believe almost any group could succeed in it, given enough persistence and the initial luck.

The conditions Batcheldor used were remarkably similar to the Thurmonds', even though the two groups had never heard of each other. What it took, said Batcheldor, was the creation of an unusual psychological situation, a very special state of mind that would manifest itself exosomatically [literally, "out-of-bodily"] through the avoidance of skepticism, tension and too much analytical reflection. Laughter, song, light conversation and cheerful utterances, interspersed with specific suggestions to the group's subconscious level, seemed a major key. Conversely, criticism, hostility, derision, impatience, pressure to succeed and intense observation were noted to have adverse effects. Why? "Well," said the psychologist, "a psychic action, like a learnt poem, should come out naturally and automatically, directed by the subconscious. It is well established that conscious attention during a skilled performance can cause the performer to stumble. Alternatively, the adverse factors can be regarded as counter suggestions."

To tune into the subconscious it is important, he said, to prevent normal conscious thinking from upsetting the psi flow. Noise and laughter are one way of doing it. It can also be accomplished, he said, by quietness, darkness and immobility, or by going into trance. Others have felt that at times even aggressive feelings could be used to block off the encroachments of analytical thought. As had other table experimenters, Batcheldor found that while some concentration was needed to ensure the table didn't "go on its own," too much could hurt psychic production.

Why the group needed darkness to operate with optimum effectiveness was a mystery at first. Batcheldor later theorized that the main reasons were probably psychological. The group had started in darkened rooms because of their initial adherence to the seemingly successful methods of seance-room mediums who claimed that light, especially the blue end of the spectrum, negatively affected the "ectoplasm" or quasi-physical matter that they figured protruded from the body like cantilevers to move tables.

The real effect of the darkness, however, was to heighten the expectation that something would happen. When, in a fully lit room, a table tipped up so that three of its legs left the floor, eyes tended to focus on the remaining leg and minds became dominated by the question, "Will it or won't it?" It was sight, not light, that interfered by introducing doubt. Darkness, on the other hand, seemed to maximize group optimism and keep concentration at the correct level.

While the group was able to do away with the darkness requirement in the latter stages, the best levitations still occurred in shaded rooms. In the dark there was less of what Batcheldor and an associate, Julian Isaacs, a philosophy student who also had studied sitter groups, liked to call "ownership" and "witness" inhibitions. Ownership resistance refers to the subconscious apprehension people have of seeing something that indicates they themselves possess paranormal skills. ESP researchers have known of such a reaction for decades, how people can be amazingly psychic until they *know* how psychic they are. The awareness that they do indeed get into "extrasensory wavelengths" sets off somewhat irrational, negative emotions. Witness fears are of the same breed. Many people have a latent fear of entering a realm they previously categorized as "supernatural" or "superstitious." Obviously, no matter how open their minds, most modern people are likely to back off from an event that seems to defy scientific laws, that partially erases a world view that the collective human ego takes pride in having mapped. When people are involved in psi activity, there is also the apprehension that is caused by the emergence into the conscious mind of mysterious subconscious elements.

Not surprisingly, most of the group's levitations began with crepitations and creaks in their tables, noises that occasionally turned into rapping sounds and spread to nearby chairs and walls, or to the floor. Often a "breeze" was felt passing over the hands of the sitters and underneath the table, more than once becoming so cool that the sitters said they felt as though they were seated in front of an open refrigerator and withdrew from the table until things warmed up.

The breeze phenomenon was usually followed by table movements, though these might take anywhere from a few minutes to half-an-hour to provoke. There would be slides and tilts that went from slow and silent to rapid and rather noisy. Whatever the force, it seemed to grow gradually as the session wore on, often reaching the awesome point where one of the participants could sit on the table's *uplifted end* without causing it to fall.

One of Batcheldor's most interesting psychological expedients for invoking PK was what he called "artifact induction." Without the knowledge of most of the sitters, he often got things started by secretly moving the table through normal muscle force. This got the group excited, believing that something was beginning to happen, and induced a strong state of "positive thinking" from which genuine PK phenomena often resulted. "The phenomena, at first superimposed on artifacts, gradually strengthen until they are clearly paranormal," said Batcheldor, who has detailed the psychological mechanics of such actions in hundreds of pages of theorizing. "This is one way that the right state arises in a group doing table-tipping without any special mental training."

On occasion, when the group had attained heightened mental states, the PK phenomena outdid themselves in bizarreness. More than once the table suddenly seemed to be "glued" to the floor — as if the same force that pushed it up had now reversed its thrust. The capricious force reacted even more strangely on control equipment, especially on a table that had been placed in a cage. It was impossible for the sitters to lift the table fraudulently by means of fingers or knees because they were outside the cage and the cage itself was fastened to the floor with four stout screws. The sitters tried to get the table to levitate, an event that would be signaled by a buzzer going off. "There were resounding bangs on the table," reported a baffled Batcheldor. "Sitters were pushed off their chairs by unseen forces — indeed as the evening wore on hardly anyone could remain on his or her chair without danger of being pushed over. Bill Chick (an original sitter) went up in the air, chair and all (not far). Once and only once, in the long sitting, the buzzer sounded, and believe it or not, at that very moment the tape recorder jammed and missed it!* There was so much 'power' about that I suggested we attempt to get the whole apparatus to levitate. It did — with one sudden bang it wrenched all four screws out of the floor simultaneously! Spectacular."

At other times small objects like matches and pebbles mysteriously "dropped" into the room from nowhere, a phenomenon Spiritualists call "apportation." Even large stones fell, one of them, four inches long, landing on a car flashlight that suddenly lit up the room, startling the unsuspecting experimenters. Subsequently the stone was given to a London museum for analysis and never heard of again. Batcheldor got a bewildered note from museum officials saying the rock had disappeared.

Still, the most regularly exciting of the group's achievements were the total levitations, accomplished with virtually every size of table Batcheldor provided. Whereas the Thurmonds' levitations were often lengthy, sometimes lasting minutes on end, Batcheldor's tended to be frequent but brief, normally lasting twenty-five seconds or less. In one session eighty-four separate lift-offs were recorded. It was Batcheldor's conclusion that with the possible exception of "adepts," man had not yet developed the degree of mental control needed for sustained levitation.

Because the levitations were often performed in complete or partial darkness, and because Batcheldor wanted to make sure the group were not imagining that they felt and saw the table rise off all four legs, he rigged red lights and buzzers to the tables in such a way that they would be

---

*Interestingly, researchers around Phil Jordan similarly reported that equipment — cameras, tape-recorders — sometimes jammed when the psychic went into trance. Batcheldor figured the malfunctioning of recording equipment during moments of paranormality may be attributed to the participants' subconscious aversion to documentation of abilities that frighten them.

triggered off in the event of a total levitation and so provide objective proof of the take-off. Some tables were also coated with luminous paint so sitters could judge their height and position in the air. Other safeguards like green and infrared lights were set up so the participants could watch each other's hands and feet.

During one session held in the first year of trials, a six-pound table was recorded as leaving the floor by nearly six feet in an especially energetic thrust; another time a fifteen-pound table completely levitated a few inches off the rug and whisked across the room. *When things were really going, the group noticed they could take their hands completely off the table and watch it carry on by itself,* a phenomenon that not only suggested a connection between table levitation, telekinesis (long-distance PK) and possibly poltergeists, but also made conventional explanations such as muscular force look silly.   •

On one such occasion, while five people stood a few feet from a forty-pound table and formed a circle around it by holding hands, the table suddenly slid more than eight feet from its original position, bucking and tilting slightly as it went. Movement without contact occurred another time when someone as hard-nosed as a physician was present. By linking hands and feet as they stood around the table, the participants were somehow able to cause it to slide right into the doctor, budging him from his watchful stance.

It was Batcheldor's considered judgment that the main reason for initial hand contact with the table was psychological and that it was not really needed. It was, he said, a matter of belief. It was hard enough for a group to believe they could raise a table at all, let alone without touching it. The touching merely served to dispel doubt. Gradually

Batcheldor's group made headway against the belief problem by using small objects like rattles, which were sometimes made to rise *without contact*. From these they graduated to metal, funnellike objects such as mediums used to employ to get "direct voices," supposedly from spirits, during their seances. At first the group practiced levitating the funnels, or "trumpets," with each member lightly placing a finger on top of the thin end of one of them as it stood upright. Then, according to detailed accounts sent back to the SPR, the group got around to raising the trumpets from across the room, just as the Spiritualists claimed they could do. The seemingly distinct worlds of mediums and parapsychologists had apparently found a common bridge.

"I think it possible that 'mediumship' is no more the prerogative of freak or abnormal personalities than is hypnotic behavior, which was originally thought to be confined to hysterics," said Batcheldor in papers that were later studied by A.R.G. Owen and the "Philip" group. "The rarity of a behavior often suggests that rare personality, but later it sometimes turns out that it is the conditions for the occurrence which are rare or unusual."†

When a fellow researcher watched the dazzling displays of the Batcheldor group and listened to the psychologist's ideas, he was so excited by what he sensed as an opportunity for major scientific investigation that he went with a few other experimenters to the SPR's Survival Research Committee with a request for funds with which to document PK phenomena, and indeed even ended up dipping into his own pocket in order to try and substantiate some

---

† Kenneth Batcheldor, "Practical Hints for Small-Group Study of PK Using Tables." (Privately published, 1966), p. 3.

of Batcheldor's newfangled theories. He was an engineer and instrument-maker named Colin Brookes-Smith, a crisp, dignified looking seventy-year-old who looked like everyone's favorite college professor. Interested for years in psi phenomena and a member of the SPR's council, Brookes-Smith was soon excitedly following the progress of two new groups of sitters who were trying to duplicate Batcheldor's feats with ordinary, nonmediumistic volunteers.

What Brookes-Smith wanted to do, it seems, was both duplicate Batcheldor's approach and then take quantitative measurements of the physical characteristics of "psyched" tables so as to get concrete evidence of paranormal occurrences on record. An adept in the field of electronics and data-tape recording, he came to the task armed with the most sophisticated gadgetry. There were "fishing rod" levitation height gauges, skotograph recorders, "reward" lights, electrodes or "grids" to check on muscle movement beneath the table, strain-gauges to check on similar movement above.

The list didn't end there. There were oscillographs and amplifiers for measuring the wave forms of changing currents, voltages or any other discharge that might possibly turn into electrical energy during the levitations; dynamometers that fed into pen-charts for measuring any paranormal forces pushing up beneath the table; bridge detectors, modulation amplifiers, Veroboards, supersensitive film — all set up to catch the elusive forces of PK. Said Brookes-Smith: "If the use of instrumentation proved successful, many advantages would accrue, not the least being that the chart recordings of simultaneous variables during the onset, display and terminal phases would be available for analysis. Human observation and testimony, moreover, would no longer be the sole criterion for or against the genuineness of ostensible paranormality."†

Although he never did get to the point of totally eliminating the necessity of human observation as evidence, the experiments were a resounding success, often in the most unexpected of ways. Equipment often had to be scrapped because of the capriciousness of table phenomena and sometimes the monitoring outfits seemed psychologically to impair the new set of sitters. But after laborious experimentation, which dragged on into 1973, Brookes-Smith was convinced the lines on his graphs spelled paranormality.

The first series of sittings was arranged in October 1968 at Grimsby, Yorkshire, under the general direction of D.W. Hunt, a dental surgeon and close associate of Brookes-Smith's. The group included an electronics engineer, a photographer and a secretary. Initially held in full light and without the encumbering equipment, the group quickly reported the total levitation of a forty-pound table, rappings and multiform tilts, many of which came when each sitter had only one finger on the top of the table. A few times that feeling of coldness swept over the hands of the participants, a phenomenon they speculated might be a dehydration process needed for the exteriorization of the paranormal forces, and on other occasions table movements were recorded *after* all hands had left it.

As has happened with so many other psi hobby groups, the Grimsby sitters disbanded after nearly a year of regular experimentation, their enthusiasm on the decline. When they got together again in September 1969, after taking a much needed break from their weekly sessions, a

†Colin Brookes-Smith, "Some Experiments in Psychokinesis," *Journal of the SPR*, vol. 45, no. 744, p. 266.

skotograph recorder fitted with special, highly sensitive film was set up on their table to see if the levitation forces would affect the emulsion of the film. A number of psychics, most prominently America's Ted Serios, had demonstrated an ability to create images mentally on undeveloped film without the use of a conventional lens and camera, and Brookes-Smith and Hunt figured there just might be some similar form of tenuous matter emanating from the participants' fingers that would, by luminous or chemical means, cause an imprint on the film during table trials. Despite innumerable attempts, however, nothing concrete showed up on the film and the project was scratched until better equipment could be secured.

Still, there was intrigue even in failure. During one of the skotograph and film tries, when the group were "revving up" their efforts in an attempt to cause knocking sounds on the equipment, a chair near the equipped table suddenly started to move slowly of its own acccord toward the group, then turned between sixty and ninety degrees. Lesser movements followed.

Soon after, Hunt and Brookes-Smith, anxious to document the apparent fact that objects could be psychically moved at a distance, had a contraption built that extended thirty inches from the table and had a hinged door at the end that lighted a red bulb when the door was opened. The group soon found they could dictate the number of times the lamp would light, even though no one was physically in reach of the triggering gauges. The light was also found to blink on and off in coded reply to verbal questions, just as rappings have been found to do. The light even solved mathematical puzzles — before the questioner had worked the answer out in his own head.

By January 1971, Brookes-Smith had a second group,

situated near Daventry, ready for scientific investigation. It was there, in a carefully constructed study, that the most conclusive evidence of paranormality was collected on complicated data-recording equipment that fed off all the gauges and dynamometers, some of which were planted in the single support colums of the tables.

The group had no problem getting quick results; often mysterious table motions were recorded only minutes after the sessions had begun. On a number of occasions the participants were able to slide and tilt a 125-pound dining room table standing on a rug. The measured force required to make the table slide horizontally was about sixty-five pounds while a tilt was figured by the research-ers to require some seventy pounds of pressure — far more than anyone could apply without being immediately noticed.

It wasn't long before Brookes-Smith was to go one step further: to specific measurement of the uplifting psi force. Often, when the tilts and levitations were later analyzed, the researcher found swayback or humpback forms on his pen-charts which confirmed that the physical force exerted by the sitters was nowhere near enough to keep the table in its recorded position. At the group's forty-seventh sitting, Brookes-Smith reported thirteen short total levitations produced in rapid succession, three of them involving a lightweight table that went three to four feet clear of the floor and produced the telltale sways and humps on the chart signals. A closer look at the feedback equipment revealed that mysterious forces on the order of fifteen pounds had in some fashion aided the table's rise, as if by rushing up from the floor. Similar results were obtained from a forty-inch octagonal table mounted on a frictionless spring-supported dynamom-eter. Up-forces of two to five pounds that lasted as long

as sixteen seconds were recorded, most of them immediately following the group's verbal commands to the table. Sometimes the transcribed data seemed to indicate
that two paranormal forces were at work, one causing the
table to adhere paranormally to the sitters' hands, the
other forcing it up from underneath.

Unexpectedly, Brookes-Smith also found through minute analysis of data-tape that on many occasions a paranormal electrical conductance was somehow taking place,
as if the psi energy was creating a current that affected the
grids lining the underside of the table. The mysterious
conductances corresponded with verbal commands and
sometimes lasted as long as fifteen seconds. (In the past,
mediums had purportedly often caused similar electrical
effects. Italy's Eusapia Palladino, for example, could
allegedly discharge an electroscope by merely pointing a
finger at it.) Excited by the apparent connection between
what his group had done and what others had previously
claimed to do, Brookes-Smith increased the sophistication
of his equipment so that it could gauge these electrical
transactions even more accurately, hooking up a direct
current-detecting bridge calibrated with a modulator-
amplifier. Again, there was a registering of electrical
conductance just before the tables shot up. "That a
psychophysical agency produces the mechanical force in
PK and that it conducts an electric current seemed reason-
ably well-established," said Brookes-Smith, who detailed
the specific experiments in a series of monographs that
supplemented his reports to the SPR.

Were the table effects, the levitations, the up-forces, the
electrical conductances, all due to "psychic fluids" or
"ectoplasm"? Were they the result of animal magnetism or
etheric energy, or of the host of other ambiguously titled
energies of the unknown?

Clearly neither Brookes-Smith nor the other research-ers really knew. What they did know was that once a foolproof electrical method of detecting the presence of these invisible energies was found, it would mean an unparalleled boon to investigators in the field.

"The quantitative force measurements have produced clear indications that by adopting suitable procedures, paranormal forces can be made available 'by the pound' in repeatable experiments almost at any chosen time," said Brookes-Smith in a commentary printed in the SPR journal. "Clearly, there is much to be unraveled and instru-mentation methods need improving, but at least a start has been made. These tentative beginnings ought to be followed up by other workers who have specialized know-ledge in both modern physical and chemical analytical methods. It might then be possible to confirm by empiri-cal evidence (or refute by its lack) that the agency pro-ducing paranormal force is a genuine though fleeting physical reality and that there is a scientific basis for the belief long held by Spiritualists and at least suspected by many parapsychologists that a temporary form of tenuous matter can sometimes be exteriorized from the human body in order to perform tasks beyond the reach of the limbs and normal senses."†

It was a plea to science, and one that went largely unheard. What he was saying was that something was out there. Man just hadn't yet the eyes to see it.

†Colin Brookes-Smith, "Data-Tape Recorded Experimental PK Phenomena," *Journal of the SPR*, vol. 47, no. 756, p. 86.

Wonderment At Kent State

"The frank realization that physical science is concerned with a world of shadows is one of the most significant of recent advances."

— *Sir Arthur Eddington*

At times it didn't seem to matter that, by 1975, the field of parapsychology had already been functioning under an imprimatur from the American Association for the Advancement of Science for some six years. When it came to anything that smacked of the paranormal, conventional science was still looking the other way. And when it came to something as freakish as paraphysical levitation, even America's parapsychologists, somewhat tenuously linked to one another as they were, missed out on opportunities to study manifestations that were genuine. Blinkered by their adherence to orthodox scientific procedure, researchers had only rarely edged beyond relatively simple ESP experiments.

Luckily, there was at least one exception, a theoretical physicist, no less. For Wilbur Franklin, who worked in the antiseptic, ultramodern atmosphere of the Smith Hall of Physics at Ohio's Kent State University, the study of phenomena like telepathy and clairvoyance was fine, but he figured that probing to the source of psychic happenings would involve first getting a handle on PK. In that pursuit he became the first United States scientist to take a look at the way Philip Jordan, the Thurmonds, and the Toronto "Philip" group caused tables to waver uncannily above their floors. Like K.J. Batcheldor and Colin Brookes-Smith before him, his intuition told him that the case of the rising tables could provide the key to a multitude of parapsychological doors.

Dr. Franklin was chairman of his department's graduate division, his main interest liquid crystals, not card-reading. Indeed, he was a somewhat unlikely candidate for such "wild" research, for he seemed the typical absent-minded, no-nonsense professor. His appearance — blond goatee, untucked shirt flopping around a thin frame, eyes that glazed as his mind forever wandered back to the blackboard equation — served to confirm the impression. His was the kind of mind that went for hard evidence, for the logical empiricist's data, not for the contrived claims of seance-room mediums.

Not that he wasn't interested in the occult. Since his first year in college he had seriously wondered about such things, especially psychic healing. In Vermont, a psychic woman had once worked magic with the diabetic condition he had, and he had sensed that something extraordinary had been at work, something that seemed to connect up with a lot of other inexplicable happenings. Maybe, he thought, it had to do with an energy of some sort, an unnamed force that could affect matter. There had, however, been no way of telling for sure, and his wonderings had nearly ceased when, at age thirty-nine, he met with Apollo 15 astronaut Edgar Mitchell, the moon-

walker who had turned his thoughts toward inner space —
consciousness research and parapsychology — after his
mystical hurtle through outer space.

Mitchell and Franklin shook hands for the first time in
the early spring of 1972, when the space adventurer
stopped off at the hilly Ohio campus as part of a nation-
wide hunt for facilities and funds with which to study psi,
which he classified as a branch of "noetic" research. Their
meeting was timely, in fact almost uncannily so. Uri
Geller, the young psychic who was causing a stir with his
ability to bend metal "mentally," was due to arrive from
Israel in just a few months for what could easily have been
a first-and-last visit. Mitchell, who had read enough history to know such "mediums" were a rare and elusive lot,
didn't want this one to get away without being scrutinized
by scientists in mainstream physics. In Franklin, Mitchell
suddenly found just what he needed: an open-minded
theorist with a respectable background that included Yale
University and Case Western Institute. For his part, the
Kent State physicist was quick to seize the chance of
checking out some of those paranormal accounts that kept
popping up and gnawing at his thoughts. His healing
experience was at the core of his interest, but he didn't
expect to find the secret to that mystery. Now Mitchell was
talking about what seemed a much simpler matter, PK
reactions with metals, and the physicist saw the possibility
of submitting these to laboratory tests.

"Back then, Mitchell was hopeful of getting a lot of
funding, in fact the figures were in the millions. We
figured we could get Geller at Kent State, and maybe even
forge something of a breakthrough," says Franklin wear-
ily. "Well, we were never able to arrange things fast
enough here to set up for him. But we got some observations of his metal-bending at SRI [Stanford Research

Institute] later, and I became convinced that the mind, or at least his mind, could interact with physical systems. So in Uri, well, we had tremendously high hopes, hopes of not only establishing the gargantuan amount of evidence science demands, but of actual insights into the causal factors behind it all."

The physicist even had some support from his university president, who had established a rapport with Mitchell and had himself been witness to some of Geller's strange phenomena. One night, as Franklin, Geller and Andrija Puharich, the physician who brought Geller to America, were leaving the administrator's home after dinner, an object suddenly fell behind Geller, not as though it had been thrown but as though it had dropped from above. When the men bent to see what it was, their eyes fell on a medallion that the president identified as one that had once been presented to him and that he had kept near his living room, not far from where they now were. As the baffled scientists stared at it, it slowly seemed to change color. When Franklin later analyzed its surface, he found that chemical changes had taken place in it. If he could only discover what made the medallion move, what caused those chemical changes — naturally enough, he felt that if he could do that he'd be well on his way to solving the problem of PK.

Those dreams of intensive research, and maybe even *the* breakthrough, turned out to be little more than a mirage, however. Mitchell's attempts to get massive funding fell disastrously short, and when Franklin took to trying for grant money, he met with rejection. Particularly frustrating was the cold shoulder that the government-funded National Institute of Health turned on him when he asked for a year's worth of funds to study Geller. His plan was to bring in three top scientists, a magician and other part-time consultants in order to establish the reality of the metal phenomenon and then apply it to healing. In a move Franklin describes as "a great disservice to society," the institute flatly and with meager explanation said no. Soon after, Geller, not terribly fond of spending his time in laboratories anyway, was gone, and the physicist's investigation into PK was seriously, and almost fatally, damaged.

For two years, paranormal subjects that he could re-search were few and far between, and his spirits sank accordingly. Then came a shot in the arm. This was word out of Toronto that a group had been trained to initiate PK using "Philip," that imaginary "ghost." Here suddenly was the possibility of a fresh approach to the tantalizing mysteries of the paranormal. "I had never seen it before," Franklin recounts, "but I knew that, if legitimate, table levitation and even the knocking sounds and the tippings could be as valuable as metal-bending. Or any phenomena. Perhaps, because of the simplicity of the man-wood inter-action, even more so." Still there was the problem of how to document it, on shoe-string funds and in a way science would accept.

Despite bad odds, Franklin decided to persist. Assistants in his lab were soon scurrying about in preparation for a new display of PK. Advised on the recent work of Batcheldor and Brookes-Smith, he followed the English lead in building tables that were electronically monitored, though limited finances prevented him from using equip-ment as sophisticated as theirs. In a small, first-floor room in the physics building at Kent State, he set up a crude strain-gauge table connected to pen-charts, electric buttons that were wired to table legs so as to document their movements graphically, and vidoe tape cameras. He in-vited members of Cleveland's parapsychology association, who included Sheridan Speeth, a cybernetics research associate and head of a psi research squad, to stand in as observers.

The results were impressive. Though, due to funding and logistics problems, the whole "Philip" group was not able to make it down, the four members who did accompany A.R.G. Owen for the week-long experiments were able to demonstrate to the observers that psychic forces were at work. Various tables tipped up on their sides, "walked" down the building's halls in bursts of uncontrolled force, and resounded with strange rapping sounds that seemed to respond to the group's simple communication code. In one instance, in clear view of the camera, a table jolted several feet with what Franklin estimated to be some fifty pounds of force. "There was only one person on the back end, and we were watching, closely watching, hands and feet," says the physicist. "Yes, we figured, though we couldn't really prove, that a paraphysical energy was at work."

Part of the problem was that the group couldn't perform as impressively on the tables laden with all the equipment. While Brookes-Smith had, from the beginning, concentrated on getting his table groups to operate in the midst of cumbersome paraphernalia, the psychological attitude this induced in members of the "Philip" group seemed to underline a danger of which the English researcher had warned. There was one instance when the gauges seemed to record some twenty pounds of paranormal "Philip" force, but this was fleeting. Speaking of past attempts at systematic evaluation of table levitation and other types of PK, Brookes-Smith had said it took months to develop the psychological attitudes necessary to work repeatable experiments in the presence of constant observation and complex gadgetry, and had speculated that many experimenters were unwittingly inhibiting and even preventing the very manifestations they hoped to witness. "It's a delicate thing, the psychological attitude," commmented Iris Owen, leader of the "Philip" group. "We felt the pressure of the ambience, and all the restrictions. Coming into that cold was very, very tough."

Franklin was keenly aware of the psychological factor and, since he was especially interested in seeing what the group could do at their psychological peak, he arranged for an easing of the scientific controls. Sure enough, the best results were obtained when the group was away from all the buttons and wires. In the relaxed setting of Dr. Speeth's home, the observers were treated to the most powerful of displays. The group tilted a chess table with such force that hard hand pressure could not keep it down, and whereas before the table had been weak and creaky, now it felt solid as a rock. So revved-up was "Philip" that when one witness, a 162-pound man, sat on the table's uplifted end, it remained at a sharp-angle tilt. There were observers above, observers below, and not a hint of fraud was found at any time during the demonstration. (Even Franklin himself had, before video cameras, boarded the risen end of one of the tables and tried vainly to press it back to the floor.)

That last display certainly seemed nothing less than a full-scale PK happening. "The whole thing was absolutely amazing — it gave me goose bumps for days," says Speeth. "We had no idea what caused it. All we knew was that there had been no fraud, and it was something that should be vigorously researched. Both Dr. Franklin and I wondered if it might be an energy, a new form of energy. The prospect was overwhelming."

The Toronto group returned to Canada soon afterward for further testing of their own, but this was not to be the last, that Franklin heard of the strange phenomenon of psychokinetic furniture moving. Only months later, in the summer of 1975, Speeth picked up the phone in his Washington, D.C. office, where he was doing some cybernetics research, and listened to a confused newspaper reporter relate an incident in New York's Tioga County in which a group of middle-aged hobbyists — the Thurmond group — had floated a dining room table. The reporter, who had witnessed some of the group's incredible feats after the first wave of publicity on Philip Jordan, heard the research associate excitedly react. "Wow! Total levitation! That could be the break we've needed. You've got to get that to Dr. Franklin! I know he'll be just as excited."

Speeth was right. His colleague at Kent State *was* excited: he set up a date for experiments within a week of hearing about the tables that were being made to float in New York State. But there was one major hitch: again, it was money. Franklin was funding what little psychic research he was doing at the time with two small grants, one from the Parapsychology Foundation and the other from Research Corporation, an institute that funds physicists and chemists. The rest was coming from his own wallet. By the time he heard of the Thurmond group, even those funds were nearly dry and he couldn't afford to fly the whole group down. Though the group had only achieved impressive results while working together, there was no choice but to limit the number of subjects to two; the group certainly could not have afforded the venture themselves, and even if they could have, most of them weren't interested. "We can do this a thousand times, do it for cameras, do it for a full-house at Madison Square Garden, but it still won't prove it to those who don't want to believe," said Betty Thurmond, who was ailing and frankly adverse to traveling. "Sometimes I wonder if it's worth getting tired for."

With Betty, the group's leader, unavailable for study in Franklin's lab, it was decided that the next best subject would be Rose Engle, the young secretary who had a few times wandered away from the Thurmond group to cause paranormal effects on her own. She would represent the rest of the group. The second subject was to be Philip Jordan. Though Jordan didn't belong to the Thurmond levitation group, Franklin was interested in his brand of PK. Together the two subjects arrived at Kent State on 25 July, met there by the excited physicist, for a mere three days of informal tests. In the end Franklin was not to get positive proof of table PK, nor to formulate any new workable theory on the energy behind it. But the occasion was to mark what was perhaps only the second time that a mainstream American scientist had been able to witness the new wave of paranormally-moved tables.

Of course, all along Franklin knew it would be a shot in the dark. Even the English researchers, after constructing every conceivable monitoring device and spending years in constant pursuit of their goal, had failed to turn up any evidence of the paranormal so strong as to pass un-challenged in a scientific journal. At Duke University J.B. Rhine had found the same problems studying table-tiltings, and had finally put his work in PK onto a more modest level. Dr. Rhine had studied a subject's ability to influence the roll of a die, an experiment that allows for all-important statistical evaluation and also, because of its simplicity, greatly diminishes psychological stress.

Again fully aware of the psychological restrictions imposed by a lab, but not wishing merely to repeat Rhine's dice-rolling experiments, Franklin kept to table levitation phenomena as his vehicle for paranormal observation and, despite his natural urge to make a scientific record of events, kept his two new subjects at the sensored, wired tables for only very brief spells. In the first session, for about thirty minutes, Rose Engle and Jordan attempted to move a thirty-five-pound table equipped with sensing buttons that triggered gauges when the legs left the floor and a much larger, circular table that had sensitive strain-gauges on top to measure downward hand pressure. Except for a suggestively mysterious chart pulse at one point, the duo failed in the same way "Philip" had months before. With the strain-gauges, Rose and Jordan were being asked, in effect, to do something they had not done before: to cause PK movement in the table from a distance. When their hands were on the gauges they were about four inches above the heavy table's surface, and they were able to create only slight vibrations in it.

Once the experimentalist approach was shelved and the gauges set aside, there was a dramatic turn in events. When Rose and Jordan, along with some other participants, were allowed to place their hands directly on the large table's surface, the whole table started to slam back and forth in an incredibly violent fashion, even threatening to destroy the electronic equipment set up nearby. Though attempts to capture a total levitation on film failed, Rose drew gasps as she made small tables and wood stools dash wildly around the lab and down the building's shiny corridors, inexplicably tipping, dragging, leaping up and attaching themselves to nearby walls, or for very short spans dangling in the air. Rushing around frantically trying for clear camera shots, Franklin had excitedly muttered, "It looks like the darn thing has been magnetized, like it has a mind of its own."

Jordan's displays were even more baffling, but easy to film. Though a score of observers watched him from every conceivable angle, often walking up to feel his bare arms, no one could figure out how he was making a heavy wood card table rise up on each of its sides in turn, rotate on one leg, tip so that its surface almost touched the lab floor. There was the familiar strong resistance that seemed to be coming up from the floor, and loud groans and knocks that were easily heard at the furthest corners of the room. It didn't even matter that there was often only one other person at the table with him — a stranger picked by Franklin to guard against collaboration on Jordan's part — or that he was asked to place his hand lightly at the center of the table where muscle manipulation would have been nearly impossible. Still the table kept leaping up, bounding before the cameras. When Jordan's hands were wrapped in slippery plastic to further prevent muscular movement, the table still rose easily, nearly totally levitating off the lab floor.

Was something shielding the table from gravity? Was it a case of energy causing paranormal ionization, charging the wood's atoms and causing a magneticlike reaction? As Franklin amusedly watched the antics, he only wished he knew; he only wished there could be enough money to find out.

But while the Engle-Jordan visit didn't offer the opportunity for documentation and theory Franklin so badly needed, it was during their stay that two assumptions widely held in parapsychology — that PK is closely related to ESP and that phenomena like table-lifting are related to psychic metal-bending — were once again tantalizingly underscored. Significantly, Rose scored highly on telepathy experiments, often being able to describe precisely the landscape being concentrated upon by lab assistants who were randomly driving around in a car a mile or two away. Those with PK ability, it seemed clear, were more apt to possess ESP as well. Another brief test held toward the end of the Kent State visit suggested that the energy behind table-lifting was in some way linked to the energy used by psychics like Uri Geller when they bend metal. This was indicated when Dr. Franklin sat with Jordan at a table and took out some thin pieces of nickel titanium alloy which, because they were made in such a way that they'd flex back to their original form after being heated, would allow an accurate, objective assessment on whether they had been bent. Never touching the end he was asked to affect, Jordan held each strip of metal in turn a few inches from the palm of his left hand — where he felt the psi force was strongest — and willed it to bend. It wasn't even necessary to heat the strips to tell if they had been altered: several of the pieces were clearly bent to the naked eye, one by what seemed to be more than five degrees. Metal-bending had also occurred while the "Philip" group were visiting, with participants' rings mysteriously bending out of shape and cutlery in the university's dining area bending by itself after the group had passed through. Thus the informal conclusion was that, yes, there was a common thread running through various forms of PK and other, more "mental" areas of psi.

But that still didn't explain where this strange power came from, what it was or how it was transferred. When Franklin sounded out the two psychics on the matter, their answers were certainly not palatable to science: they linked the power to "spirit forces" and nonmaterial, otherworld entities beyond the human psyche. While they both agreed there was a "power flow" coming from their own beings, the sensitives felt that when they were raising tables they were possibly getting help from invisible friends. They didn't think the ghost of a dead person was lifting the table on its misty back, but Rose Engle suggested that spirits might be changing the "energy constructs" of the rooms in which the table floated and unleashing floods of psi energy that humans could use.

The suggestion seemed to make sense. Both psychics had run across phenomena suggestive of "ghostly" existences, especially Jordan. After all, he had made himself into a spirit medium and he specialized in going into trancelike states to communicate with such. During old-fashioned seances and "energy circles," where people hold hands to generate a "current," Jordan had often assumed a wholly different personality which he claimed to be that of a deceased doctor and had appropriately nicknamed "Doc." When "Doc" was around, Jordan's face contorted in a most unnatural way, his arm movements changed style, and his voice became much lower. While in deep trance, his powers of ESP were incredibly acute.

Nor was "Doc" the only presence Jordan felt around him. In fact, he claimed he was surrounded by an entourage of "guides" who constantly communicated with and through him. When he was away from home, performing on the road, his hometown neighbors, a couple named Mr. and Mrs. Richard Clark, said they often heard a "rumbling around" in his apartment, a phenomenon Jordan associated with his "guides." Once, during a table levitation session at which Jordan was under hypnosis, a newspaper reporter had claimed to see an oval-shaped, mistlike form hovering across the room, and when the psychic was brought out of trance he said it had seemed to be his deceased mother.

This spirit question was nothing new to Franklin. An endless number of mediums had claimed communication with spirits, especially the Spiritualists, who frequently worked with rapping, rising tables as a means of "talking" with the dead. Other, more modern table levitators, most notably Olof Jonsson, the Chicago psychic Edgar Mitchell had employed during his celebrated ESP experiments in space, had also drawn a connection with spiritlike beings. Jonsson, an engineer by trade, had once actually been filmed totally levitating a rather heavy kitchen table for Copenhagen parapsychologists and another for an investigative team from *Paris-Match*. Like Jordan, Jonsson had a history of dealings with spirits, which he said had represented themselves to him, in youth, as fairies and wood sprites. That so many of those who caused PK effects believed in the existence of spirits was disturbing to researchers like Franklin, and certainly too bizarre to research scientifically.

Still, the possibility that it was spirit beings and not human energy that caused paranormal events could not be discounted. There were, after all, disturbing parallels between seance phenomena (where spirits are held responsible for paranormalities) and human PK reactions (held to be caused by living, material beings). Both seemed to overlap in hopelessly complex fashion. For example, in seances those same cool breezes in evidence at table raisings also accompany the arrival of an alleged spirit. Similarly, rappings and violent furniture movements often occur during spirit sessions, and participating mediums often experience the same sense of mental fatigue that PK psychics sometimes encounter. In addition, PK psychics and spirit mediums both employ altered states of consciousness from time to time to abet the production of phenomena. So similar are PK and mediumistic (spirit) phenomena that it seems they both might be different variations of a basic source. And thus, if indeed such things as spirits *do* actually cause seance phenomena, there is a good chance these hypothesized beings are also behind the levitation of tables.

But even if there were spirits, the physicist didn't intend to pursue that end of things. Science was finding it hard enough substantiating the minor aspects of psi without having to consider notions of immaterial beings. Instead, like the majority of other orthodox scientists who entered the psychic realm, Franklin was more comfortable working on the premise that with PK he was dealing with something originating from the human being, perhaps a force field linked to or identical with the spiritual essences and energies so many occultists have written of as pervading all matter and space. It was a plausible notion, and one that seemed susceptible of scientific enquiry. For ages, clairvoyants like Jordan have claimed to see such energies in the form of the human aura, a colorful band of light that enshrouds the body and functions as a counterpart to the physical body, serving, according to psychics, as the medium for psychic phenomena and spirituality. Greek and Indian holy figures were often artistically rendered with such hazy luminosities around their bodies and heads; Christ was painted with an auric halo. Through Kirlian photography, a process developed by Russian electrician Semyon Kirlian in 1939, this spiritlike encompassment has supposedly been captured on film and thus made available for laboratory scrutiny.

In a darkroom in the physics building, Franklin had arranged his own Kirlian device, which consisted of a photographic plate into which was directed high frequency, low amperage electrical current. When a hand was placed against the plate, the resulting photographs were beautiful — and perplexing. They showed explosions of dazzling colors around the human form, eerie glows and miniature galaxies and sparkling flares of blue, violet, gold and green that seemed to dance from the skin, just as the clairvoyants described. In Russia the aura had been determined as "bioplasma," a cross between some form of spiritual energy and a plasmalike construct of excited electrons, protons and other minute particles that spread several feet beyond the body.

That such aureole energies are related to psychic events has never been proven, but there are clues to suggest it. On one occasion when Franklin took Kirlian pictures of Olga Worall, the renowned psychic healer, he found two intriguingly unusual effects. When her hand was at rest — when she wasn't concentrating on healing — the pictures showed a uniquely beautiful purple glow on the inside of her hands. When, soon after, she was photographed during a healing attempt, the "power on," that purple haze left the inside and instead was pictured surrounding the outside of her palm and fingers, as if it had been externalized through her will. Douglas Dean, a Kirlian expert formerly of the Newark College of Engineering, got similar results, finding that at rest there were only slight flares coming from the thumbs of healers but that when they went into a healing state those flares jumped out with fascinating brilliance. Furthermore it has been found that the deeper, slower rhythms of the brain, which are operative when a person is in a state of relaxation or meditation, also seems to have a brightening effect on the aura. Interestingly, Mrs. Engle, Jordan and the other table-movers had all worked with altered states of consciousness and had, during those times, noticed that their auras were brighter.

With so little else to work with, Franklin decided to go with his hunch that auras could be a factor in levitation. He was never able to prove it but he came across some fascinating evidence while making the attempt. On the last day of the experiments he took Jordan to the darkroom for some Kirlian shots of his hands, wrists and arms while he was trying to levitate a small stool. As the stool began swerving and tilting under Jordan's touch, the psychic and an observer claimed to have watched Jordan's aura glowing brighter and brighter as it shrank into the stool's wood. "That will show brighter, just like the healers'," Franklin said excitedly.

Nor was that all. Later in the session, observers were amazed to note small white sparks leaping from Jordan's hands to those of a participant. They seemed to be an electrostatic effect coming from his hands as the Kirlian current flowed through them. Indeed, if that effect was of a paranormal nature, then it could be assumed that Jordan's PK was coming from his energies and not solely from any spirit.

Inconclusive as those test were, they were about as far as anyone could go. Nevertheless, the nature and origins of the psi energy remained uncertain. Electromagnetism? Regular static? Ionization from the fingertips? Magnetism? None of these quite fit the PK bill. "I think it's beyond the realm of known forces, yet at times crosses over to a number of them," says Franklin. "It seems spiritual in nature, a toss between the physical and spiritual perhaps. It's probably something all humans have. If we find out what this influence is — well, the whole field could open up. But first we must tackle this step-by-step before going further and confusing the issue." He said there was no use wondering too much about possible spirits since, after all, not even human PK was yet proven to science. Franklin obviously felt investigators must first work on the premise that PK was the result of human energy before probing more arcane possibilities.*

---

*Franklin was careful never to officially pronounce table-tilting as PK since he had not carried out, due to funding, adequate documentation on an objective level.

It was the intelligent position to take. Clearly, the range of PK reactions had only begun to be defined, and the Kent State tests chiefly served to show how little was known about table levitation and how many questions it posed. For all anyone knew, PK would eventually not only unravel the other perplexities of psi and make it possible to enunciate physical theory relevant to psychic happenings, but would also shed light on the mysteries of spirit seances and the like. For the time being, however, caution was in order.

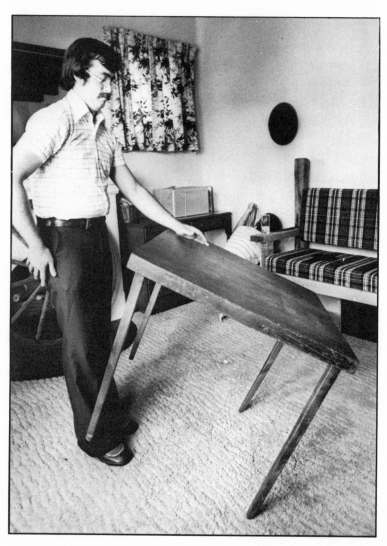

Above, Philip Jordan causes a wood card table to tilt upward on his side while touching its surface very lightly. During such demonstrations, strange rappings usually emanate from the wood and a cool breezelike "ether" is sometimes felt. At right are excerpts from a rather unclear — and yet unique — home movie taken of the Thurmond group before they disbanded. In one sequence, four persons are psychically guiding a 65-pound dining room table up off the floor so high it is threatening the chandelier hanging above. The table remained hovering for about 60 seconds despite just light hand contact with the top of the table. On the far side of the table are the hands of a fifth participant who had to eventually leave the levitation because the table tilted out of reach. The other excerpt shows a female member of the group taking a bucking ride on the table as it tilts upward and dashes around the room. (Photos courtesy of Suzanne Dalton and the Thurmond group).

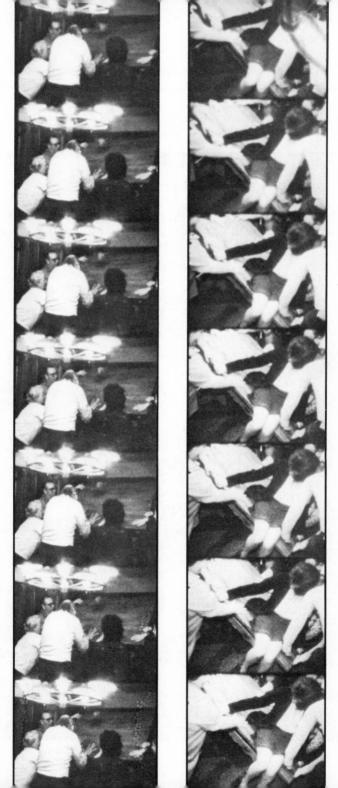

At bottom, K.J. Batcheldor, left, the English clinical psychologist, participates with his table group as another member goes for a ride. Though photographs do little to illustrate the force at work, actual presence at such sessions allows one to feel a tangible upward force that couldn't be caused by muscle movement. The top photo shows members of the Toronto "Philip" group taking a break from their table-rapping sessions. They have created an imaginary ghost to provoke PK phenomena that have been scientifically documented.

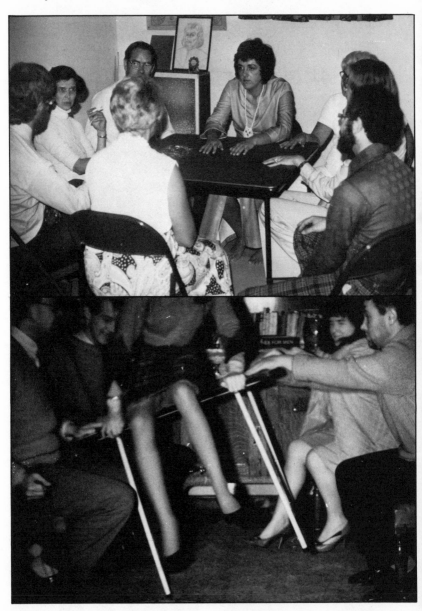

At right is Toronto mathematician-biologist-parapsychologist A.R.G. Owen, one of the world's leading poltergeist experts and director of the "Philip" group. Below, English engineer Colin Brookes-Smith, who through elaborate tests showed psychic force can cause tables to float, poses at one of the many apparati he used to document levitation. This device closely monitored unconscious muscle pressure and sliding movements.

At right is psychologist K.J. Batcheldor of England, whose extensive experimentations with PK showed psychic feats are not necessarily confined to just mediums and psychics but can also be accomplished —impressively — by normal people. His experiment groups were able to totally levitate a variety of objects. Below is one, a metal "trumpet" his group levitated by merely touching the top. (Though the photograph fails to show it, the fingers are resting on top and are not holding it up from inside.) In later experiments, Batcheldor's group got to the awesome point of levitating this trumpet from across the room — through just positive thinking.

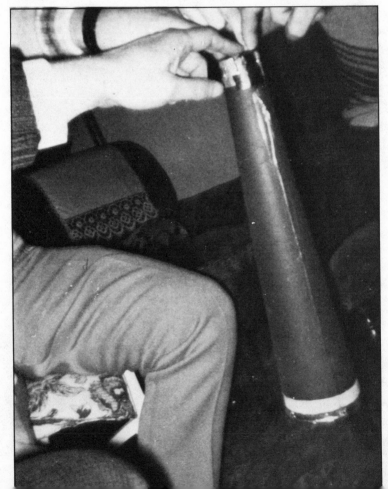

At right is Dr. Wilbur Franklin, a physicist at Kent State University and a metallurgical expert who has amassed perhaps the most impressive evidence to date that Uri Geller is genuine. (Photo by David Tinney). Below is a Kirlian photograph showing the white auras around a person's fingertips. Such photos purportedly show an unknown energy surrounding human beings and perhaps responsible for PK.

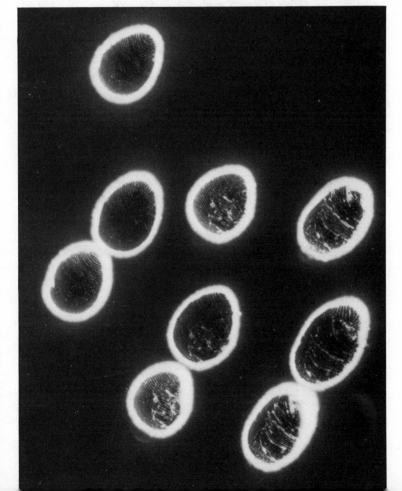

Section Two: Connections, Past and Present

Israeli psychic Uri Geller.

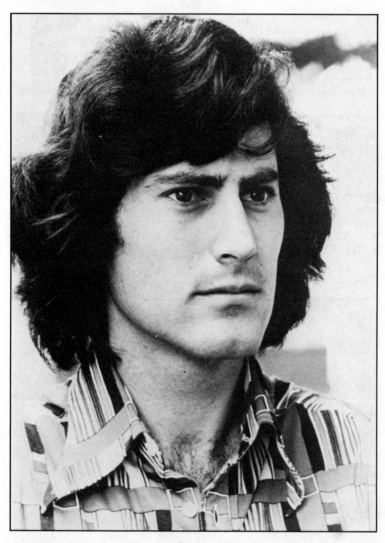

The Poltergeist

"We will say that 'powers' are a class of entities — I mean the powers which make us able to do what we are able, and everything else what it is able."

— *Socrates*

If the current opinions of scientists like K.J. Batcheldor and A.R.G. Owen are correct, if further down the psychic road, which science has as yet barely ventured upon, their hypothesis that table phenomena are caused by human forces and not "spirits" is proved, a vast new world of intellectual discovery could open up. One mystery that might at last be brought into the range of clear understanding is that which concerns ghosts and poltergeists.

In virtually every country, and no matter the race, religion or culture of its people, there have, century after century, been accounts of "haunted" houses where inexplicable raps suddenly erupt, objects fly in from nowhere, furniture seemingly moves of its own volition. In perhaps as many as a third of such cases these strange happenings seem to occur only in the presence of a specific person, who is then sometimes referred to as the focus of a "poltergeist," a word coined in Germany during the Reformation and meaning a noisy spirit or ghoul.

In the past, those afflicted with such were often cast off as demented witches and malefic wizards, and even recently poltergeists have been widely interpreted as signaling demonic possession. Now that's starting to change. Instead of blaming such mysterious activities on spooks and imps that sit in wait behind every mirror, parapsychologists are wondering more and more whether at least some hauntings might not be the result of unconscious PK, what pyschoanalyst Nandor Fodor called "a bundle of projected repressions."

The theory has a nice rational ring to it, especially for those uncomfortable with the frightening notion that nonmaterial beings are behind hauntings. If PK can be performed on a conscious level, parapsychologists ask, then why not at a subconscious or unconscious level? If a person has an overabundance of either psi energy or psi-stimulating frustrations and anxieties, why can't these be released through a psychic event the same way strong emotions can be released through some violent physical action, like banging a fist against the wall?

Indeed the facts themselves seem to point to unconscious PK as the source of some ghosts. A strikingly high percentage of poltergeist cases has been found to occur when the focus (the person who is the special object of the poltergeist's attention) is in a state of strong emotional upheaval, often marked by severe anxiety, hyperventilation, dissociation (or schizophrenia), mania and hysteria. If psychoneurotic problems are not cleared up, it's conceivable that subliminal tension can coil like an overwound spring, eventually unfurling and lashing out in a way that, if enough interior or exterior psi energy is available, causes objects suddenly to move and sounds to break out wherever the poltergeist focus goes. On the supposition that everyone possesses the capacity for PK, it's not unreasonable to think a "blowing off of steam" could take such form.

This seems to be what happened in the case of Dr. Simon Oakley, a Cambridge professor who was arrested in 1718 and jailed for debt. From his dank cell Dr. Oakley often wrote of the strange experiences he had in prison: loud knocks and thumps pounded out in eerie rhythms, chairs mysteriously moved, the bed heaved up and down through no known cause.

A jailhouse phantom? Oakley thought so. According to several accounts, the professor checked out the other prisoners to make sure he wasn't the victim of a hoax and spent a good deal of time testing the gamut of normal explanations — all to no avail. Though there were no investigators back then to thoroughly check for hallucination on the part of those who witnessed the jail phenomena, the case does make the "overwound spring" theory sound plausible. Any man of dignity who suddenly finds himself in the supremely degrading circumstances of prison is likely to seethe with unreleasable anxieties.

There are even more direct links between poltergeists and certain types of psychological strain, one of the more interesting being evidenced in the case of an Englishwoman, Miss H. Power, who lived during the late 1800s. According to her detailed testimony, it happened while she was sitting in her living room one day, boiling inwardly because a book she was reading was rubbing against the grain of her profoundest religious beliefs. Suddenly, while in her frenzied emotional state, her handbag went flying under an end table, rapping and ticking sounds broke out around the room, and a drawing board fell over, all in rapid sequence. In some way her emotions appeared to have externalized PK energy.

That an emotional state like Miss Power's could cause

PK is no longer considered such a farfetched idea, especially in light of Russian experiments with star psychic
Nelya Mikhailova, who has been tested by no less than two
Nobel Prize-winning scientists for her ability to make
glasses, matches, apples and a host of other objects move
through sheer willpower. When Mikhailova was biologi-
cally monitored during PK demonstrations, an interesting
observation was made: it was discovered she was operating
in a state of *controlled rage*.

Because a high number of poltergeist visitations involve
girls between the ages of ten and twenty, parapsychologists
are also looking at the psychological and biological roles
sex maturation may play in them. The writer of the famed
thriller *The Exorcist* had good reason to center the demonic
activity of his story on a teenage girl. Historical accounts
reveal that women are more than twice as vulnerable to
the poltergeist syndrome as men, the odds climbing much
higher for females traversing the frustrations and pains of
puberty. Just about all well-versed students of poltergeists,
most notably the distinguished English parapsychologist
Hereward Carrington, have made the connection between
poltergeists and puberty. "An energy seems to be radiated
from the body in such cases, which induces these phenomena, when the sex energies are blossoming into maturity
within the body," said Carrington, an eclectic scientist who
had studied table levitation and various other areas of the
paraphysical. "It would almost seem as if these energies,
instead of taking their normal course, were externalized
beyond the limits of the body."†

Some of the best documented accounts of poltergeists,
which have come from respected scientists, police officers
and hard-nosed reporters alike, have involved the emo-

†H. Carrington, *The Story of Psychic Science,* (London, 1930), pp. 145-146.

tion-sex factor. A classic example was the "ghost" that started to perform its antics on 22 November 1960 in Sauchie, Scotland, around an eleven-year-old girl named Virginia Campbell. Her case made headlines across Europe mainly because of the clearly objective nature of the evidence it presented. Before the manifestations slowed down, a few weeks after their onset, three physicians, a minister and a schoolteacher had all witnessed stunning paranormal phenomena firsthand; and by the time Cambridge's A.R.G. Owen finished a meticulous investigation of the case, he was both convinced of the poltergeist's authenticity and sure that the strange force was indisputably connected with the young girl.

Two of the main differences between poltergeists and haunted house ghosts concern rapidity of events and length of visitation. Though poltergeists are usually very temporary (whereas ghosts may not leave their haunt for decades), they pack much more action into their visits, are more dynamic and violent. The Sauchie case was no exception. It started with loud, angry-seeming knocking noises that the shy Virginia heard one evening as she was preparing for bed at the home of her thirty-year-old brother, Thomas, who was taking care of her while her parents were attending to business elsewhere, probably in connection with their recent move to the small village. Sitting downstairs when a frightened Virginia first called out that something strange was going on, Mr. Campbell and his wife didn't take it seriously and sent the girl back to bed. But the sounds Virginia had complained about started up a second time, in fact so loudly Mr. and Mrs. Campbell later compared them to the sound of a heavy rubber ball being thrown against the floor. It was as frightening as it was inexplicable; they knew that Virginia was mature for her age and not given to pranks. The noises eventually made their way down the stairs and into the living room in a manner the girl could not have physically caused, and finally died away after, more confused than frightened, she had dropped off to sleep.

The next day around teatime the action got underway again, this time complete with visual effects. As Virginia was sitting in an armchair, a nearby sideboard suddenly leaned about five inches from a wall and then mysteriously moved back. As the Campbells watched they noticed Virginia was in no way touching it.

That night the poltergeist, as it evidently was, came around again at Virginia's bedtime, thumping so loudly it raised the curiosity of the neighbors, who were soon gathering at the scene. At midnight, with those frightening sounds refusing to abate, Mr. Campbell called in the Reverend T.W. Lund, minister of the local Church of Scotland parish. Like the others, Lund was completely taken aback by the phantasmal noises, which were manifesting themselves as rappings in Virginia's wood bedpost by the time he got there. All during the disturbance the youngster lay motionless in the bed, understandably scared, her hands in full view and her body positioned in a way witnesses claimed could not possibly have caused the acoustical commotion. When the investigating minister grabbed the bedpost, he felt a strange vibration that ran through the wood with each tick and rap. Next, the invisible agency jumped to a large, fifty-pound linen chest in the room, rocking it from side to side with what the preacher and others described as a jerky, uneven series of tiltings. Soon such spectacular events had the nervous townsfolk figuring an evil spirit was the cause, and within the next few days an exorcistic ceremony was held. It proved ineffectual.

In the majority of poltergeist cases, the noises are not restricted to any one place but seem to follow a particular person (the focus) wherever he or she may go. This constitutes yet another difference between the poltergeist and most ghosts and lends support to the theory that the former is an energy emanating from the individual, not a discarnate spirit entity. In Virginia's haunting the poltergeist preferred to appear at the Campbell home but was not averse to following her right into Sauchie Primary School, much to the consternation of her teacher, Margaret Stewart, who was totally unfamiliar with Virginia's "affliction" and had had no previous dealings with things occult.

During a silent reading session on 25 November, Miss Stewart's watchful eye was suddenly attracted to Virginia, who was fiddling with the top of her desk when she was supposed to be into her books. It irritated the teacher at first, but upon a closer look at the fidgety youngster she understood why. The desk top was mysteriously lifting up — and the startled girl was trying her best to keep it down. A few minutes later the whole desk levitated, rising about three inches from the floor before settling back down just slightly out of place. The next week there were similar occurrences when Virginia sauntered up to the teacher's desk to ask a question while her classmates were busy writing. Suddenly, inexplicably, Miss Stewart's chalkboard pointer started to vibrate and roll. Then the teacher's heavy desk jerked out of place.

When Virginia was visited by Drs. W.H. Nisbet, William Logan and Sheila Logan at the home of another relative who lived miles away in another town, once again the poltergeist showed it had tagged along. The awed doctors testified that at the end of November they were witness to a wide array of thumping and tapping sounds that erupted around the girl, together with a bizarre noise that sounded as if a muffled saw was at work in a wall.

Finally, around the end of January, and after a few welcome periods of remission, the poltergeist halted its displays, one of·the last involving a dish of Christmas bulbs that moved around the edge of a desk at school as Virginia walked by.

"In my opinion the Sauchie case must be regarded as establishing beyond all reasonable doubt the objective reality of some poltergeist phenomena," said Dr. Owen after checking to make sure that the occurrences could not be explained in terms of hallucination or such factors as atmospheric vibrations and earth tremors. In an award-winning, 436-page report, *Can We Explain the Poltergeist?* (New York, 1964), he stated: "There is no evidence indicating the separate existence of 'the poltergeist' as a discarnate entity. The phenomena are consistent with production by forces emanating from the child or else resident in space·and 'triggered off' by some influence emanating from her."

In the same book, Owen said there was no medical evidence to prove the outbreak was linked to energy from the girl but pointed to the many emotional factors that may have been at the root of the trouble. Virginia, he observed, had been going through a period of acute psychological stress, as was indicated by the fact that she had begun to talk frequently in her sleep. Her shaky emotional state, though showing no signs of fundamental abnormality, was attributable to her family's recent relo-cation to an unfamiliar setting, where her naturally re-served disposition only made things harder for her. Virginia was also bothered by the fact that her parents were often away, and she was, to top it off, going through a period of rapid pubescence. There were even some indications that the poltergeist activities coincided with the girl's quasi-menstrual cycle, a biological condition that makes a young girl especially sensitive. According to Owen, who had created the "Philip" group in Toronto for the specific purpose of seeing if the mind could create a "ghost," it is even conceivable that rapid pubescence could itself provoke a poltergeist event.

America's most renowned poltergeist researcher, William G. Roll, an Oxford educated parapsychologist who heads the Parapsychology Research Foundation in Durham, North Carolina, also cites "a very clear association" between human beings and some types of hauntings. Dr. Roll, who unlike Owen has actually been present during poltergeist occurrences, thinks many outbreaks could be the result of some sudden change in the nervous system. He points out the frequency of epileptic fits in cases he has recorded, as well as indications, often, that the focus's nervous system is impaired. Likewise he has frequently found that distinct emotional, or what he calls parapathological, factors are involved. And the implications of that, with regard to psychology and even philosophy, are far-reaching.

"The poltergeist is a big frontier for science, and a revolutionary one," says Roll, who still carries a heavy accent from his native Sweden. "It shows the relationship between the animate and inanimate world, that there is no real separation. The main interest is that these abnormalities, like anomalies in any other area, will throw light on the normal world and the workings of the mind."

A prime "abnormality" came Roll's way during 1967 in the form of a Cuban refugee named Julio Vasquez. Vasquez, nineteen years old at the time, was the center of a remarkable poltergeist outbreak that left no doubt either that it was paranormal or that certain high-strung individuals attract poltergeist forces.

The scene was a novelty and souvenir shop in Miami, Tropication Arts, Inc., a place crammed with shelves of alligator ashtrays, hand-painted beer mugs, imported cocktail glasses. In December 1966 the firm's owners, Glen Lewis and Alvin Laubheim, were disconcerted to note a sharp rise in the amount of damage taking place. Broken mugs and glasses were found on the floor in unprecedented numbers. The initial inclination was to put it down to extraordinary sloppiness on the part of the shipping clerks, but soon the owners realized they were dealing with something quite different. Employees watched as objects popped off shelves by themselves, often falling not straight down but at impossible angles. Shortly after, an investigating reporter and a local police officer were witness, on separate occasions, to the levitation and flight of highball glasses and beer mugs. It wasn't just a case of shaky shelves, and there was no sign of a prank. Before long, even a magician was called in who, after watching objects move in an alarmingly paranormal manner, joined with others in concluding that this was no trick.

It didn't take a Sherlock Holmes to figure out that the Cuban Vasquez was closely associated with the events. Nothing happened when he wasn't around. When he was, all hell broke loose. Accompanied by Dr. J.G. Pratt of Duke University and assisted by the note-taking of author Susy Smith, Roll was able to log some 224 paranormal incidents, more than seventy occurring after he had gotten to the scene. All of them took place while Julio was on the premises. So active was the Miami poltergeist that Roll was even able to set up semi-controlled experiments during an outbreak, tests that further confirmed that the energy at work was connected with the Cuban.

The parapsychologist set up target and "decoy" objects for the poltergeist to knock over and was able to watch stationary objects move. Whenever Vasquez was out of the room, Roll noted his target objects stayed perfectly still.

The refugee's being behind it all certainly made sense. He was suffering from both physiological and psychological disturbances. Within three months of the onset of the attack, he had come down with measles, chicken pox and mumps. Upon psychological questioning it was found he was experiencing strong negative emotions. His step-mother had just demanded he leave her house, and that seemed to have initiated strong feelings of anxiety and rebellion. So deep were his angers and frustrations that he also displayed suicidal tendencies and was having morbid nightmares. Clearly, the poltergeist seemed a way of releasing some of the tensions. "After many of the objects moved I asked Julio how he felt, what he felt," says Dr. Roll, "and he said the object movements felt good, that with every disturbance it felt like he had been relieved of some weight."

Roll's target observations made him conclude that the force causing the warehouse damage possessed a curvilinear field. The PK energy was not running into an object and bowling it over like a train but appeared to be carrying it along in a falling trajectory until it was itself closed off from its source or became too weak to keep the object in motion. With the help of a mathematician, an engineer and assistants, who accurately charted the objects' rotations and the distances they moved, the parapsychologist determined that the force did not follow the standard inverse law that holds for forms of electromagnetism, which are characterized by a linear field. The poltergeist energy faded *faster,* resembling processes like radioactive decay. The energy also seemed most powerful when Vasquez's back was turned to the objects, which moved in a counterclockwise direction.

While Roll has started to get a feel of the characteristics of the poltergeist energy, the exact origin of such energy remains one of psi's most baffling mysteries. In one case study Roll and his associates were able to pin the source of poltergeist activity to two energy sources near the focus — a couple of psi transmitters apparently physically detached from his body — but were unable to go any further. Were they two "energy bodies" formed as offshoots of the focus's own energy? Or two spirits feeding off him?

Roll is willing to call poltergeist outbreaks instances of RSPK — recurrent spontaneous PK — but usually stops there, unwilling to speculate on whether the PK energy comes just from the living or gets a boost from the no longer living. While parapsychologists generally agree that most poltergeist cases probably do indeed involve human energies, there are cases where either or both material and nonmaterial entities could be involved. The spirit theory can not be disregarded. There are too many poltergeist cases involving voices coming from nowhere, apparitions, a focus going into trance and assuming a "spirit" personality. Also there are often suggestive parallels between the phenomena and the behavior or personalities of the recently dead which make one think the dead are in fact returning. *✳ subjective unc personality*

Those who believe spirits are behind poltergeist incidents could argue that a disembodied being is tapping the overabundant energy of the troubled focus to play games from a perch in the "astral plane." One could, in this context, view poltergeist focuses as the targets of parasitic victimization, as in cases of possession. Or the poltergeist focus can be looked on as an energized person whose newfound powers have opened a hole in our reality and let through entities from other planes.

On the other hand, any researcher who wishes to attribute poltergeist effects to unconscious human PK could argue that, in cases where an apparition is seen, the subconscious, under the impulse of emotional stress, is causing a form of dissociation, splitting the person's energy body into entities that function separately. According to this train of thought, the world is composed of different levels and densities of psi energy. When various brands of energy interact, an energy entity, or "thought form," could develop a psychic life of its own, temporarily haunting the living as a partial personality with limited intelligence. By the terms of this notion, called the "psychic crystallization theory," poltergeists or "ghosts" might be the result of mind blending with a psi substratum. *ssess* Taken to its logical conclusion, the crystallization theory could account for the ghosts of haunted houses not as spirits but as the "thought forms" or memories of a person who has died. Samuel Lentine, a physicist at Rensselaer Polytechnical Institute, has investigated such "thought forms" and claims they can be created by mixing psi energies in the same way you can create certain chemicals by mixing other chemicals. Lentine, blind since childhood, found during meditation that such humanly-created entities can actually exist by themselves for short periods, causing a whirl of energy about them. "It's not exactly the safest of experiments," he says. "The forms sometimes leave your control and, like anything else, can have negative effects. For that reason I've more or less stopped working with them and am not sure one should get into it until we have more knowledge." Shades of alchemy, voodoo — and of course ghosts. *and Tulpas.*

The same thought-form theory may hold for seance phenomena, which in so many ways combine the characteristics of levitational PK, haunted houses and poltergeists. During the typical seance, hands are held together in a procedure that parallels that of a group getting together to levitate a table. Once the energies are flowing, noises erupt, objects may move, and some have claimed even to have seen spirit faces and hands enshrouded in an eerie luminosity. Many times voices are heard and seemingly intelligent messages transmitted to participants from those purportedly "on the other side."

Whether, in a seance situation, the group or medium is merely creating exotic but human PK or is indeed conjuring spirits could be debated till doomsday. Though many a researcher has spent a lifetime combing haunted homes and seances, no one has been able to piece together a theory that would pinpoint the exact relationship between hauntings and the various aspects of psi. Though scientists like UCLA's Thelma Moss have tried, the phenomena of haunted homes and other spiritistic situations seem too capricious to lend themselves to objective review. The same problem is inherent with poltergeists; the phenomena are much too fleeting, and rarely does a poltergeist focus maintain PK abilities after the poltergeist's activity has ceased.

It is for this reason that those who want to find out more about these phantom energies must take a harder look at those psi phenomena that have already been studied in controlled or semicontrolled situations under the heading "human PK." And the reason is not simply that consciously induced PK is repeatable. Curiously, the three phenomena witnessed in levitation displays — cool breezes, noises, levitation itself — have also shown up, in some form, during poltergeist hauntings. So striking are the similarities between the two that it seems both must somehow originate from the same type of energy and that an investigation of one would necessarily shed light on the other. The following miscellany of psi phenomena underlines that supposition.

RAPS, BUMPS AND OTHER NOISES

The most consistent connection between what goes on in both PK table sessions and haunted homes are the rappings, tappings, creaks, groans, knocks and scratching sounds that reverberate in wood. In virtually every case of table phenomena, the first signs of paranormal activity take the form of such noises, just as they do with poltergeists.

In several well-recorded poltergeist outbursts, the onset of the attack has been preceded by ticking and scratching sounds in walls, sometimes described as suggesting fingernails tapping and dragging across the undersurface of the wood. During an attack experienced by two teenage brothers in Glasgow, Scotland in the fall of 1974, slight taps and clawing sounds were clearly heard to come from the bed headboard in their room. As in so many other cases, steadier and louder rapping sounds came next, eventually swelling into loud knocks followed by furniture movements. In many other such cases, like that of the famous 1663 Tidworth spook, cracking sounds and groans have accompanied the scratching and rapping, all four variations strongly reminiscent of the sounds that start up in Philip Jordan's card table.

Then there's the matter of communication with the rappings, a phenomenon prevalent in hundreds of poltergeist reports. When investigators encounter such sounds, many start trying to learn the origin of the disturbance by asking the rappings questions on a one-tap-for-yes, two-for-no basis. Many have claimed that during the most active period of an occurrence they can actually sustain an intelligent "conversation" with whatever agency causes the sounds, at times soliciting answers that go beyond the typical yes-no rapport. A few investigators have reportedly received answers to questions only they themselves could have known. It's as though the agency can read minds. *or that they are the agent.*

Such descriptions match up perfectly with the happenings recorded during "Philip" sessions in Toronto, as well as in cases reported by the likes of Dr. Andrija Puharich, an Ossining, New York parapsychologist who, using a seismographic pick-up and an oscilloscope, found table rappings to be of a definitely paranormal nature. Significantly, not only have Owen and Puharich both reported communication through the rapping code, but they also considered the raps to be a form of human PK. Although a lot of witnesses have trouble imagining how anything but a spirit could answer through such a code, intelligent responses via such taps could be plausibly explained as a combination of ESP and PK — as the result of some person in the room perceiving the answer through telepathy or precognition and unconsciously transforming it into a PK energy pulse that vibrates through the wood.

Over and above the basic similarities between poltergeists and table raps, however, stands an area of significant difference between the two. For one thing, poltergeist raps and knocks are usually louder than table noises. And for another, there seems to be something mischievous if not downright malicious about them.

In the January 6, 1976 issue of the *National Enquirer*, the widely distributed gossip-news tabloid which has taken a keen interest in psi, was a report on a five-week long poltergeist outbreak in east central France that allegedly involved knockings so loud an investigating police officer said it was as if someone was pounding a fist against the wall. Investigators were quoted as saying that the young girl at the center of the activity, identified only as Danièle, could never have produced such bangs without breaking her hand in the process.

According to the report, which sensationalized the incident as the work of the devil, the phenomena started up on 15 September 1975 when Danièle's father, a truck driver, was disturbed out of his slumber by loud, hammer-like blows that eventually turned so noisy they disturbed the sixteen other families living in the apartment complex. While that was going on, Danièle was supposedly choking with coughs and sobs, two characteristics said to indicate demon possession. When police couldn't find an answer after fifteen days of search, a Catholic exorcist, Canon Armand Blancherbarbe, reportedly was successful in halting the phenomena. Of course this successful exorcism cast no light on the exact *origins* of the disturbance.

TABLE AND FURNITURE MOVEMENTS

Just after midnight one cold winter day in 1968, psi investigator William Roll was meandering through a ghost-plagued Kentucky home when the impossible happened before his eyes. As he entered the kitchen, shadowing a twelve-year-old boy he suspected as being the focus of a poltergeist, a kitchen table suddenly rose into the air, off all four legs, rotated a bit, then descended onto surrounding chairs. No one was seen touching it.

The event was extremely rare in that it was one of the first times a respected researcher had witnessed a complete series of heavy furniture movements firsthand, and levitation of such a heavy object is, of course, an exceedingly infrequent occurrence. But in other ways it was quite typical of poltergeist happenings, for in nearly every clearcut poltergeist case furniture of some kind is seen mysteriously to move.

One of the most famous instances of poltergeist table movements was reported on in the prestigious *Atlantic Monthly,* the Boston magazine that prides itself on its sobriety. It happened in 1868 to an eighteen-year-old Irish servant girl named Mary Carrick. According to the detailed account, tables suddenly lifted in her presence and other furniture — chairs, stools — uncannily moved across rugs when she was nearby. The description was fascinatingly similar to recent accounts of PK table-tiltings and levitations, which are often sprinkled with descriptions of tables uncontrollably running and sliding about a room.

The same things were said to occur around a nineteenth century French poltergeist focus named Angelique Cottin. Dining room tables, couches and chairs would literally jump aside as she went by, in a way that led reporters to nickname her "the electric girl." Significantly, Miss Cottin's jumping chairs and tables are strikingly similar to the mysteriously moving chairs described in accounts of the Batcheldor and Brookes-Smith table experiments in England.

LEVITATION

In the more spectacular of hauntings, the strange levitations or flights of anything from pebbles and stones to animals and human beings have been reported, many of the instances being reminiscent of the way psychically-moved tables hover and dash around a room.

In Boston in 1693 there was the powerful poltergeist that afflicted seventeen-year-old Margaret Rule, who many claimed had herself once bodily risen during an attack. In India during the 1930s, newspapers were filled with a similar account, that of Damodar Bapat, a poltergeist focus who reportedly rose into the air in front of several reliable witnesses.

Because levitation is so awesome to see, many who have come across it have immediately labeled it the work of some tremendously powerful and evil beings. Around 1680, English investigators reached such a conclusion in the case of a twenty-one year-old girl who, in the midst of a poltergeist attack, was seen hovering above the floor. The famous Francis Fontaine of France was similarly pronounced "possessed" because of her strange, uncontrollable levitations, as was a group of nuns in Hoorn, Holland, whose purported ability to climb trees with incredible swiftness and to hover in midair was looked upon by residents as proof they were bewitched.

Total levitation in one form or another is a classical trait of a haunting. From parts of the world as far apart as Russia, Spain and Brazil have come accounts of bottles floating, fruitbowls rising before the stunned eyes of onlookers, and small objects flying into rooms as if from another dimension. When science gets around to understanding how PK causes tables to rise, it should be in a position to better explain all those tales of levitational spirits and ghouls.

COOL SENSATIONS

An account of a haunting just doesn't seem complete if there is no mention of clairsentience, especially with respect to the cold spots and icy breezes associated with haunted places and poltergeist victims.

As with table levitation, cool sensations usually preface the major displays of poltergeist phenomena, sometimes appearing simultaneously with rapping sounds. In many cases the frigidity is felt not only by the afflicted focus but by objective witnesses as well, and in a way that often rules out normal causes such as air drafts, air conditioning or psychological suggestion. In many instances the chilly air seems to hover about the limbs of those present, sometimes seeming to be only inches away from the body of one individual, at other times engulfing the whole group. In the case of a haunted house, the coolness is often confined to a specific region of a room and can almost be felt like a sort of invisible curtain. Some parapsychologists have claimed that the differences in temperature in one small area have been as much as twenty-five degrees. A thorough scientific analysis of the matter, however, has been lacking.

Many psychics claim the coolness results from an alteration of energy, a toning down of some "vibrational" rate. They note it as one of the best indicators that something paranormal is in progress whether it be in haunted homes, poltergeist outbursts, PK experiences or circle seances. One au courant parapsychologist named J.T. McMullan, a scientist at Northern Ireland's New University of Ulster, has even suggested that such frigid effects, whatever their origin, may be responsible for some of the energy needed to move objects in PK and poltergeist situations. McMullan points out that paranormally levitating a table weighing 25 kilograms to a height of one meter would require a minimum expenditure of 250 Joules (58.5 calories), far more energy than known sources in a human agency could transmit. Indeed, he says, this is underscored by the minute amounts of energy involved in encephalography. Enough energy to move a table could be made available, however, if one considers the calories that would theoretically be released when the gas in a room was cooled. According to thermodynamic equations, if the air in a room 3 x 4 x 5 meters (60,000 liters) was cooled just 1° centigrade while at a specific heat, the result would be the additional availability of more than 50,000 Joules, enough to raise that 25-kilogram table through some 200 meters. Thus the cold spots could be a key to some of the energy employed in such situations, though the theory can not yet be taken seriously simply because of cases where no coolness prevails. There is also the problem of how all the newly released energy would be controlled.

What is confusing about the phenomenon for those who adhere to the unconscious PK theory is the frequent prevalence of these cool regions in areas unoccupied by humans. Those who offer spiritistic explanations claim the coolness is not always created by human energies but sometimes by the auras of spirit "guides" and other nonphysical entities. One central New York State psychic, Grant Marshall of Johnson City, a former Spiritualist, says chilling breezes even followed him around his home, sending shivers through those present. Though people like Marshall fear they mean some Stygian spirit is on the prowl, scientific investigators, once they get around to researching such things, will probably link them to a flux of energy created by human forces, a view that makes sense in light of the cool sensations often felt during events classified as PK.

There is also the opposite pole of this temperature phenomenon, poltergeist situations that breed intense heat. There are many stories of inexplicable fires breaking out around a focus or leveling a haunted house. Again, there are parallels to other psi situations, cases of PK mediums, for example, causing skin burns or even steam to rise from the body. Theoretically, it makes sense. When the psi agency is causing rapping noises, it's because molecules are being speeded up. If such motions are steadily increased, friction could build to the point of generating an appreciable amount of heat. In the case of the Thurmond group, the dining room table often warmed to a paranormal degree and, according to participants, the heat once or twice even softened the wood's finish to the point where their fingerprints left impressions on its surface.

ELECTRICAL MYSTERIES

For some reason the mystery force behind PK and poltergeists seems able to affect and sometimes even initiate the flow of electricity.

Often in haunted house accounts there are claims of strange illuminations and of electric lights going on and off, as if the psi agency is manifesting itself as a carrier for electrical current or for forces that block electromagnetic flows. In August 1975 the news crew at WGR, a large radio station in Buffalo, New York, got a taste of an electrical anomaly when it investigated a severe poltergeist outbreak centered on a middle-aged woman who, at the time, was undergoing a tense emotional experience. The case, reported on by disc jockey Thomas Donahue, allegedly included instances where an old radio played even though it wasn't plugged into an outlet. The poltergeist had started up the Christmas before, causing holiday lights to flash on and off by themselves through no known means. Significantly, the disturbance also included the knocking about and partial levitation of a dog, and a series of events during which a bouquet of artificial flowers flew from Donahue's hands as he was scouting around the woman's home.

Others have also noticed the electrical aspect of psi. During experiments with the "Philip" table group it was found the imaginary ghost could on occasion cause effects like the flickering of lights. Still others have been known to cause electrical resistances to flow through filaments. A Southern stage performer named the Astonishing Neal, known mainly for his ability to "see" while blindfolded, has caused camera flash cubes to go off through sheer concentration, and a New York Spiritualist, the Reverend Robert Howell, has on several occasions demonstrated the ability to make light bulbs glow while held in his hands. Yet another psychic, John Scudder of Homewood, Illinois, has been witnessed lighting up 300-volt fluorescent tubes, simply by holding them in his bare hands.

This ability to create psi phenomena on command certainly seems to point to an energy that is an integral part of man's being and gives a boost to the unconscious PK theory. While convinced spiritists could say that what PK psychics are doing is tapping the energy of separate, invisible beings, the energies appear more directly associated with the minds of the living. Even spiritists might admit that the psyche could conceivably split into two or more entities to cause poltergeist PK, or that, as others have ventured, man's mental apparatus could be viewed as part of a world soul, a nonlocalized intelligence that flows through all matter and may perhaps be disrupted by an especially energized mind which can then cause distant psi reactions. Then there's the relatively simple idea that unconscious thought might influence a human force field (or aura) into causing the kind of proximate environmental disturbances wrought by the poltergeist.

Buoyed by recent findings in the area of PK, parapsychologists, who as scientists obviously prefer natural to supernatural explanations, will surely turn toward the former as a way of approaching the unapproachable, a way of applying reason to those things that go bump in the night. We can't state categorically that there aren't spirits out there, and maybe, as some researchers believe, the poltergeist focus causes eerie disturbances by becoming a temporary spirit medium. That, however, is something that won't be known until science examines the minds of some of those who are "haunted" and explores phenomena like brain waves in the light of its findings.

Music Of The Mind

"The stuff of the world is mind stuff."

— *Eddington's epigram*

"Welcome," says the slogan, "to the next phase of human evolution on this planet."

To those whose eyes first glance at that apocalyptic sentence, printed on the inside cover of pamphlets for Silva Mind Control, it may sound more than a trifle sensationalistic, another pretentious catchphrase of the psychochic, another gimmick riding the revolutionary tide of inner space. Constantly bombarded with hard sells on biofeedback and alpha training, mantra chanting and the scores of other quickie meditation methods bordering on the miraculous, a wary public has developed a justified skepticism.

Strangely enough, however, the Silva slogan may actually have a basis in fact. Though science has only started to understand the complexities of mind and how it is affected by processes like meditation, some researchers already speculate that manipulation of altered states of consciousness will not only increase man's control over his body and brain, as the alpha-sellers assert, but may also breed a swarm of newfound psychics. The reason: it's at the deeper, "evolved" levels of mind that many psi events like thought transference and mind-moving-matter often take place.

It all has to do with brain waves, those electrical patterns recorded through the electroencephalograph (EEG) and categorized, according to frequency, as either in the beta, alpha, theta or delta ranges. When electrodes are pasted to a person's scalp and fed into the EEG, the resultant peaks and valleys that appear on the machine's graph paper can fairly accurately gauge what kind of energy is going through his head. If it's a normal awake level of brain activity that's being monitored, a form of consciousness that incorporates concentration, tension and problem-solving intellection, the predominant wave will be beta, at 13 to 26 cycles per second. If the subject is in a state of deep, nondreaming sleep, the EEG will swing over to the opposite end of the spectrum, where delta rhythms of 0 to 4 cycles will be recorded.

In between the extreme levels of beta and delta are the more moderate states of theta and alpha. It is toward these two states, and especially alpha, that people on the consciousness circuit are aiming.

Something rather mystifying happens when the brain dips to these levels. While beta reality centers on the physical world of sight, sound, smell, touch and taste, the deeper ranges are more spiritual in nature. Alpha, at about 8 to 13 cycles, is typified by alert, free-flowing relaxation, an uncommonly pleasant state in which time and space seem nonexistent. The theta frequency, generally figured to be from 4 to 8 cycles, is associated with creativity, extreme drowsiness and dream states. Down in this world of semiconscious reverie, vivid images may float by. Suddenly the mind seems to expand in a way unimagined before. No longer does one need the forgetful phase of sleep to transcend reality, nor LSD to shoot the mind at the stars. And no longer does one have to be a medium to pick up thoughts from the outside.

"The discovery that human intelligence can learn to function with awareness at alpha and theta frequencies will go down as the greatest discovery of man," claims Jose Silva, the plump, smiling founder of the Mind Control International method. "This discovery is sure to change our conceptions of mind, psychology, psychiatry, psychoanalysis, hypnoanalysis and of the subconscious. Students functioning at these altered frequencies seem to have more energy, and it is here that one perceives information he didn't even know he had access to and becomes full of energy."

Silva, a middle-aged Mexican American who with his neat business suit and his hair cropped to bristles hardly looks the part of either guru or sorcerer, first delved into matters of the mind in 1944. Though he had no formal training in the field, he tackled the intricacies of psychology as a hobby after becoming fascinated with the army's psychological testing of inductees, and his interest grew rapidly. An electronics engineer by trade, he continued his extracurricular mind venture until it included parapsychology, hypnosis and brain waves, which had been discovered in man just twenty years before.

While operating his own electronics firm in Laredo, Texas, Silva began working with his children to see if some of those strange intellectual disciplines he had been reading about in Eastern philosophy could enhance their intellectual capabilities. Sure enough, their schoolwork soon showed remarkable improvement; their memories grew stronger, their intuition sharper, their attitudes at once more perceptive and more relaxed. But that wasn't all. Often during his sessions with them, he noticed they would answer questions even *before* he asked them — as if they were using the legendary "sixth sense."

Spurred on by this success, he spent years refining his techniques. Then, in 1966, at the urging of some college students, he developed a program intended for the general public and gave his first paid course in Amarillo. Less than ten years later, more than 400,000 people in seventeen different countries had caught onto his forty-eight-hour, no-machines method of reaching alpha and supposedly even lower frequencies, its popularity exceeded only by Transcendental Meditation (TM) in an era when meditation suddenly became a household word.

Silva's course involves a plethora of consciousness techniques, culled from just about everyone who ever entered the inner space arena and designed to accomplish the same ends as those attained by Eastern methods. There are countdown exercises, hand anesthesia, autosuggestions á la Norman Vincent Peale and Emile Coue.

First, students are taken through what is best described as progressive physical relaxation, then guided toward a mood of alpha relaxation; finally they master techniques that enable them to lower consciousness at will. By the end of the course, graduates have supposedly learned to "project" their minds into human bodies for psychic healing purposes, into animate and inanimate matter like plants and metal, and even onto other planets and galaxies. They are taught to construct imaginary laboratories in their minds where they can charge up their new psychic forces and construct mental screens on which "self-actualizing" images can be projected and clairvoyant messages can be received. While the eventual purpose behind all these wild-sounding methods is to help the psyche solve mundane problems to do with bad habits, illness, tension, poor memory and so on, what sets it apart from any other organized technique is the last session of the course, when students, allegedly functioning at alpha frequency, are gathered together for what amounts to a mind-reading session. Grouped in foursomes with classmates they didn't know before the course began, students are given the names, ages and addresses of persons who are in some way ailing but whose ailments are not known to them or the instructor. Then the students take turns "going to level" and, via the mental screen, exactly diagnosing each ill.

Though there have been no scientifically conclusive studies of Silva's "clairvoyants," his method, which has already found some imitators, does seem to produce genuine psi effects in some cases. Students see symbolic forms that suggest specific illnesses, black clouds around the subject's chest, for instance, which suggest heart trouble, or they know what areas of the body the subjects are afflicted in because they feel sensations in those areas of their own bodies. In some informal tests success rates as high as seventy percent were recorded. Many Silva "graduates" report that after learning the meditation-hypnosis technique they have often astounded themselves by "knowing" who is on the phone as soon as it rings, or what someone is about to say. All this is supposedly accomplished by ordinary people with no obvious psychic talent. While many scientists refuse to endorse the Silva method as a road to ESP, since it's been so little studied and couldn't anyway claim alpha frequencies as the unquestionable cause of its successes (complex psychological factors might be involved), nearly everyone who has acquainted himself with Silva's techniques thinks there's *something* to them.

That such reportedly phenomenal results could derive from the descent to alpha should not be too surprising. At lowered frequencies, with mental static and internal dialogue tuned down or out, it seems logical to assume that a person would be more receptive of a telepathic or clairvoyant energy. If, as many scientists theorize, such ESP messages are always bombarding the human psyche but go unnoticed, alert mental control, together with a housecleaning of beta "noise," might clear the way for paranormal communication.

In Russia, where parapsychological research has gone beyond "if" to the "whys" and "hows," the link between alpha waves and psi ability has been expounded by several of the nation's top scientists, some of whom have actually gone on record as relating lowered consciousness to telepathic success. It has been found that the best ESP subjects are those with an above average alpha rhythm. While the majority of American parapsychologists are careful to avoid any such conclusions, some researchers, like Dr. Charles Honorton of the Maimonides Medical Center in New York City, have connected ESP to relaxed emotional states, mild dissociation and passivity — words that perfectly describe the alpha state. That researchers like Dr. Honorton and Stanley Krippner have also found prophetic and telephathic messages running through dreams, when the psyche is roving at very deep levels, seems to confirm the connection.

"It's extremely important for the receiver to be in a peaceful state," says Dr. Lutsia Pavlova, an electrophysiologist at Russia's Leningrad University. "Man is normally incapable of maintaining this state of 'operative rest' for an extremely long time, free of involuntary motion and distracting thoughts."†

Like Silva, Russians believe suggestology and meditation can reduce mental activity and simultaneously rev up psychic power. In fact the Russians, guided by Dr. Pavlova and Dr. Genady Sergeyev, a military mathematician, have gone so far as to link ESP with brain wave patterns scientifically, through the use of the EEG. In the late 1960s the two scientists electronically monitored the brain reactions of telepathic senders and receivers, and they found that when the sender was beaming out a thought or image to the target subject, almost simultaneously the brain waves of the receiver showed drastic fluctuations, lighting up with each transmission. Other researchers found that if subjects were on roughly the same EEG wavelength, success in telepathy increased dramatically.

Because of the similarities between ESP and PK, including the possibility that both employ the same type of psi energy medium, students of parapsychology often wonder whether the same mental conditions necessary for thought transference also govern the mind's ability to affect matter psychically. Their question: if ESP is more prevalent at lowered brain frequencies, do alpha and theta also serve to induce PK?

If you ask Jose Silva, one of the few American researchers seriously to consider this important query, the answer is yes.

At his Laredo laboratories during 1975, Silva had test subjects drop down into alpha to attempt, among other things, to get a PK reaction with water. For fifteen minutes at a time people in altered mental states were set

---

† Sheila Ostrander and Lynn Schroeder, *Psychic Discoveries Behind the Iron Curtain* (New York 1971), p. 24.

before glasses of ordinary tap water and told to "mentally treat" the liquid, projecting their minds in the manner taught in his course. Next he went out and picked a few tomatoes, placing some of them in untreated, control glasses of water. and the others in the "prepared" water.

The result, according to Silva, was that tomatoes in the "treated" water lasted five times as long as those plopped into the control glasses.

Similar results were tabulated at Canada's McGill University a few years before, where it was found that a "healer" could cause a slight spreading between the hydrogen and oxygen atoms of water through sheer willpower. There, water that had been psychically charged with "positive thoughts" was found inexplicably to enhance the growth of barley plants.

"Something has apparently been altered to cause this effect," says Silva. "But we really don't know what it is. Right now all we can go by is what's happening."

This insightful researcher does have some tentative notions about the mechanics behind the phenomena, however. Silva found, for instance, that the best results in water experiments occurred when the brain wave frequency was hovering around 10 cycles a second. That, he thinks, could be an essential clue. He points out the existence of energy waves located in the cavity between the earth belt and the ionosphere and how some of the fields there also vibrate at 10 cycles a second. Maybe, he says, the mind is tapping that geophysical energy during a psi display, as if it were coinciding with a "life-giving" frequency that physically exists.

What Silva seems to be talking about are the "Schumann," or ELF ("extremely low frequency") waves, electromagnetic waveguide fields that serve as spherical condensers around the earth. If such ELF fields do play a role in psi, the age-old problems of how ESP can instantly travel great distances around the globe, of why telepathy often fluctuates with geomagnetic conditions, and of how psychic energy can penetrate nearly any physical material would seem to be partially solved by the very nature of such atmospheric energy.

Researchers at Laurentian University's Psychophysiology Laboratory are starting to work along these same lines. Laurentian's Dr. Michael Persinger, a psychologist with a solid background in geophysics, notes that when the cortical voltage of the brain oscillates at certain frequencies that coincide with those of earth fields, an energy interaction could very well take place.

"When one talks about energy exchanges with psi phenomena I have to stop and note the fact that, so far as we know, there is no biogenic energy that can travel from the body to such unusual distances as occur in telepathic behavior," Dr. Persinger told a conference of top Canadian scientists in 1975. "Consequently, assuming the phenomena are real, the energy involved with ostensible telepathic events must be coming from somewhere else. Our first investigation indicated that perhaps the energy is coming from the medium. Alternatively, however, we suggest there is a resonance taking place between the brain and the ambient ELF fields."[†]

What of PK?

"Well," says the Canadian, "if indeed the environment can be tapped for ELF, then an energy exchange will result. We have made some calculations which indicate that if a person has some peculiarity in his brain so that its power peaked at 7.8 (cycles or Hz.), then he would have

---

[†] Michael Persinger, "ELF Waves and ESP," *New Horizons* special report: proceedings of the first Canadian conference on psychokinesis (Toronto 1975), pp. 233-235.

the possibility of absorbing ELF wave energy and using it in his body. Now there's a great amount of energy available in the earth's spherical waveguide. According to the present theory, individuals who have brain energy output peaking at both 7.8 and 14.5 Hz. should be the ones with exceptional PK powers."†

Other scientists have likewise found lowered frequencies, especially theta brain waves, to be linked to PK ability. Russians discovered their EEGs recording strong theta brain waves when famed PK medium Nelya Mikhailova was moving objects mentally, and Germans have found the same. At Toronto's Society for Psychical Research, the preliminary work of Dr. Joel Whitton, a physician and close associate of A.R.G. Owen, has added further credence to those claims. He discovered that when the brain of English psychic Matthew Manning was monitored during metal-bending feats, ramp-shaped forms on the EEG graph pointed to a predominant theta production. (Then, to top it off, there's the link between hauntings and theta. When a subject is observed under a prolonged state of theta, psychologists describe his behavior as characterized by selfishness, impatience, intolerance and childishness — all perfect adjectives for a poltergeist.) Whether this is because lowered frequencies allow the psyche to release more energy or just because a toned-down brain wave frequency is more conducive to positive thinking is not known.

If the connection between brain waves and PK is conclusively proven, the theory that everyone has PK potential gets a major fillip. Many scientists believe that unusual theta brain wave readings (like those of Manning) and PK aptitude originate in the area of the thalamus, the brain's

† Ibid.

sensory clearing house and emotion transmitter, or in the old "animal brain" (das Ur Gehrin), a region thought by most psychologists to have long ago grown defunct. If there's any truth in that, then the development of psychic ability may one day be looked upon not so much as an advanced stage in "evolution," but rather a rediscovery of an ability we all once possessed — and somehow lost.

Mysteries Of The East

"The soul, in other words, has created a world for you to inhabit, to change — a complete sphere of activity in which new developments and indeed new forms of consciousness can emerge."

— *Jane Roberts' "Seth"*

The hiatus between East and West goes far beyond the basic governmental, religious and philosophical factors commonly underscored. It encompasses, in so many ways, not just curious differences in life style and concepts of God, but also the very way deep thinkers on both sides look upon mind and its relationship with physical reality. While the West is just now finding fascination with the spectacular things that can happen when consciousness is altered or when a good psychic performs, to the fakirs, yogics and shamans who have roamed certain parts of the East for thousands of years man's mental power over matter has been just an everyday fact of life.

There can be few better examples of the East's time-honored grip on psi than Hidy Ochiai, a sinewy five-foot-two-inch, 125-pound mystery from Japan whose brilliance in karate has caused experts and ranking karate organizations to label him perhaps the best martial arts adept in the United States today. An international grand kata champion with a seventh degree black belt in the unique art of Washin Ryu karate, Ochiai draws wonderment for more than just his masterful handling of kata and his total physical control. There are also the remarkable energies he has learned to create through his mind. Indeed, for the last ten years he has been baffling national TV audiences in the United States with demonstrations which appear, under close review, to be PK manifestations invoked through Zen meditation.

Before many major karate competitions, the thirty-five-year-old native of Tokyo struts out on the mats and calmly sets down a thin wood board that sprouts dozens of sharp, jaggedly aligned nails. Breathing deeply and throwing himself into a semi-trance, he stares into nothingness as he tenses the muscles through his back and stomach and quickly lays down on the torture board.

Next, assistants rush up with 250 pounds worth of concrete blocks, placing them on his bare abdomen. Then comes a man with a ten-pound sledgehammer. The crowd chants a countdown to zero. And crash! the blocks are reduced to small, sharp splinters that fly across his chest. Ochiai springs up from the board and does a victorious flip through the air to show he's alright. Incredibly, neither on his back nor on the front of his body are there any hints of injury.

At first the demonstration may strike skeptics as just another nailboard stunt carried out by one of the scores of magicians who have in recent years taken to laying on gimmicked boards as a crowd pleaser. Plainly, however, Ochiai is not a magician and neither his board nor body is secretly rigged. Unlike the vast majority of those who have imitated the feat, he does not use blunt, closely placed spikes or any form of physical protection. When observers wander up close to feel for themselves whether the spikes are for real, all it takes is a gentle brush of the fingers to puncture the skin to the point of drawing specks of blood.

"Three physicists and two mathematicians from New York University, they tried to figure it out — you know, measuring the weight of bricks, the sledge, the pressure on each nail," says Ochiai, his years of severe training under Zen monks seeming to shine out of his intense dark eyes. "Finally, they tell me it's impossible, given all the circumstances. Then, see, they ask, 'Mr. Ochiai, how do you do it?' And I tell them I have learned to control my whole existence, everything, by my mind, to know the world as one. But they don't understand. They don't know about C'hi."

Most people in the West don't. C'hi, or Ki (pronounced "key"), is the term Easterners, going back centuries, have used to describe a mysterious, primordial "force" they claim is a sort of counterpart body, an energy that concentrates around human systems and flows throughout the cosmos. The descriptions are reminiscent of what has often been called the human aura. Around the body, sages and seers have claimed, is an energy structure that flows like invisible electromagnetic rivers to hundreds of points on the body, acting like a paraphysical version of the lymph and blood networks. From this mysterious idea evolved acupuncture, the method whereby thin needles are directed into various "energy areas" to correct imbalances in the purportedly prephysical field. As far back as 3000 B.C. ancient Taoists spoke of the forces of Yang and Yin, supposedly the positive and negative "currents" that flow through and around us all, causing illness when they are out of balance. While the acupuncture points were long visible only to those with extrasensory sight, they have now purportedly shown up as bright flares in electrophotographic pictures of the human body, and correspond neatly with the exact locations described by mystics hundreds of years ago. The Yang and Yin may be part of an invisible organizing field, one that will some day be captured on photographic film and viewed in its entirety.

When the C'hi currents are properly tapped through meditation, they supposedly can be used to shield the body miraculously against physical harm. Interestingly, when Ochiai is in the deepest region of his altered state, a level he descends to just before the sledgehammer hurtles down, his students have on occasion claimed to see what looks like a hazy light flowing around his spine. Though several informal attempts to document that alleged phenomenon have failed, those who have encountered it could, in a clairvoyant flash, have actually gotten a glimpse of that power Ochiai so often speaks of conjuring.

"It's body and mind," says Ochiai casually. "People here [in the United States] sometimes forget the mind part. I find everywhere I go those who ask why I do it, why I get on the nail thing. It's because I feel my job, what my master told me, was to get a message across, to talk about the psyche. But they don't listen. After I started doing the demonstration in this country, many tried also to do it. But they can't, so many of them lie between chairs or fake the nails, right? They put the cement blocks on the stomach, make it so the bricks absorb the shock, you know? It's not the real thing. They never even think of C'hi, so they keep being amazed how I do it. Who knows? Maybe I'm floating or something."

The thought of paranormal forces at work is intriguing not only as a start in explaining the nailboard phenomenon, but likewise in rationalizing the other seemingly impossible demonstrations that Ochiai and other karate adepts perform. For example, Ochiai can also split unusually thick wood boards with what seems just a light tap of the wrist and has allowed students actually to crush cement blocks on his unprotected head. The usual physical explanations of what might be happening seem inadequate. Says Ochiai, "When I was on TV once, the actor, Telly Savalas, commented that I must have strong bones, thick skin. That's not all it is. It's not the total answer for where it comes from, what does these things."

When Ochiai jumps in the air to give a karate kick, another strange characteristic is observable. His body, compacted of tough, bulging muscles, jumps lithely several feet above the floor, then slowly — a little *too* slowly — descends. The best way to describe the downward pattern is that it resembles a levitated table suddenly making its way back to the floor. In Russia, a number of parapsychologists have wondered whether the great ballet artist Nijinsky employed the same touch of levitational power when he made his feather-soft descents. The dancer, along with yogics who perform horizontal jumps, seemed briefly able to defy the earth's gravity. (Significantly, Nijinsky had a record of psi experiences like automatic writing and astral projection and had studied the yoga methods of altering consciousness.)

One of the most baffling feats Ochiai performs is what he calls the "apple split." Quite simply, what he does is place a piece of the fruit on the neck of a brave karate student, have himself totally blindfolded, and then slice the apple with a razor-sharp Samurai sword without so much as nicking the skin of the volunteer. While imitators have cheapened the feat by doing the same thing with large objects like watermelons, which easily fall into two pieces when a sword cuts but part way through, Ochiai's apples don't fall apart until the sword has cut through every piece of the skin. How does he "see" it while blindfolded? How can he judge to such a precise degree? Again, the paranormal: Ochiai claims that his mental energies flow with the sword, with the apple, as if he has "become one" with the outside world. He also "feels" the person's energy, he says, so he knows exactly how to position his volunteers.

Given Ochiai's background, which reads like something out of Carlos Castaneda, these mystical explanations have weight. Trained with meditating Zen monks since age six and a devoted student of the respected master Kanabe Saito, a sake-drinking sensei whose great knowledge of the world and the mind was both practical and arcane, Ochiai learned things in his long apprenticeship that he still can't explain logically. In his youth, whenever confronted with a difficult question, he was taught not to ask for a solution to it verbally but to meditate for an answer. The correct answer, he says, often came in moments of thetalike trance, as if Saito were standing at the center of his inner psyche revealing it.

Ochiai also seems to touch on the psychic when he describes the injuries he sustained during vicious fighting competitions in the temple, where he was once required to remain alone for twenty-five days and nights while twelve black belts roamed the building ready to attack him at any moment. When he broke bones during such tests no doctor was ever called in to administer a splint. He was simply told to heal his own wounds mentally through an ancient visualization technique. In his mind he would "see" his injured areas and try to heal them by intense concentration. Time after time, apparently, it worked.

"Once I was sliced here with a Samurai sword," says Ochiai, pointing to a foot-long scar extending from his right side to his stomach. "But in my mind, while still fighting, I told the pain to go. The blood, it stopped. It's hard to explain. That sort of thing is illegal here, that kind of test, and even in Japan now the law has stopped those fights. But there was really nothing to fear as long as you acted as Saito said, like a warrior. Nothing can touch you then." Not even white-hot coals, which some of Ochiai's fellow adepts prefer to nailboards for displays of their incredible talents.

The C'hi can even protect against intense heat, according to Eastern meditators. Again, when yogics and fakirs go strolling barefoot across twenty-five-foot beds of 2,500-degree coals, something along the lines of protective PK seems to become activated. In 1935 England got its first look at that mystery when parapsychological researcher Harry Price imported a Kashmiri Indian named Kuda Bux to show some university professors how mind can overcome matter, however severe the circumstances. After a lengthy period of oblation and prayer — the Kashmiri equivalent of meditation — Bux casually strutted across coals so hot they could literally have melted steel. The scientists were agape: his feet showed no signs of skin burns after nearly five seconds of contact with the coals.

Just as baffling in recent years has been Vernon Craig, a Wooster, Ohio businessman who claims to be the first American to have fully duplicated the feats of Hindu fakirs. His mind-boggling feats have won the forty-three-year-old at least two endurance records in the Guinness Book of World Records.

Craig, a practitioner of yoga, is much like Ochiai; he can somehow wind himself down so that he feels no pain and can protect his muscles and skin under what would otherwise be mutilating circumstances. Those who saw him on the Mike Douglas Show in 1974 watched him set one of his records when he allowed four obese volunteers whose weight totaled 1,142 pounds to stand on his stomach and chest while he lay on a bed of sharp nails. Another time he lay on the nailboard for twenty-five hours and twenty minutes, a feat one magacian, Howard Bamman, past president of the International Brotherhood of Magicians, proclaimed as inexplicable in stage terms. That same protective capacity is in force when Craig slowly walks across twenty-foot-long beds of hot coals without developing so much as a blister, something that has stunned scientists who have seen it.

Craig, an experienced student of Hindu mysticism, finds psi the easiest explanation. "I nearly leave my body when I do these things — I step away and watch," he says. "That way there's no pain. It has to be something that comes from the mind. How else can you physically explain it? When I've crossed the coals I've had electrodes to my head, and though I'm in an awake state the doctors say they find a lot of theta and delta waves. That must have something to do with it, because what else is left?"

Travelers' logs from Pakistan, India, the region of the Tungus people of Siberia, Honolulu, New Zealand, Africa and other places are filled with similar marvels. What the West is calling PK today seems to correspond to feats performed elsewhere from time immemorial. Adepts of various disciplines have been reported able to swim in ice-cold water for extended periods of time, handle red-hot fires, and even dip their hands in boiling oil, all with no harmful physical consequences. In preparation they take in deep, rhythmic breaths of air during a process called, in the case of India, pranayama, believing this in some way evokes supernormal powers.

All this is consonant with Hindu mysticism, which says in effect that mysterious energies are centered at seven bodily locations called chakras. The various chakras are located near the spine, in the area of the kidneys, pancreas, thymus, thyroids, pituitary and pineal glands (the one near the pineal gland is thought by some to be the mystical "third eye"). Though they seem to correspond to some of the endocrine glands, the chakras are looked upon as above and beyond the physical, areas that determine the spiritual nature of man. Clairvoyants have described these centers, which in some ways seem analogous to the Seven Seals written about in the Book of Revelation, as whirling vortices of beautiful colors. So respected are such energies for their awesome powers that the central area of the force, the Muladhara chakra, located near the base of the spine, was visualized by ancient Hindus as a sleeping serpent they called the "Kundalini." In karate, forces like the kundalini are visualized as lightning bolts that can be invoked by means of spiritual disciplines.

According to the famed Paramhansa Yogananda, perhaps the most accomplished Eastern ascetic ever to lecture in the West, India has produced masters able to levitate their own bodies. Some believe that specific ability is connected with the Anahat chakra, the energy spot that Indian legend says allows one to "walk on air." When Yogananda, the first great Indian master to settle in the United States, was asked to explain the phenomenon, he cryptically answered, "A yogi's body loses its grossness after use of certain pranayamas. Then it will levitate or hop about like a leaping frog. Even saints who do not practice formal yoga have been known to levitate during a state of intense devotion to God."† What pranayama is remains a mystery, but there does seem to be a connection between air and psi events. At UCLA, Dr. Thelma Moss,

---

† Paramhansa Yogananda, *Autobiography of a Yogi,* (Self-Realization Fellowship, Los Angeles: 1946), p. 71.

the Kirlian aura researcher, has secured electrophotographs that purport actually to show a mysterious pattern
on film that could be the manifestation of the surrounding energies described in Eastern literature. On film it
comes across as intricate designs, "forests" and weird
squiggly shapes one would not expect to see in a scientific
photograph of the air. Perhaps it is connected in some way
with what Christians call the Holy Spirit, and with what
has been called "orgone" and "od."

After years of research into shamanism and yoga,
parapsychologist Andrija Puharich decided an invisible
envelope he has called psi plasma is formed around the
human body. Deep meditation, what yogics call samadhi,
could dramatically effect the psi plasma, according to
Dr. Puharich. In certain mental states, he says, the psi
energy could decrease the gravitational constant of an
object, shielding it from the gravity of the earth. In theory
such a field might be related to an all-encompassing
"mental field" that serves as the medium for phenomena
like ESP.

Whatever the force, it can obviously work away from
the body. When English journalist Paul Brunton came
back from a trip to India in the 1920s, readers were
amazed to find in his written account of it the case of a
fakir who could move metal bars across a table through
mental powers. Likewise Swami Rama, founder of the
national Himalayan Insitute and known mainly for his
spectacular ability to make his own heart stop (a feat he
has performed in front of scientists), has also demonstrated an ability to cause a fourteen-inch needle, mounted
horizontally on a vertical shaft five feet away, to rotate
paranormally. It happens after he enters a deepened state
of mind.

But while the tales of Eastern mysteries are many,

reliable documentation is scanty. Sadly, most ascetics are not the least bit interested in proving powers they have long regarded as just an integral aspect of existence. Their main concern is attainment of the divine, and some Easterners even feel psychic events can divert a mystic from that path. Though the old-time sages of the East were very probably the first to master psi ability on a large scale, their utter lack of concern for historical records or for rudimentary scientific evidence has sent parapsychologists who wish to know more about phenomena like PK and its role in history to those places where at least some semblance of records has been kept.

Psychic Phenomena Through The Ages

"History has been a picture; she is about to become a mirror."
— *Victor Hugo*

Perhaps it can all be traced back to the very dawn of civilization, back to those footsteps in time mysteriously imprinted in the sands of the Nile. Though no one can really say when PK phenomena were first experienced, some recent researchers claim paranormal abilities like levitation were first employed between 60,000 and 2,500 B.C. in that arcane land of the first magicians, Egypt, where in the middle of the nation stand those fantastic structures we call pyramids.

The pyramids always generate awe, especially when visiting eyes fall upon the most spectacular of them: the Great Pyramid of Gizeh (or Cheops). What we know is that the structure pokes out of the sandy horizon just west of Cairo as a monstrous hulk of rough-hewn limestone and granite, a pile of meticulously placed stone that stands 77 yards higher than the towers of Notre Dame cathedral in Paris, occupies an astounding 82.111 million cubic feet of open space, and is built with some 6.5 million tons of stone. What we don't know is how such an ancient people constructed it.

Many scholars, acting on the speculations of old historians like Herodotus, would have us believe the 480-foot monument was constructed by more than 100,000 slaves who, at the whim of Pharoah Khufu, dragged blocks each weighing between two and 16 tons all the way from the Turah quarries and set them in place with such incredible precision that one can pass a penknife along their sides without finding where some of them join. The method, claim conventional historians, involved between 30 and 600 years of back-breaking labor as the Egyptians yanked the blocks up ramps and onto elaborate scaffolds by means of mere ropes and pulleys.

Somehow, we are told, this enduring wonder of the world was erected to the demi-millimeter so that its facades aligned perfectly with the four cardinal points of the compass even though compasses weren't around back then. Using primitive methods, ancient architects constructed the pyramid so that its angles dissect the continents and oceans into equal parts, its base divided by twice its height gives us the celebrated figure π (3.1416) and its height corresponds in precise proportion to the distance between the earth and the sun (a distance unknown to man until the early part of this century).

To some it doesn't make sense. How could Egypt's economy, dependent on the narrow Nile delta, support so many laborers at one time? How were the blocks cut from the quarry without sophisticated equipment? How could a country of scorching sun and endless sand produce all the wood needed for the rollers, which would quickly wear out under the tonnage of the transported stone? Where did all the rope come from? And, most importantly, how were those gigantic blocks hoisted so high?

The questions might continue, but to a mounting number of researchers the conventional answers don't apply. With an increasingly searching eye, modern man is wondering how far primitive methods could account for a structure that even the most sophisticated constructional engineering couldn't readily duplicate today.

Similar enigmas involving the transportation of tremendously heavy blocks of stone are to be encountered elsewhere on the globe. There are ruins in Guatemala and Yucatan that bear a striking resemblance to the Egyptian pyramids, and the pyramid field of Teotihuacan where each structure is aligned with the stars. There's Cholula, where a pyramid larger than Cheops was built around the time of Christ.

On Easter Island hundreds of ancient statues stand as a testament to the incompleteness of modern knowledge, some of them weighing more than 40 tons and rising 60 feet. How gigantic stone hats weighing 10 tons each were transported over the island's rugged terrain, then hoisted upon the statues' heads, are questions that must be filed "unsolved." The same questions arise with regard to other places like Stonehenge, England, and Sacsahuaman, Peru. How were those blocks carried over long distances and set precisely in place?

In the forefront of new ideas on the subject, at least among psychics, is the supposition that some unknown energy force raised the heavy stones of yesteryear, perhaps through a large-scale manifestation of PK, a levitational ability lost through the ages. One of the subscribers to such a theory was the famous psychic Edgar Cayce, the "sleeping prophet" whose phenomenal ability to diagnose and cure illnesses has been the subject of a spate of books. Cayce was once asked during a trance how the Great Pyramid was built. The stone, replied Cayce, was simply floated, a proposal seconded by G. Patrick Flanagan, a California physicist who has extensively studied the pyramid's structure. In light of the record we have of Egyptian psychic healing, Cayce's answer is intriguing.*

Others, following the sometimes dubious lead of Erich Von Däniken, the radical-thinking author of *Chariots of the Gods?*, conjecture that beings from outer space swooped down to help humans erect these ancient structures, possibly by channeling some psychokineticlike power into the stone. Surprisingly, the notion was not lost on space scientists, who are beginning to lend ear to such extraterrestrial talk.

"Ideas of how the ancient, mysterious pyramids may have been built using levitation have presented evidence to support the theory that extraterrestrial beings have used PK (psychokinesis) on earth and have taught earthmen how to use psychokinesis,"† writes scientist Adrian Clark, who was associated with the Skylab project. He goes on to quote Rameses III, who spoke of working with large stones and "giving them life" while building a large wall. Is levitation what Lenormand was referring to in *Chaldean Magic* when he wrote that in olden times "the priest of On, by means of sounds, caused high winds to blow and thus raised into the air huge stones to build their temples which a thousand men could not have lifted"? We can only guess.

Far less speculative than the levitation-of-stone hypothesis is the first mystical use of a table. It followed centuries after the last block was placed on Cheops and featured, of

---

* In *The Probability of the Impossible* (New York: 1974), Dr. Thelma Moss of UCLA writes on p. 68: "In Egypt, before the Christian era, ancient rock carvings show healers treating patients by placing one hand on the stomach, the other on the back."

† Adrian Clark, *Psycho-Kinesis* (West Nyack, N.Y.: 1973), p. 83.

all people, a man who stands as a pioneer of modern geometry — and whose main interest history has largely ignored.

The man is Pythagoras, whom our texts refer to as a great mathematician-philosopher, disregarding his extensive psychic pursuits. He was born around 570 B.C., in a remarkable era that also produced Buddha and Confucius, and was schooled in both the mysteries of Samos and Egypt and the secrets of the mystical Persian magi. Lauded for his famed "Pythagorean theorem" and early dubbed a genius, Pythagoras drew far less academic applause for his other theories, which included one about the mystical connotations of numbers and symbols.

After laying out an array of model numerals and symbols in his yard, Pythagoras, assisted by disciple Philolaus, would often set up a small table he had constructed and place wheels under its legs. By putting their hands lightly on top of the table, the two men found it would move in a surprisingly powerful fashion, many times going straight to numbers and symbols scattered about the yard. Like those who work with the table rappings, Pythagoras would ask the table a question and interpret its movements in accordance with a code. No doubt contemporary scholars were outraged by his explanation of these movements: he said they probably spelled out messages "from another world."

Another student of the Persian magi, Simon Magus, followed centuries later with much more impressive displays of what was probably PK. Magus, referred to in the Acts of the Apostles as the "miracle worker of Samaria," presented a spectacular example of levitation and mystical ability, and, like Pythagoras, he paid the price.

According to several lengthy accounts, Magus was able to cause both his own body and surrounding furniture to float through the air, a feat he supposedly learned from Egyptian priests. If old accounts are reliable, Magus was one of the best psychics of all time. He could make heavy furniture levitate without touching it and make incredibly loud noises erupt from wood. Because of these "abilities," many considered Magus a practitioner of black magic, a suspicion aggravated by his founding of a small sect of gnostics. Around the same time, a neoplatonist philosopher named Iamblichus was astounding people with his feats of levitation, but he never captured the limelight as Magus did, probably because he was more discreet. When the apostle Peter heard of Magus's stunts, he hurried along to challenge the Samaritan to a battle of power. Historical accounts claim Magus readily levitated himself in front of the apostle, who considered the psychic potently malefic. Peter quickly knelt down as Magus hovered above him, and eventually brought him down with a well-aimed prayer.

If Peter was upset with Magus mainly because of his paranormal feats (he also had a reputation for taking bribes), then maybe he was forgetting the great acts of his own master, Jesus Christ, who was second to none when it came to levitation. Or at least so the Bible says.

The first possible allusion to Christ's powers of self-levitation occurs in Matthew 4:56, where he meets Satan on top of a temple. The Angel of Darkness had quite plainly challenged Jesus to prove himself by drifting down to a crowd gathered on the streets below. Said Satan: "If thou art the Son of God, throw thyself down."

The Nazarene declined to exhibit psychic powers on that occasion, but later on he supplied direct evidence of them. His disciples were once crossing the sea on the way to Bethsaida, according to the famous tale, when suddenly the sky unleashed a vicious storm that threatened their small boat. Noticing their peril from the mountain on which he was meditating, Jesus hurriedly set out to help, walking on water to get to them (Matt. 14: 22-23; John 6: 16-21; Mark 6: 45-52) and guide them out of danger. Further levitational inferences, however vague, can be drawn from the accounts of his ascension after death, a miracle supposedly also accomplished by Elijah and Moses. Further evidence of Jesus's strange powers is to be found in the biblical accounts of his miraculously curing the sick, in a manner that today we might call psychic healing. Then there was his halo, the visible sign of his inner radiance. Many parapsychologists are wondering if this was similar to what we are now seeing in pictures of the human aura, if that luminous atmosphere around Christ was some kind of force field. Speculation has also focused on Rembrandt paintings that depict Jesus dematerializing in front of thunderstruck disciples. Whether Christ possessed powers akin to those exhibited by current psychics seems to be a question that it's now appropriate to ask.

Followers of Christ kept up with the tradition of miracle-working and many of them are known to history as levitators. One of the earliest levitators was Elisha, who supposedly made an axe float on water (II Kings 6: 4-6). Less than a century later, around 980 B.C., pseudo-history has it that the sick St. Dunstan, archbishop of Canterbury, levitated into the air bed and all just before his death. And then there was St. Teresa of Avila, who claimed in her autobiography that she had often levitated during spiritual rapture, sometimes floating with such power that other nuns had trouble getting her down.

The list of religious levitators is long: Mary Magdalen Postel; St. John Mary Baptist Vianney; the Curé of Ars; Mère du Bourg, founder of the Sisters of the Saviours (of the Blessed Virgin); Sister Mary Jesus Crucified; St.

Bernard Ptolomei; St. Philip Benitas; St. Albert of Sicily; St. Dominic, founder of the Dominican order; St. Ignatius Loyola; St. Philip Neri; St. James of Illyricum; and a Dominican priest allegedly seen rising above the ship *Newfoundland* minutes before it sank.

The most startling and best documented occurrences of religious levitation concern a strange monk, St. Joseph of Copertino, who amazed everyone from laborers to the Pope with his ability to somehow float high as the treetops during moments of ecstasy.

Born Giuseppe Desa in Apulia, Italy, in 1603, he was known as a rather feebleminded, fanatic youth, often given to starving and flagellating himself to show his piety. In his early twenties he was accepted as a Franciscan priest and soon after became known as "the flying monk."

Desa often entered into deep prayer, an altered state of consciousness that blocked out the rest of the world and led to a mood of exaltation. While in one such state he suddenly lifted off the floor of a cathedral and landed amidst the candles on the altar. (It's interesting to note he did not receive burns, a fact reminiscent of the shamans and yogis who have psychically developed protection against similar harms.)

As the levitations continued, word of the incredible monk spread through the whole of Europe and brought hundreds to his door to witness the amazing stunts. Among the baffled onlookers were Johann Friedrick, duke of Brunswick; the German philosopher Leibnitz; the daughter of Charles Emmanuel I; the duke of Medina de Rio-Seca; Princess Marie of Savoy; Cardinal Fachinetti; the Grand Admiral of Castile; and dozens of priests and doctors.

Some of the monk's many supposed feats are spectacular indeed, like his flying to the top of a tree while reveling in the beauty of a spring sky, his startling workmen by levitating a cross they were struggling to erect, his healing a demented nobleman by grabbing his hair and levitating him. He seemed able to turn his power on at will once he'd discovered it, a fact that greatly displeased his superiors.

When things seemed to be getting out of hand, Desa was sent before Pope Urban XIII, whereupon, seized with joy, he floated in midair until ordered down. A worried Pope sent him to Assisi to calm down, but the levitations continued. When he died in 1663, his corpse supposedly levitated for fifteen minutes, doctors struggling all the while to get it down. He was rapidly canonized — for doing the very same thing that had caused others to be branded as demonic.

Another well-documented case is that of a poor monk named Martin de Porres, who was born in 1579. The New Catholic Encyclopedia reports that this Peruvian monk, who had to overcome the stigma of being illegitimate, could perform psychic healing and astral projections, as well as being able to levitate off the ground. He too was canonized — eventually.

De Porres was once said to have ascended four yards off the ground through no visible means, a feat witnessed by two priests and a startled surgeon while they were standing in front of the Dominican Monastery of the Most Holy Rosary in Lima. (This feat was duplicated by Joseph Benedict Cotolengo who made news a few decades later when he mysteriously levitated on a street after giving thanks to God for saving him from a robbery attempt.) Though it took some time for the religious hierarchy to embrace a man whose father was a Spanish nobleman and whose mother was black, by the beginning of this century de Porres's exploits had convinced it that he was worthy of beatification.

Similar feats of self-levitation, or volitation, run through every magico-religious system on record, and are particularly common among the shamans, yogics, lamas and fakirs who have wandered Asia for the last 3,000 years. Their accomplishments, achieved through meditation and ascetic self-control, are depicted in Stone Age drawings and have left their influence on a wide range of spiritual disciplines, most notably those of Hinduism and Zen. In Tungus seances, self-levitation was attributed to master "bird-souls" who were said to be able to float feet upward despite the weight of sixty-pound costumes they wore during their rituals. In India, self-levitation has been for centuries claimed as an ability of yogics who work themselves into a psychic frenzy through breathing exercises (pranayama) before defying gravity. (Such events have allegedly been filmed by Dr. Georgi Lozanov, head of Bulgaria's Institute of Suggestology and Parapsychology). In ancient China the two daughters of Emperor Yao supposedly practiced self-levitation; in Greece, religious mystery men of the countryside were reported able to make themselves float. In Western folklore stories of sorcerers and witches who could conjure their powers to propel them from the ground are commonplace.

The most widespread manifestations of levitation and other forms of PK occurred during the second half of the nineteenth century when a flurry of mediumistic spiritualism swept across America and Europe. It left in its wake a public craze for levitation and table-tilting that infected not only intellectuals like Carl Jung, Robert Browning and Victor Hugo, but even such august personages as Queen Victoria and Abraham Lincoln. In the span of just a few years, more than twenty thousand people proclaimed themselves psychic in America alone, some of them producing phenomena so impressive that science felt compelled to take its first real step toward studying PK.

The whirlwind started innocently one raw March night in 1848 as John Fox and his family put the lights out in their small, box-shaped tenant house in New York's Wayne County and snuggled in for the night. Suddenly, there was an eruption of strange sounds, rapping noises, which started fast, fizzled out, then started up again. Not given to superstition, John figured it was the wind, or maybe a neighbor hammering tacks. But his wife Margaret was more apprehensive: her family had a history of strange events, and she worried that the home was haunted. She rustled out of bed to check on her two youngest children, Kate, fourteen, and Margaret, twelve, and hurried back to bed as the sounds continued into the night.

To the family's distress, the noises continued throughout the next few months, during which time two important factors were discovered. One was that the raps "responded" to questions by a code of one-rap-for-yes, two-for-no. The other was that the noises occurred only when either the two girls or their older married sister Leah were present.

Since A.D. 1,000 similar rappings had been associated with what has been called the "poltergeist effect," but nothing on record had matched the frequency with which the Fox raps were heard — nearly every day. It wasn't long before the sisters were the talk of the state, for everywhere they went, the rappings followed. In a short while furniture started to move in their presence. And the manifestations grew in frequency.

Naturally some claimed the raps were the work of a

cabal of spirits, some that they were the product of fraud; some said they indicated a power unknowingly possessed by the young girls. In an attempt to find out, crowds gathered several times at Rochester's Corinthian Hall to hear the noises, hundreds of people later leaving in awe. As public interest swelled to the proportions of a furor, the state's intellectual and political leaders, spurred on by complaints from nearly every quarter, finally took action. On 14 November 1848, the first of three committees was sent in to investigate.

The investigation units, which included names like Frederick Whittlesey, vicechancellor of the state, and A.P. Hascall, a former congressman, exercised every conceivable precaution against fraud. The girls were stripped and checked for gimmicks. Doctors placed stethoscopes on their necks to check for ventriloquism. Cloth was tied around their knees to prevent them cracking their joints. Their hands and feet were held.

But it made no difference. The noises, the loud rappings and knocking sounds, continued to come from surrounding walls, some witnesses claiming that rapping sections seemed to swell under their hands. Though pressed to find just the opposite, the committee ruled there was no *earthly* way such phenomena could be produced. As reported in the *New York Weekly Tribune* of 8 December 1849, the working hypothesis was that there had to be "something manifesting an intelligence beyond persons visible."

The debate grew. While one segment of the population demanded that the girls be exposed as frauds or cast out as satanic, hundreds of people were inspired to produce phenomena like theirs. Startled by the number of those claiming they too could cause paranormal raps, the School of Medicine in Buffalo, in 1851, formed its own committee to look into the matter. Its members quickly concluded that the rappings were made by clandestine movements in the girls' knee joints. However, because they failed to explain how the noises actually came from walls a good distance away from the sisters or why their knees showed no signs of injury from such abuse, their report was lightly regarded, even by the diehard skeptics; and soon after the Buffalo debacle, the girls received a vote of confidence from none other than New York newspaperman Horace Greeley, who after a personal investigation reported that the phenomena probably were supernormal.

By the time the girls were in their twenties, their following had increased to such an extent that they were able to organize an actual religion based on psychic phenomena, which they called "Spiritualism,"* as well as collect large sums of cash as famed professional mediums. Indeed, their displays had caught the fancy not only of lonely widows but of the politicos of Capitol Hill. Suddenly, there were rap-seances everywhere.

A strange thing happened when, for convenience on the road, the girls started carrying wood tables on their tours with which to create raps when a wall wasn't available. They were surprised to find that when they placed their hands on the tops of the tables, these would often lift, causing a table-leg to tap against the floor and sometimes completely levitate and move around the room. It wasn't long before table-tilting and levitation began to edge out rappings as the popular occult preoccupation of the day.

This spread even faster in Europe than in the States.

*In this work, the religion "Spiritualism" is differentiated from "spiritualism," the latter meaning about the same thing but not connotating a formal religion.

After an American journalist, Mary Hayden, put on a
table-tilting stunt during a trip to England in 1852, an
invitation for "tea and table-tilting" became the standard
social lure for an afternoon of entertainment. Prince
Albert and Queen Victoria were not above the new fun,
though they took it to be more than just a game. Like
others, they would ask questions and wait for a table leg to
tap out a coded reply, all the while accompanying the table
as it moved weirdly around the room. Though it certainly
seemed possible that the tiltings might be the result of
unconscious muscle tension, that didn't deter the spread
of the craze. Hokey stores started to market special "spirit
tables"; Ouija boards became popular.

The era became the Age of the Medium, its psychic
phenomena so varied and numerous they defy synopsis.
Fantastic — and often fraudulent — reports filtered in
from all over. "Mediums" were soon materializing "spirits"
out of dark closets, getting "ghosts" to play the accordian
or guitar, conjuring mysterious hands out of thin air,
causing bells to ring without touching them. In Ohio,
farmer Jonathan Koons drew large crowds as he went into
trance and allowed "spirits" to talk through him, play
tambourines and levitate handkerchiefs. It all started to
sound not only ridiculous but more than a touch insane.

Still, so impressive were some accounts that the U.S.
Congress considered a bill to study spiritualistic phenomena on a scientific level. By December 1862, the psychic
craze was in full bloom, even, as previously noted, reaching the White House, where purported "spirit" phenomena were witnessed firsthand by President Lincoln. At one
White House seance held in the Red Parlor a medium
went into a trance for the First Family, producing a
barrage of phenomena that were climaxed by her going
over to a large piano and somehow causing it to move up

and down as she played a tune. It remained in the air, apparently, even with the President sitting on top.

Nor was the psychic boom confined to just occasional displays in front of the famous, the rich, the powerful. In France, Victor Hugo, author of *Les Misèrables* and *The Hunchback of Notre Dame,* began by scoffing at things like table-tilting, but as he watched all sorts of seemingly psychic occurrences involving simple pieces of furniture, his interest grew. It even got to the point where he'd let table raps make some of his everyday decisions. Hugo believed one could communicate with "higher forces" through a tapping table; even greats of the past like Dante, Aesop and Shakespeare would come through, he claimed.

As word of such noteworthy conversions to the new "faith" circulated, other writers like William Butler Yeats and Henry Holt started to investigate the psychic realm for themselves, searching out seances, table sessions and mediums who could present some form of "proof." Yeats saw furniture shift inexplicably, drawers fly across the room, pictures move on walls while mediums were in trance. Holt watched a student touch the side of a night-stand at New Haven's General Russell's School and make it float.

Spiritualism interested a young psychology student from Basel, Switzerland, who watched with both amusement and skepticism as relatives held rapping and table-tipping sessions while he was home on vacation in 1899. Surely, he thought, the tiltings were only muscle movement, the rappings some kind of subconscious, perhaps even tele-pathic, release.

But then a curious thing happened, one he couldn't quite account for logically. It started with a loud snap from the kitchen, as if someone had barged in and fired a shot. When the brilliant young student entered the room, there was his grandmother's old walnut dining room table, mysteriously split apart.

Two weeks later a similar noise burst from the sideboard. Inside the boy noticed a displaced bread knife, its blade unaccountably snapped in several places. From then on the youth, Carl Jung, put more stock in what he had previously considered merely ridiculous.

While Jung later devoted a great deal of time to probing ESP and synchronicity (the study of the paths of coincidence) most other scientists would have nothing to do with such "madness." The new occultism bothered the famous English physicist Michael Faraday so much that, scientific shotgun in hand, he made it his business to totally discredit it, with table-tilting as his prime target.

Moved with a passion reminiscent of Harry Houdini's hatred of mediums, Faraday stepped center stage in 1853 and announced he would expose table-tilting as unadulterated hokum. His game plan was simple: he constructed a table that had two tops with small rollers in between, and with it prepared to show that table-tilting was a purely natural phenomenon. The upper surface was supposed to move in an easily discernible manner if muscle pressure was applied during a tilting session. After only a few tests, none conducted with the most famous of the day's levitating psychics, Faraday quickly drew the conclusion that all the table movements were entirely the result of muscle pressure, a position temporarily adopted by another table researcher, Camille Flammarion. A short while after the experiments, Faraday reportedly had occasion to witness a man completely levitating off the floor while sitting in a chair. He decided to ignore this event, it seems, and keep his skepticism intact.

A more formidable critic was Houdini, conjuror of

conjurors, who mounted a broad attack on the religion of Spiritualism (despite the fact that he was deeply attracted to it) that was to last more than thirty years. He had apparently convinced himself that occult "happenings" were all trickery. Although accounts of Houdini's investigations have been so exaggerated as to make it hard to sort out fact from fiction, we do know that he exposed many mediums who were frauds — and severely damaged some who were not.

By the time the amazing escapologist entered the act, Spiritualism had indeed taken a turn for the phony: mediums throughout the world were taking pictures that allegedly showed spirits, spooks were writing answers on slate boards in dark seance rooms, phantom faces were materializing out of the air. For some odd reason Houdini felt very threatened by it all.

Admittedly, he was able to shoot down some of the more flagrant frauds, often setting them up for a trap and then, as in the case of the famous New York City "medium" Henry Slade, getting them to sign appropriately humiliating confessions. Having caught Slade in some obvious sleight-of-hand, Houdini forced him to admit that he used fakery in getting furniture to move (the "medium" had lifted a chair with his foot) and in obtaining "spirit" messages via a chalkboard, stunts that were drawing hundreds of old ladies to his door while incurring the wrath of the scientific community.

Houdini disposed of other psychic conmen in the same manner, forcing them out of business. But when he came up against phenomena he couldn't logically explain, he resorted to personal attacks, even in the case of some seemingly authentic mediums who were not out to make money. There was something paranoid about his obsession to "expose" the occult. He could not, for example, stand hearing about the most spectacular and credible mediums of the day, such as D.D. Home, whose levitations were the talk of Europe. Obviously unable to duplicate Home's feats, Houdini contented himself with attacking Home's personality, using spurious information to do so.

He quite rightly attacked one famous psychic from Italy for her frauds, but he failed to mention incidents in which the effects she produced seemed genuine. Like Faraday, Houdini dwelled on the easy-to-explain, skillfully avoiding the rest. He said table-tipping was the result of objects hidden up sleeves, trick dresses that latched onto table legs, or balancing acts performed with confederates. Quite conveniently, he forgot to mention the total levitations some of his aides witnessed in daylight, never going on record as duplicating them himself under the same circumstances. It was fraud because it *had* to be fraud, was his thinking.

In like manner Houdini found easy explanations for table-rapping sounds: they were accomplished, he said, by knocking knees, tapping fingernails, or trick gadgets. He ignored the real mysteries, such as taps that sounded out across a room a good distance from the medium. He was, in fact, engaged in a private crusade, and he relied on his international reputation to carry him to victory.

But despite his gross shortcomings as an investigator, Houdini performed a real public service in putting a stop to tricksters who were creating "spirits" out of cheesecloth and "ESP messages" out of their own imaginations. Flim-flams were everywhere on the loose and comprised a good number of the thousands who had declared themselves mediumistic. In Buffalo, two brothers named Davenport — Ira and William — had been reaping piles of cash from their fake seances, establishing a national reputation when they were accomplishing nothing more than amateur sleight-of-hand. It was like the UFO situation: once one person spots a strange light at night, thousands do. And where there is money to be made, an outburst of "interest" is certain. Serious scientific inquiry into the psychic realm was nearly strangled at birth as a result.

But behind the chicanery was a solid core of phenomena that could not easily be dismissed; authentic-sounding reports consistently arrived from every corner. From England was word of a psychic named Colin Evans, who reportedly levitated himself in North London's Rochester Square in front of a score of witnessess. In Barr, Massachusetts, news of a Mrs. S.F. Cheney, who could self-levitate, was quickly circulated. At the same time Polish researchers were claiming to have found a psychic, Stanislawa Tomczyk, who made objects ascend without touching them. In Germany scientists had concluded there must be some invisible fluid throughout the universe, for they could not otherwise explain the levitations witnessed in their labs.

The move toward seriously studying psychic phenomena was advanced by the surge in popularity of the Reverend Stainton Moses, founder of the English Spiritual Church, and Madame Blavatsky, who intrigued everyone with a variety of psychic displays, especially loud rappings. Both formed schools of thought that helped offset the surge of disbelief provoked by the likes of Faraday.

Madame Blavatsky, a tough-talking, heavyset Russian, often pictured at a seance table with a cigarette dangling from her lips, won over thousands with her convincing mediumship and her comprehensive knowledge of mysticism, which she used to meld occult experiences from around the world into the metaphysical doctrine of Theosophy. The Reverend Moses, joining Madame Blavatsky in refining spiritualistic techniques, contributed to the cause by his readiness to submit his paranormal abilities to scientific examination. He was known mainly for his ability to levitate objects without physical contact, a feat favorably reported on in 1873 by psychic researcher E.W. Cox.

One of Moses's most ardent supporters was author Sir Arthur Conan Doyle, who at one time was a good friend of Houdini. Doyle tested Moses on a number of occasions, later reporting that on 2 June 1872, he and Moses were sitting at a six-by-nine-foot mahogany table when inexplicable things began to happen. He said the table, set on a thick Turkish rug in his own home, rapped out violently, swayed, and then moved without being physically touched. According to Doyle, the table slid seven inches while he and the medium were feet away, then completely levitated three inches off the floor.

Meanwhile, in another part of Europe, a remarkable orphan girl named Eusapia Palladino was soon causing academic tremors with her displays of table levitation, attracting the attention of scores of scientific investigators who had trouble figuring out whether she was a spectacular psychic or a crude fraud. (She was probably a little of both.)

Eusapia got her start when a Naples family that had taken her in started playing with spirit seances and rapping sessions. Before long the family discovered that this semiliterate, wayward girl possessed more than her share of preternatural powers. Loud knocks broke out around her; furniture strangely moved.

As a young girl she amazed everyone with her ability to make tables of all sizes mysteriously leap off floors, feats that were quickly noticed by England's Cesare Lombroso, a famed psychic researcher who had had his fill of fraudulent table-tippers and had set out to prove her a fake. But after investigating her, Lombroso had a quick change of heart, becoming convinced she was genuine. Once news of his conviction spread, swarms of other scientists followed suit. The Society for Psychical Research, formed in London around 1882 to study spiritualistic phenomena, promptly sent a team of experienced skeptical investigators to check out the volatile Italian medium. The committee included notables like Everard Fielding, son of the Earl of Denbigh, W.W. Baggally, an arch disbeliever in levitation, and Hereward Carrington, a well-known parapsychologist who, as an accomplished magician, had gained an illustrious reputation for exposing scores of frauds.

The investigators set up a small room as their lab, taking strong precautions against possible fraud. In the room they placed a small cabinet with a variety of objects in it which would thus be well out of Eusapia's reach during PK testing, yet in easy view should an attempt be made to manipulate them surreptitiously. In the middle of the room they put a heavy table.

Eleven sessions conducted with the medium yielded the following tally: 470 instances of "paranormal phenomena," 305 of them occurring while Eusapia's arms and legs were directly watched and held; 34 times when the table turned and levitated completely; 59 times when curtains hanging from the cabinet bulged inexplicably; 28 times when objects moved around inside the cabinet; 41 miscellaneous movements (couch and chair motions, etc.) which could not be logically explained.

Eusapia sent the investigators back to England convinced she wasn't a fraud.

But Eusapia Palladino didn't come as "clean" on other occasions, or so her critics claim. When her talents weren't on form, she was reportedly inclined to help them along by subjecting the table to a little kicking or elbowing. At

Cambridge University she amazed a group of scientists with a number of levitations, but later on, when the "forces" ebbed, she started flagrantly shoving objects around; she was afraid that the witnesses would go away disappointed and bring an end to her fame.

When she visited Columbia University for informal testing, Eusapia was able to produce scant results with a table and the observing scientists, wary of what had happened in England, dared not give her full credit for what she *had* produced. When Everard Fielding investigated her a second time, he found her using some fraudulent means which she was quick to blame on "spirits" who were taking over her body to discredit her while she was in trance. Though scientists like Charles Richet, a Nobel Prize winner, figured there was some unknown energy behind her displays, her need always to perform spectacularly brought a permanent taint to her name.

Fortunately for the cause of serious investigation, such problems were never encountered with the most famous and spectacular psychic of them all, a man by the name of Daniel Douglas Home. He too encountered skepticism at first. But despite ardent efforts to discredit him, his levitations, performed through several decades, never gave the slightest hint of fraud.

Home had been born in Scotland in 1833 but reared in the United States, where he stayed until leaving for England at twenty-two, at a time when, thanks to frauds, crackpots and the Civil War, parapsychological interest in the States was declining. Home's ability had first been noticed through the clairvoyant images he was privy to as a boy and rapping noises that he heard throughout adolescence. After a prominent theologian named George Bush and a Harvard professor, David A. Wells, proclaimed their belief that he was a gifted psychic, the young man was off and running toward a sensational career as a psychic. At one time or another his feats were to strike awe into Napolean III, Czar Alexander II and the English aristocracy, among countless others.

Home's feats thrilled the nineteenth century imagination. He made a grand piano float while Countess Orsini of Italy was playing it. He levitated dining room tables for the rulers of France. He made musical instruments float around inside a cage while he stood across the room.

In December 1868, Home pulled off what has to be considered the most spectacular single levitation of the century. At London's Ashley House, demonstrating for a group that included Viscount Adare, vice-chancellor of state for the colonies, Home suddenly rose into the air and, according to all the witnesses, floated out of a window eighty feet above the street, then wafted into an adjoining room by somehow sliding under a window opened only eighteen inches. When asked to repeat the performance, he allegedly did so straight away.

On other occasions Home would hold hands with a circle of people whom he had never previously met, then suddenly drift up to high ceilings. Still other times he would levitate while seated at a seance table, and end up on top of the table with the chair still under him. His powers were such that they would come at totally unexpected times. Once he was in the parlor of some aristocratic friends, reading the afternoon newspaper. When his hosts entered the room, their jaws dropped. Though he hadn't even realized it, Home was floating several inches above the couch, cushioned on air.

Such feats involved him in a lifetime of controversy. In Rome he was banished as a sorcerer and threatened with physical harm. In America he had to withstand the vitriolic attack of Harry Houdini.

Home's personality only served to aggravate the situation, for he was, by most accounts, a vain and haughty man. Charles Dickens and Houdini publicly implied he was not only an obnoxious personality, but a homosexual to boot. Poet Robert Browning openly hated him, perhaps principally because the poet's celebrated wife, Elizabeth Barrett, had taken an ardent interest in Home's ability to levitate objects and go into a spirit trance. Though Browning admitted he could not explain how Home made heavy objects float in front of his very eyes, his jealousy led him to attack the medium as "that dungball," a description later elaborated in his poem "Mr. Sludge, the Medium." Another writer, Nathaniel Hawthorne, watched Home's displays of levitation and admitted there was no way he could explain them. But Hawthorne, equally rankled by the psychic's personality, swept them aside as unimportant in the overall scheme of things.

Before he died at fifty-three, however, Home did manage to attract an impressive group of supporters. Poet William Cullings Bryant stood by him, having witnessed his total levitation of a table, a feat performed in full light, for a special committee at Harvard University. William Makepeace Thackeray was more vocal in his defense of the medium. As editor of the popular *Cornhill Magazine*, Thackeray allowed a highly laudatory account of Home ("Stranger Than Fiction," circa July 1860) to appear in his publication, going so far as to add a footnote personally vouching for Home's authenticity. Defenders included English historian H.T. Buckle, playwright Edwin Arnold, Voltairean rationalist Lord Brougham, and scientific investigator Sir David Brewster, who once thought table-tipping was mere muscle movement but changed his mind after watching from every angle as Home completely levitated a heavy table.

In the end what put Home above most mediums was not only the enormous volume of his paranormal successes, but the manner in which he presented them. He never accepted money for his performances and, unlike the majority of levitating psychics, actually disliked working in the dark. He was also more than willing to submit to rigid controls during his feats, a characteristic that precipitated the most spectacular about-face in recent scientific-occult history.

Sir William Crookes was unquestionably one of the most highly esteemed scientists of the day, a diversified, creative man among whose achievements were establishing the august journal *Chemical News,* inventing the radiometer and discovering the element thallium. Great excitement was generated in scientific circles in July 1870 when, through the *Quarterly of Science,* Dr. Crookes announced he was going to investigate spiritualistic phenomena, a move he was sure would eventually expose the whole business as a hoax. His decision was loudly applauded by academia, which was greatly relieved that such a revered man was stepping in to end all the nonsense.

Their relief was short-lived. It ended when Crookes, after a year of extensive experimentation, announced a startling conclusion. Home, he stated, was genuine. Perhaps natural laws, he warned reluctantly, would have to make room for a new influence he called "psychic force."

The conclusion was especially irksome in light of the thoroughness of Crookes's precautions against fraud and his ingenious devices for detecting PK, some of which are still used today. He used spring balances on tables to test for muscular exertion during levitation, placed objects to be levitated in cages so that they could not be made to float by ordinary means, and strapped Home to a rig attached to a galvanometer, which electronically monitored his every move during levitation.

Despite all these controls, Home still functioned superbly, causing the caged objects to rise and furniture to move by itself across the room, levitating tables and chairs while his arms and legs were tightly held.

Many of the experiments were carried out in Crookes's "seance room," a compartment specially built to preclude fraud. The room had a solid concrete floor to prevent ordinary vibrations from causing furniture movements, windows fitted with iron shutters, and a massive table constructed so that even strong physical manipulation could not cause it to rap or budge.

Again, despite all these precautions the levitations continued, the heavy table floating so impressively that it made another renowned scientist, Francis Galton, reel with excitement.

"I can only say, as yet, that I am utterly confounded with the results, and very disinclined to discredit them," wrote Galton in a note to Charles Darwin dated 28 March 1872. "Crookes works deliberately and well."

In another note, dated 19 April 1872, a time when Crookes was expanding his experiments, Galton reported to Darwin that the whole procedure was "thoroughly scientific" and certainly "no matter of vulgar legerdemain."

Darwin's response indicated an anxious perplexity. "I can not disbelieve Dr. Crookes' statements, nor can I believe his results," wrote Darwin, who later expressed complete faith in Galton's observations.

London's Society for Psychical Research took a close interest in the tests, especially because Crookes, though under heavy criticism from orthodox circles, had decided to investigate other physical mediums, a move which convinced the society that he meant business. In 1887 the society set up a special organization specifically to look into cases of supposed levitation. Because it wanted to be sure unconscious muscle movement wasn't involved, the society investigators went after only those cases where there was no attempt at physical contact.

A report titled "On Alleged Movements of Objects Without Contact Occurring Not in the Presence of a Paid Medium" was soon issued, consisting mainly of instances compiled by Frederic W.H. Myers. It contained a treasure of baffling information on tables and chairs that levitated and tilted without human touch, and furniture that started "walking around rooms." It was followed up in Poland by a scientist name Julien Ochorowicz who, after studying a psychic named Stanislawa Tomczyk, concluded that furniture could be levitated from a distance.

While research into the mystery of table levitation continued into the twentieth century, it lost much of its steam. Interest cooled not only because of the frauds that littered the previous century, but because when there *were* authentic cases, science was at a loss to explain them. Between 1914 and 1920 the bulk of investigation was shouldered, in Belfast, Ireland, by a mechanical engineer named W.J. Crawford, who had picked up Dr. Crookes's flickering torch.

Dr. Crawford centered his studies on a young psychic named Kathleen Goligher, who allegedly made tables hover above the floor for several minutes by merely placing her arms lightly on their surfaces (sometimes talking and singing to them for better results). Crawford testified that the rooms she performed in often turned uncannily cold during the levitations. While most of the time Goligher generated what seemed like a rubbery force that pushed the table upward, sometimes she could cause the opposite effect, making the table so heavy no one could pick it up.

Crawford set up scales during the displays of table phenomena, arranging them so as to record the weight of the sitters. After a series of prolonged surveys he revealed that the medium's weight seemed to increase during complete levitations approximately by the weight of the table. This finding led him to develop the controversial "cantilever theory," which held that a psychic force protruded from the psychic's body during levitation, bouncing off the floor and angling up to raise the table. He also speculated that these "forces" could form "psychic rods" to move objects at a distance, a theory fraught with so many mechanical difficulties that it was never taken seriously. Crawford's work further suffered when another investigator claimed to have found Goligher doing something fraudulent. Neither the charge nor the theory was pursued.

Around the same time, well-known researcher Harry Price had also taken up with a few levitators, most prominently with an Austrian by the name of Rudi Schneider. Price placed Schneider's hands and feet in special electronic "gloves" constructed to follow muscle movements, an apparatus that didn't prevent the psychic from levitating furniture from across the room.

Price, president of the National Library of Psychical Research, went on to study a young psychic, Stella C., who on one memorable occasion caused a levitated table to splinter into a pile of matchwood, and American psychic Eileen Garrett, who supposedly made a 112-pound table rise halfway to the ceiling.

In America the bulk of the parapsychological research was conducted by J.B. Rhine of Duke University. Dr. Rhine, who introduced the word "psychokinesis," touched only lightly on table-tilting, preferring instead to test such abilities through dice throws (which are easy to evaluate statistically.)

The Scientific American made a more casual approach than Rhine, dispatching an investigating committee in the 1930s to study Margery Crandon, "the witch of Beacon Hill." Though readers anxiously waited to see whether the magazine would find that she really could levitate furniture and get messages through rappings, the publication ended a short study without venturing a conclusion.

The reports thinned out as the century wore on. Thomas Mann, Germany's premier writer of the century, caused a slight uproar when he reported success with table-tipping and witnessed several "poltergeist-like" levitations, but that quickly petered out. In Chicago some claimed that Olof Jonsson, famous for his ESP experiment with ex-astronaut Edgar Mitchell, was able to levitate himself, but no one ever bothered to study him. Nor did anyone study a group from a small Southern college who said they could levitate heavy tables (see appendix). In Bulgaria scientists were halfheartedly studying Mikhail Drogzeno-vich, a fifty-three-year-old farmer who "could sit on air" in full view of reputable witnesses, sometimes nearly five feet off the ground.

But aside from the infrequent reports that filtered into parapsychologists' hands, and the work of English scientists K.J. Batcheldor, Colin Brookes-Smith and D.W. Smith, levitation had been more or less pushed under the rug, whence it was to re-emerge only very recently.

All eyes were on the psi metal-benders.

The Geller Flap

"Ego! It is the great word of the twentieth century. If there is a single word in our century that has added to the potentiality of our language, it is ego. Everything we have done in this century . . . has been a function of that extraordinary state of the psyche which gives us authority to declare we are sure of ourselves when we are not."

— *Norman Mailer: Existential Errands*

Thanks in part to the public's TV-stimulated responsiveness to psi phenomena, there is now a storm in the world of parapsychology that makes the storms caused by Eusapia Palladino, D.D. Home and J.B. Rhine's Duke University experiments seem small by comparison.

At its eye, of course, is enigmatic Mr. Uri Geller, thirty, a wonder-worker with a natural flare for massive publicity, a healthy-sized ego and, if most of his serious investigators are right, an awesome ability to perform PK. Geller is the boyish-looking Israeli who has strewn the television platforms of just about every American and European talk show with spoons, forks, keys and spikes that he supposedly bent with just a flick of the fingers and a blink of the eyes. He's that guy, the innocent-sounding entertainer, who has sent scientists, magicians, journalists and parapsychologists into sand-bag trenches, from which, on occasion, they snipe at their own kind.

The story goes back to 1971. At the time, Geller was

doing the smoke-filled night circuit of Tel Aviv, driving packed audiences to frenzy with his ability to "read" thoughts, start broken watches, make metal necklaces and rings mysteriously bend. There wasn't much being said about the strange, handsome ex-paratrooper and his unprecedented stage act. But then, in the fall of 1971, Uri ran into a bushy-haired, mustachioed neurologist-parapsychologist named Dr. Andrija Puharich. It was soon apparent to Geller that he might be on the brink of fulfilling his dreams of fame and fortune. Finally he had met, in the American doctor, somebody who wanted o take inventory of his freakish abilities and report them to the world.

Ever since the death of Arigo, the celebrated psychic surgeon from Brazil, Puharich had been looking for a powerful subject who, like this "surgeon of the rusty knife," could survive the booby traps of science. Geller turned out to be the man. Puharich spent more than a year in Israel cataloguing the most inexplicable events associated with the psychic and began talking to people not only about spectacular ESP demonstrations that he'd witnessed and spoons that turned to wet noodles, but about materializations, dematerializations and messages from another dimension. Even some of his good friends were made to wonder: Had he suddenly lost his mind?

Edgar Mitchell seemed to think so. At the Institute of Noetic Sciences in Palo Alto, California, Mitchell, the moonwalker-turned-parapsychologist, got some of the first direct reports from Puharich and, like others, planted his tongue firmly in cheek. Even if such things were true, thought Mitchell, America wasn't yet ready for them. Scientists were only starting to accept those findings from Russia that indicated man's mind could move objects, or that some unknown force, seemingly controlled by the human psyche, could affect the mercury in a thermometer or the roll of a die. But bend metal? Make the hands of a clock advance? No way.

Still, Puharich persisted. He kept emphasizing the fact that the psychic had developed to the point of performing at will, and that, at least in his then mood, he would submit to lab scrutiny. Next thing anyone knew, Mitchell, accompanied by Dr. Wilbur Franklin of Kent State, was at Puharich's Ossining, New York home for a session with Geller, there to witness things that neither Mitchell nor Franklin could readily believe.

"I remember one time, we all went off somewhere in a car," tells Franklin. "And there was a stop sign near the place we were staying. When we went past it later on, it was out of shape, twisted. We were pretty sure we would have noticed it before, and Mitchell is an astute observer, maybe the best I've seen. Puharich looked at it and I remember he just nonchalantly commented that there must be a lot of energy around. We knew we could not tell many people about things like that."

Soon after, in the summer of 1972, Mitchell, certain there was something truly strange going on, decided Puharich was right: it was something science just had to take a look at. It seemed so *tangible,* so repeatable. And off went Mitchell to the Stanford Research Institute (SRI) at Menlo Park, taking with him psi's new golden boy.

At SRI's sprawling seventy-acre compound, a veritable town-within-a-town located thirty-five miles south of San Francisco, the reception was on the cool side. With most of its cash flow coming from contracts with the United States Department of Defense and other sensitive institutions, SRI certainly was in no need of scandal, and research brass knew from what Mitchell was saying that they were probably about to involve themselves in widespread controversy. But Mitchell and Puharich eventually got through to two young SRI physicists, Russell Targ, whose forte was laser and plasma research, and Dr. Harold Puthoff, who specialized in quantum physics. After some institutional wrestling, SRI said that, yes, it would help out in the project as long as Mitchell collected most of the funds.

As carefully yet as quickly as possible, before the unpredictable Israeli might change his mind about the whole setup, Puthoff and Targ, along with Mitchell, readied magnetometers, electrical balances, videotape cameras. For ESP experiments, lab assistants assembled an isolation room shielded against all paths of normal sensory input. The experiments were designed so that, in order to cheat, Geller would have needed an army of accomplices hidden in the walls and a battery of sophisticated equipment that he surely could not have carted in unnoticed.

For the next five weeks, the physicists witnessed crazy happenings like those Mitchell and Puharich had filled them in on. Though they had problems with Geller's personality — he grew a bit impatient as the experiments dragged on — the psychic came through with ESP transfers that defied all statistical odds, deflected compasses with a wave of the hand, and made spoons bend by merely rubbing them between his thumb and index finger. While his telepathy and clairvoyant abilities were fairly easy to document, his PK aptitude proved a tougher proposition. Often the scientists had to wait an hour or two before metal started to bend and Geller was temperamentally unamenable to doing an experiment over and over, which was what SRI needed. When the experiments ended, a bureaucratic tug-of-war ensued over how the findings should be released, and though the scientists involved were sure Geller was the real thing, a shroud of semi-secrecy surrounded their efforts to prove it.

That semisecrecy was short-lived, however. And the stunning news that SRI was dabbling with psychic phenomena was soon leaked to journalists. Though SRI had feared just such an eventuality and tried to suppress all major information about the experiments until they'd had time to write a careful report, Uri and Puharich's hurry to prove the former's powers blew their discretion to the winds. When *Time* requested a meeting with the psychic, even before a shred of scientific data had been released, Geller and Puharich quickly consented to it, despite the scent of a lynching in the air. It was, perhaps, Geller's most notable mistake. At *Time*, the running joke was that the psychic was not only going to bend metal but was also going to treat the staff to a seance with the tooth fairy. There was reason for the skepticism. One of its reporters, John Wilhelm, claimed that he had personally caught Geller cheating, and there were reports from other sources, including one of Uri's former girl friends, that, like Eusapia Palladino, he resorted to trickery when the paranormal energies weren't aflow. At SRI it was said that Geller himself admitted sometimes using trickery and had once been persuaded by an Israeli stage manager to use a confederate in the audience during "ESP" demonstrations. Some claimed, too, that his spoon-bending was a result of clever sleight-of-hand. Such rumors seriously tainted Geller's "feats," even those that have been clearly genuine. They also discouraged some of his early advocates: one such, a scientist, said the psychic had no sense of ethics, no regard for the truth. It was an unfair remark.

For the meeting, held that February, the magazine slipped in two magicians, James (the Amazing) Randi, a flamboyant Canadian professional, and Charles Reynolds, an amateur at legerdemain, disguising them as reporters. Then the writing staff, led by senior editor Leon Jaroff, took Uri through a nightmarish session widely described as having been more like a police grilling than an open-minded demonstration. Journalistic objectivity was noticeably absent from their search. "If you're the kind of person who believes such things are even possible, then I have nothing to say to you," commented editor Jaroff later on. "Why, if Geller can do those things just by knitting his eyebrows, it destroys everything I hold dear."†

When it was obvious which way *Time* was heading, SRI followed quickly with a preliminary presentation of its findings. On 9 March 1973, Puthoff and Targ stood before the Physics Colloquium of Columbia University. Their prepared statement was terse but dramatic: they had observed certain phenomena, said the two physicists, for which there were no scientific explanations.

The scientists had invited Leon Jaroff to the session, where a film of Geller bending a stainless steel spoon and guessing the roll of a die was to be shown, but Jaroff chose not to attend. The SRI announcement, in fact, only served to bolster the magazine's skepticism. *Time* dragged Geller over the coals with a venomous news item in its March 12 issue that portrayed the confused foreigner as a conniving stage magician with a slick new trick. Everything Geller did, said *Time,* could have been done through sleight-of-hand. The newsweekly conveniently omitted to mention that he had bent a key for its reporters, and that the key supposedly continued to bend after it had left his grip. Instead, the magazine said its clandestine magicians were able to duplicate the Geller stunts or at least explain them

† Saul-Paul Sirag, "The Skeptics," *Psychic* magazine, October 1975, p. 16.

in terms of quick fingers and clever psychology. (Randi claimed to have seen Geller take a target object and press it against a table to make it bend.) Besides, said *Time,* Geller had left Israel under a cloud of suspicion. Geller was understandably enraged. "I think I was set up," he barked. "I think if I had levitated in the air for five minutes in front of them, the magicians would have still said it was some trick."

As if that was not a sufficiently devastating blow, Geller next met with humiliation on one of America's top-charted television programs, the Johnny Carson "Tonight Show." Randi, the elfin, bearded conjuror who was probably most responsible for the negative tone of the *Time* piece, had decided he would follow Uri around in a full-scale effort to discredit him, and when Carson, himself a former magician, allowed Randi to supervise Geller's appearance, the Canadian magician threw himself into the project with a vengeance. It was a match of egos. Geller had his eyes on Hollywood lights; Randi, who likewise seemed preoccupied with fame, felt it his duty to stop him. It seemed Randi had stepped into Houdini's shoes.

Employing just the right combination of rigid stage controls and subtle psychological harassment, Randi walked away from NBC that night with what was to be his most prized victory: Geller was a total flop. For an embarrassing twenty minutes, the nervous psychic struggled to pick up messages clairvoyantly and to bend metal. Nothing happened.

It looked as though he was destined to be just another flash in the psychic pan. But then came a reprieve from England. In the October 1974 issue of *Nature,* the British science journal, was an article by-lined by Targ and Puthoff that defended the authenticity of at least some of

Geller's displays. *Nature* is one of the most respected of all science periodicals, and the article caused considerable waves in the scientific community.

Another heavyweight publication, *The New Scientist,* countered with an article by Dr. Joseph Hanlon, who claimed the SRI experiments had been sloppily conducted and later put forth some bizarre explanations for the Geller effects, his tired assumption being that if it could have been a trick, it must have been a trick. Hanlon said that in experiments where Geller claimed he was defying odds of several million to one, he may have received the "ESP" messages through a radio implanted in his teeth or somewhere else on his person. Scientists on the other side hastily came back to point out that if Dr. Hanlon had seriously looked into the matter, he would quickly have found his radio-in-the-teeth theory untenable. Geller, they said, had no fillings, a fact that had been checked by SRI.

While scientists argued, Geller and a handful of magicians who followed Randi's lead headed for a showdown. The magicians moved with an urgency many close observers thought was prompted not only by jealousy over the inexplicable things Geller seemed able to do, but maybe even by a touch of fear. Were the conjurors afraid that an authentic psychic would tarnish their reputations? Was there actually an apprehension that psychic phenomena, or what was once called "genuine magic," would usurp their artificial magic?

It seemed so. Randi and another leading skeptic, Milbourne Christopher, a Hall-of-Fame magician who headed the Society of American Magicians' occult investigation committee, turned frustrated and bitter, as was clearly evidenced when they discovered they couldn't do the things Geller did after being asked to perform with controls similar to those that had been imposed on the psychic. On NBC's "Tomorrow Show," Randi angrily tossed a pen and paper in the air when he dismally failed to duplicate an ESP experiment Geller had spectacularly succeeded in just nights before, while Christopher, appearing as a co-guest, stayed away from trying anything. Randi also met with embarrassment at Brooklyn's Maimonides Medical Center where he attempted to show parapsychologists how Geller "fraudulently" bent keys but succeeded only in clumsily scratching a desk. When reporters scrutinized Randi's claims, his temper flared.

"I asked Randi about the key Geller had bent at the *Time* demonstration," says Saul-Paul Sirag, a writer and member of the Physics Consciousness Research Group in San Francisco. "[Charles] Reynolds had claimed Randi and he saw Geller make suspicious movements with the key. I asked why the *Time* story had omitted all mention of the key — was it because he and Reynolds hadn't been able to duplicate the bending? [The magazine had said its secret-agent magicians could duplicate all the Geller "tricks."] Randi didn't know. Besides, he said Reynolds was going around bending keys for people in bars. I said that the light in the bars must be quite dim, because Reynolds hadn't bent any keys for me. Randi couldn't accept this needling. 'OK, Charlie can't bend keys! I can't bend keys! Only Uri can bend keys!' He sounded as if he was about to burst into tears, and he abruptly hung up the phone."†

On other occasions, however, when Randi's personal feelings were more subdued and when he wasn't running around referring to Geller as his "foe" and calling scientists "chumps," he performed a legitimate service for the cause of objective investigation. It was badly needed. After

---

† Sirag, op. cit., p.20

all, several observers had claimed to have witnessed elements of fraud in Geller and even Edgar Mitchell feared that the Israeli's ego might drive him to employ sleight-of-hand if his legitimate powers were stubborn and his superstar standing at stake. Randi was quite professional in his thoroughness. After studying hours of film showing Geller television appearances, he devised several methods of duplicating the PK effects by trick means, and he managed to fool a number of unobservant scientists by slipping pre-bent spoons into his act or bending keys with skilled muscle manipulation. Indeed, he was so excellent that within two years of meeting Geller he had completely convinced certain objective investigators like psychologist Andrew Weil that Uri was a hoax.

But Randi's quick hands were no match for even amateur magicians who observed him imitating Geller's feats; they immediately knew how he was doing them. When Randi vehemently refused to perform his imitations under even semicontrolled conditions, magicians started leaving his camp, and when his ego asserted itself with blasts against Geller that were exaggerated and unfactual, many others suddenly started wondering if perhaps Geller was genuine after all.

The most detrimental finding against Randi and Christopher's position came in June of 1975 when Artur Zorka, an investigator for the magicians' occult investigation committee, set up the first rigidly controlled yet psychologically fair magician's test for Geller. Unlike Randi, Zorka, assisted by another magician named Abb Dickson, did not go about trying to upset Uri and rack his nerves, but instead concentrated on watching him closely. After the demonstration, held in Atlanta, Georgia, Zorka raced back to the society's executive board with the startling conclusion that Geller wasn't using any known trick and that none of the methods devised by Randi and Christopher was to the point.

Zorka came to this surprising conclusion simply because he had no other choice. He had checked for hidden chemicals and every possible mechanical device, as well as supplied forged steel for the experiments, a metal specially chosen because of its unusual resistance to physical pressure. According to the testimony of the two Southern magicians, Geller took one of their forks during the session and *caused its handle to shatter into fragments.* They also said Uri handled one of Zorka's keys and made it curl in his palm, as though it was melting. Not a hint of fraud was detected, though the two conjurors claimed they had their eyes trained on the psychic's hands at all times, and from every angle. Copenhagen magician Leo Leslie similarly concluded that "Uri Geller is genuine" after closely scrutinizing a feat in which the psychic paranormally fixed a watch that had been ingeniously rigged not to run.

There were other, even stronger indications that Geller was authentic, that, despite Randi's claims, there was such a thing as PK metal-bending. Metallurgical tests (see Chapter 13) showed odd microscopic effects on the fracture surfaces of the metal he had bent; dozens of scientists and researchers started to claim that he could bend metal placed in a vacuated bell jar or in someone else's hands; and one investigator claimed to see a spoon bend forty degrees after Geller had set it down. Geller also affected magnetometers, broken watches, photographic and video film and Geiger counters, in many cases at a distance.

Whatever the precise nature of the Geller force, indications are it's a different manifestation of the energy at work in levitation. While both these forms of energy have striking similarities with electromagnetism, gravity and electricity, neither of them fits the category of a known physical force.

That metal-bending and levitational energy might even be identical can be hypothesized from some of the few scientific experiments that have dealt with PK. In one SRI test, Geller affected the weight of an object placed on a sensitive electrical scale that was shielded with glass. By just holding his hand a few inches above the bell jar, he altered the object's weight in a way the scientists could not explain. It was reminiscent of the way some psychics alter the weight of tables. On occasion he was said to have involuntarily caused objects such as ashtrays and pens to levitate before the eyes of observers while he was bending metal or performing clairvoyantly.

There was also an obvious similarity between the activities of Geller and those of the "Philip" group in Toronto and indeed of poltergeists. Like Geller, the Owen group had also bent metal. Conversely, like the Toronto and other groups, Geller caused ghostlike reactions unintentionally. At London University's Birkbeck College Professor John Hasted, a top English physicist, was baffled when objects flew through his home and clock hands mysteriously advanced for months after Geller had paid a visit.

But what was the Geller energy and where did it come from? Unfortunately, the volatile psychic was becoming increasingly hard for scientists to work with under lab conditions. Like Phil Jordan, he seemed much more interested in the show-biz side of things, and he had his sights on a movie. Reportedly he often missed appointments with scientists. While he was intelligent and charming most of the time some who had known him before he became famous concluded that the whirlwind of publicity had gone to his head. "People get upset that I commercialize this ability," he said in self-defense, "but why not? Why can't I make money from my talents just as others make a living from their abilities? I feel I have already shown that what I do is for real." He had a point.

Despite Geller's intransigence, however, some scientists were able to piece together what may some day prove to be valuable clues as to the nature of PK. At UCLA, Dr. Thelma Moss, an expert on Kirlian photography, found that energy streams seemed to shoot from Geller's fingers to objects he was trying to affect as if they came from his aura. That wasn't all. Her electrophotographs showed a remarkably bright energy field round a key Geller was attempting to bend, and it seemed to be responsive to his fluctuating mental state. Significantly, he used a technique similar to that used by the Thurmond group in Owego, New York. He visualized how he wanted an object to look before attempting to make it look that way, just as the Thurmonds and Rose Engle first "imagined" heavy tables into the air. The Thurmonds, of course, related their visualization techniques to the projection of white light, as they had been taught to do in the Silva Mind Control class. Were they both using the same "light," and was Thelma Moss photographing it?

It was possible, but the idea that PK energy comes from an individual's aura leaves a lot of unanswered questions. How did Geller make metals bend hundreds of miles away, as he had done during a performance for the BBC? How did he cause broken watches to tick, also at great distances? How did he cause metal to bend after leaving its vicinity?

Neither Geller nor Puharich has been able to answer those questions satisfactorily — at least not to the satisfaction of science. Puharich supports Geller's claim that he is influenced by superintelligences who, from their location in another space and time, have set up computers to keep track of human evolution on earth, and Geller has often described himself as a "channel" for higher forces. These forces, which Geller, Puharich and at least one other researcher have claimed to see manifest as UFOs, were supposedly last in contact with the planet in ancient Egyptian times.

The odd claim that Geller is semicontrolled by extra-terrestrial beings has only served to heat up the debate at all levels. Magicians point to it as evidence that both Geller and Puharich have taken leave of their senses; parapsychologists often see it as the sign of a messianic complex in Geller, product of an enlarged ego, or maybe the same kind of rationalization that causes so many to impute inexplicable events to "spirits." The astrally inclined say the two men may be the victims of a trick being played by entities on the spirit plane, one that causes them to hallucinate.

And so the confused debate continues. PK? Trickery? Messages from on high? While ostentatious psychics pose the questions, the truth is likely to remain elusive. Perhaps science would do best to turn its attention to quieter psychics who have been creating PK effects as spectacular as Geller's, including the bending of metals.

A Spate Of Bent Metal

"It is possible that fourth dimensional space is the distance between a group of solids, separating these solids, yet at the same time binding them into some (to us) inconceivable whole, even though they seem separate from one another."

— *P.D. Ouspensky: Tertium Organum*

Elaine Fortson leaned back in her chair, slowly twisting a ring laden with what seemed to be a bunch of defective keys. "A lot of times I find they just bend by themselves, while they're in my purse," said the meticulously dressed, effervescent Ohio housewife. "We found other members of the family, especially my twelve-year-old daughter, could also do it. She has made spoons and keys bend by just asking the objects to move. Of course, you've got to figure it's some kind of energy, probably of a spiritual nature, and probably something everyone, to an extent, must possess."

It's phenomena like those just described by Mrs. Fortson that have convinced physicist Wilbur Franklin, who incidentally has watched the forty-year-old Akron woman and her daughter perform in his Kent State University offices, that Uri Geller is certainly not the only one with the ability to distort objects such as nail files, combs, spoons, keys and even mirrors through mind power. Dr.

Franklin, probably the first American scientist to search out other metal-benders, has seen and heard enough to know the phenomenon is not as rare as was thought when Geller made the international scene. He has watched a twelve-year-old Ohio boy plasticize a spoon, a Canadian table-tipper bend a fork held by a skeptical colleague from his own department, and several others operate paranormally with hard metals, causing effects that would usually require intense heat or extreme force.

"Suddenly, after all the Geller headlines, reports started coming in from all over. South Africa, Canada, Japan," says the scientist. "We still have a great deal of testing to do, and because of [inadequate] fundings it has been hard to get anywhere with it; but it looks like scores, and I mean scores, of others can cause the so-called 'Geller effect.' And to me all the incoming data strengthen the belief that psychokinesis is at work in such cases, and that maybe it's an ability that, like so many other talents, can actually be learned, at least with some people."

All told, the tally of alleged metal-benders has gone far beyond the "scores" Franklin estimates to exist, and is thought to be at least in the hundreds. In California, newspapers have reported a spate of child metal-benders, and in Switzerland scientists have recorded a new breed of "physical psychics" able to affect anything from sealed spoons and forks to watches and electric saws.* In England, where metal-bending has reached a faddish proportion that rivals the outbreak of table-tipping a century ago, mathematician John G. Taylor of King's College, London

---

*In fact, after Uri Geller made a Swiss television appearance the winter of 1974, Swiss parapsychologists learned of more than 40 individuals who reported metal-bending and paranormal clock restorations (in which watches and clocks that had been inoperative suddenly started up again, if only temporarily). The majority of those reporting the phenomena had been under psychological tension at the time of the alleged PK.

reports that new metal-benders have been coming forth at a steady rate of about two a week since 1973, when Geller captured British headlines with a series of stunning television successes. At first Dr. Taylor had counted forty-six English psychics who could bend metal, a rate of about one person in a million. But within a year of that estimate, he judged the number to be at least ten times larger. Metal-bending had developed, he said, into a "mini-epidemic." Ordinary people with no previous psychic experience suddenly found themselves witness to all sorts of metal that bent in their own homes during or shortly after Geller appeared on TV and radio shows. Soup ladles drooped during his performances; gold bracelets broke; and in at least one case a woman reportedly became pregnant because her metal birth control device bent out of form. "I put four forks and four spoons on a table in front of the television while Uri stroked a fork," said one perplexed Middlesex woman. "I did not believe it would really happen. But then I looked down and saw that one fork and three spoons had been twisted out of shape. I tried bending one myself but I found I could not do it."† Others found that broken watches and other defunct mechanisms started up again while Uri was on the air, and the same thing has happened even when some unknown psychics broadcasted.

(In February 1976, Samuel Lentine, a physicist at Rensselaer Polytechnic Institute and a self-claimed psychic, suggested in an interview on Schenectady radio station WGY that those in the audience with broken watches should place them next to the radio. Minutes later, he claims, the station's switchboards were jammed with people calling in to report that their watches did indeed start up

---

†John Taylor, *Superminds* (New York: 1975), p. 18.

again during the talk show, and one woman said a spoon had bent before her eyes. It would seem that these people's own energies, plus those of Lentine, had provoked this display of mass PK.)

At first it seemed as if a force was emanating from Geller himself to cause long-distance effects, since the initial bendings coincided with his broadcasts. Later, however, Taylor, a forty-three-year-old author of books on the new physics and the black holes of outer space, observed a number of people cause the same results on their own in controlled situations, some of them never having seen Geller in action. One researcher, Canadian medical doctor William Q. Wolfson, even found that metal bent if it was merely placed in proximity to a piece of paper on which the names of various PK psychics had been written and still others noted that much of the metal-bending occurred not during live Geller broadcasts, but during video-tape replays. In these specific situations, it seemed Uri was merely a psychological catalyst that got the psi forces of others going.

As Taylor's inquiry into the matter progressed, he found his best subjects to be children between the ages of six and seventeen. So spectacular were the results with the more youthful subjects that he wondered if metal-bending ability might not be something that tended to wither with age. One child could reportedly shape paper clips into animal shapes without touching metal. Another could bend by about forty degrees a metal towel rail one-quarter-inch in diameter and constructed of mild steel with a chromium plate finish — an object the child simply could not distort through physical means. Yet another could cause all the nearby cutlery to bend and break, at times without even trying. It didn't matter if the objects were silver, lead, zinc, tin, copper, aluminum, iron, tungsten or sodium iodide crystals, or if they were placed out of reach in sealed laboratory tubes; they still warped by as much as 180 degrees under the children's gaze. On occasion, poltergeist effects accompanied the children's feats, and once they started bending metal their ability to do so was apt to pop up when least expected.

Interestingly, the metal-bending studied by Taylor and Franklin was similar not only to the feats of Geller, but to those of other PK mediums, including table levitators. The same physical side effects were observable, for example occasional headaches and fatigue. Also the English metal-benders were successful, like so many other psychics, in deflecting compasses, causing watches to advance, and making magnetic and nonmagnetic objects, including wood, spin on enclosed pinwheels. Then there were distinct psychological similarities. If the atmosphere in which the subjects worked seemed markedly skeptical, or if they were made uneasy by the constant scrutiny of their every move, their feats often diminished in frequency and strength. As in the case of both conscious and poltergeist-affected furniture movements, the relation between success and mental attitude varied. With some metal-benders the best results occurred when the subject was calmly exhorting spoons and forks to "please bend" or "come on and curl up;" with others tension and anxiety seemed to speed the process.

Meditation also seemed to figure in metal-bending phenomena, as it does in various other PK feats. In a brief, informal experiment conducted by this author, a Wisconsin artist who had had a record of psi experiences as a child was asked to lower her consciousness through about thirty minutes of yoga breathing exercises. She imagined white energy flowing into her forehead with each inhalation and flowing down the front of her body to her hands, which were placed in the vicinity of her sternum. When she felt sufficiently "charged," another subject, who had also been meditating, pointed his fingers toward her hand as if to transmit additional energy. A thick stainless steel spoon was then lightly pressed against the pointer finger of the artist's left hand. It immediately bent about five degrees, even though she was in fact hardly touching it. Just prior to this, she had claimed to see a "shadowy presence" in the room, and after the experiment rapping noises were heard in her home.

The links between metal-bending, other forms of PK and phenomena of a more spiritistic nature have come to seem even stronger of late, mainly because of the emergence of English psychic Matthew Manning. A shy, intelligent twenty-year-old whose long brown hair and well-groomed beard have evoked comparisons with Christ, Manning approaches his psychic abilities, which rank with the most powerful on recent record, from a refreshingly scientific angle. Far from wishing to follow in the flashy footsteps of Uri Geller, Manning is quietly trying to find out as much as possible about the mechanics of his widely diversified paranormal gifts.

He first encountered strange psi energies at age eleven, when a poltergeist raised havoc in his home, located in the peaceful college town of Cambridge. Night after night during the winter of 1967 his parents would find that objects had strangely moved out of place. Silver tankards, coffee tables, cutlery and a host of other items, some rather large, were found quite a distance from where they were supposed to be. Manning's parents naturally suspected that one of their three children was playing tricks, and they set about trying to pin the perpetrator. Before they retired to bed, Mr. and Mrs. Derek Manning would booby-trap doors leading to the "haunted" rooms with cotton threads and sprinkle talc on the floor around the most "active" objects so that any human trickster would unwittingly leave telltale footprints.

Not only did these efforts fail to produce a human suspect, but the strange happenings stepped up their frequency during the next few weeks. During a two-month period tables and chairs were found unaccountably over-turned and disturbing knocks and raps were heard throughout the house, these last fading away gradually.

Though local parapsychology experts, including A.R.G. Owen, then the top European authority on poltergeists, told the family the problem had probably run its course and would not return, a second, more powerful wave of occurrences struck in 1971 after the family had moved some seventy miles away to the village of Linton. This time it started in Matthew's bedroom, confirming suspicions that the boy was the source. One night, strange knocking and scratching sounds emanated from his wardrobe cup-board, and shortly afterward his bed began to vibrate violently before actually levitating off the floor. It even began following him around. At Oakham, where Manning enrolled in boarding school, beds in the communal bed-room moved out of place, objects came flying into the room, and students often complained of an "etherlike" cold that swept around Matthew. During protracted out-bursts, witnesses claimed to see objects float across rooms as if intelligently controlled. At certain times of peak activity, the young poltergeist focus caught glimpses of apparitions, and on at least one occasion a wall in a locked room was found scribbled on when the door was opened one morning, the scrawls indicating the signatures of people who were dead.

Oddly, the phantom forces stayed with the boy far longer than they do in most poltergeist cases, the violent movement of objects and the knocking sounds dying down only after the boy discovered he could perform automatic writing, a process by which someone writes intelligible messages without the conscious control of his own mind. Though there was argument as to whether the strange writings were the product of Matthew's subconscious, many times it seemed that some discarnate entity was controlling his pen. At one point messages alleged that they were coming from the recently deceased Bishop Kephalas Nektarios, a leader of Britain's Greek Orthodox community, and when researchers investigated the writings they found they contained information only high officials of the bishop's church could possibly have known.

While Matthew engaged in automatic writing, the poltergeist disturbances stopped completely, as if the energy that caused them had found this other form of release. Happy to have found a remedy, an escape from the poltergeists, he kept working with pen and paper and soon despite his lack of innate artistic talent, was doing automatic sketches and drawings of strange brilliance. In a way that of course defied logical explanation, he started reproducing the drawings of such masters as Van Gogh, Rembrandt and Dürer, and with such accuracy that they looked like photographic reprints, which, it was verified, they certainly were not. (Fraud has never been associated with this psychic's name). To draw like Van Gogh, all Matthew had to do, it seems, was will to do so and a "crackling energy"directed his brush.

In 1973 Manning found a new psychic toy. One night, being then seventeen, he was watching a TV special, "Uri Geller: Is Seeing Believing?" in which the Israeli psychic was demonstrating his metal-bending techniques when suddenly his mother exhorted him to see if he could match Geller. He didn't expect anything to happen, but to please his mother he grasped a stainless steel spoon and, while Geller was on the tube, started to rub it.

For a good ten minutes, not a thing happened. Then the boy's father walked into the room, and as happens in so many cases of this kind, the sudden distraction, the break in concentration, did the trick. Suddenly Matthew felt the spoon drooping like heated wax, and it continued to bend until it resembled a hairpin.

Later that evening, Manning's father gave him a six-inch nail, a quarter-inch in diameter. It was made of tough galvanized metal, and when the young man tried to bend it physically, even with the aid of a vise, his efforts failed. Matthew then tried to affect the hard metal psychokinetically but tired after a fruitless fifteen minutes and headed for bed. On the way up the stairs, he noted something very strange: a hand on his wristwatch had bent up and jammed against the glass cover.

Encouraged by this unexpected result, Matthew decided to keep trying with the nail; before going to bed he rubbed it a bit, then placed it under his pillow. By next morning it had worked — the nail had bent about thirty degrees. Soon other objects around the household started to bend even when he was quite a distance away.

In March of that year Matthew was visiting Peter Bander, the well-known English publisher and psychic researcher, when the most dazzling psychic metal phenomenon took place. A little earlier Uri Geller had given rise to considerable controversy by bending a pair of Clejuso handcuffs on arrival at Frankfurt Airport, a feat most people, including one of Bander's friends, were sure had to be a fraud. Clejuso handcuffs, experts knew, were made of a special metal that just did not bend, and to prove the point Bander's skeptical friend delivered a pair for the researcher's personal perusal.

When Manning saw the handcuffs he decided to try them on, wearing them as he watched TV that night. He "felt" something was going to happen. Sure enough, when Bander tried to take the cuffs off, something seemed to have affected their rigid structure. They were stuck, inexplicably jammed around Manning's hands. "I went cold, then hot," recounted Bander. "My mouth became dry and I felt my composure cracking. Inside the locking device, the notched bar had bent to what I estimated as some fifteen degrees."†

The friend who had lent the handcuffs arrived later in a flurry of irritation, threatening to turn Bander's home upside down until he could find the machinery they had used to bend the bar. He claimed such an effect could be accomplished only through use of hydraulic equipment, but that explanation hardly applied. After all, the bar was located in the lock with only 0.1 millimeters to spare on each side of the casing — far too small a space for any equipment to operate in.

When the cuffs were finally removed and sent to the forensic laboratories of the Metropolitan Police for analysis, the mystery only deepened. After X-rays and other forms of metallurgical analysis, experts stated categorically that no physical force had been exerted on the bent metal.

What such a force might be has, of course, befuddled all investigators. Even Manning, whose inquisitive attitude and close-up observations make him a viable authority, is confused. "All I know is that it is a nonphysical energy that has physical effects,"† says Manning, who believes feats

---

†Matthew Manning, *The Link* (New York: 1974) p.11.

†Interview with Matthew Manning, *Psychic* magazine, vol. 5, no. 5 (December 1975), p.52.

like metal-bending are of human origin but is not so sure when it comes to some of his other phenomena. "When I 'switch on' I sometimes get a feeling of being filled with a crackling abundance of energy. Others present can also sense it in the room. I think this energy attracts 'spirits' who can use it as a way of communicating with the living. It can also be used for poltergeist activity and other forms of extrasensory phenomena. It could be described as mind power but I feel the actual energy is being generated in some part of my brain rather than the mind or so-called 'spirit.' I certainly don't think anything external is controlling me."†

Scientific testing has indicated Manning's "brain theory" may be correct. When a physician in Toronto monitored the psychic's brain waves, he noted an odd, low-frequency pattern that seemed to connect his psi functioning to the "animal brain" or "Ur Gehrin," a part of the brain thought to be defunct in humans. Scientists who have scrutinized the Manning phenomena have also speculated that perhaps his abilities were literally sparked just before his birth, when his mother suffered a jolting electrical shock that sent her sprawling across a room. In a number of other cases, psychics have reported similar electric shocks before the age of ten.

Whatever the origin of Manning's energies, so powerful is the force field involved that he jammed Kirlian devices when scientists attempted to take a picture of his aura. In fact experts in Holland and France found the energy was so intense that he could "put on the power" and somehow cancel out the equivalent of 35,000 volts being fed through Kirlian machines. When investigators *have*

†Anne Dooley, "The Phenomena of Matthew Manning," *Psychic* magazine, December, 1975, p.46.

been able to get his Kirlian picture on film, the results have been stunning. His aura has been described as more brilliant than any others. Manning has also been found able to reduce this effulgence at will, to mere pinpoints of concentrated light that resemble stars exploding in space. Again, such effects have been described as unique.

Other clues to the source of Matthew's extraordinary powers were unearthed by the Toronto Society for Psychical Research in June 1974, when twenty-one top scientists from Europe and North America convened for one of the first conferences devoted solely to PK. Before these plenary sessions were under way, Manning was found able to deflect a compass and bend some thirty keys. As Geller has done on occasion, Matthew also was found able to induce PK effects at substantial distances, as if he was hooking into some form of all-pervasive energy flow.

One of the witnesses to his Toronto demonstrations was Professor Brian Josephson, a Nobel laureate in physics. After watching the psychic in action, he told a reporter for the London *Daily News:* "We are on the verge of discoveries which may be extremely important for physics. We are dealing here [i.e., in respect to metal-bending] with a new kind of energy. This force must be subject to laws. I believe ordinary methods of scientific investigation will tell us much about psychic phenomena. They are mysterious, but they are no more mysterious than a lot of things in physics already. In times past, 'respectable' scientists would have nothing to do with psychical phenomena; many of them still won't. I think that 'respectable' scientists may find they have missed the boat."†

†Matthew Manning, *The Link* (New York: 1974), p. 16.

Other Figures, Other Forms

"Beneath an infinite number of secondary differentiations, caused by the diversity of social interests, of scientific investigations or religious faith, there are two types of mind, and only two: those who do not go beyond (and see no need to go beyond) perception of the multiple — however interlinked in itself the multiple may appear to be — and those for whom perception of this same multiple is necessarily completed in some unity."

— *Pierre Teilhard de Chardin: How I Believe*

Because so very little is known of the mechanics of paraphysical energy, scholars in this new and controversial field are best advised to review as many instances of psychic phenomena as they can as a prelude to validating insights into the nature of the force. While ESP provides the commonest manifestations of what certainly appears to be a nonphysical energy ("energy X," as it's now being called), science is slowly coming to realize that PK, though still much rarer, may be the most fertile way to approach it. The results of such study could be far-reaching. As the great Yugoslavian inventor and electrical engineer Nikola Tesla put it, "The day science begins to study nonphysical phenomena, it will make more progress in one decade than in all previous centuries of its existence."

Here are merely a few of the many recent psychics whose names have been associated with PK. Their abilities illustrate the wide variety of PK manifestations and some of them provide science with excellent opportunities for profitable investigation, as do the following PK experiments.

TUMBLING DICE — "We know, yes, that PK exists. But one has to be so careful — it's so hard to prove."

The cautious words were those of the legendary J.B. Rhine, the aging North Carolina psychologist who during the last fifty years has come to assume in parapsychology the stature of Sigmund Freud in psychology. It was Dr. Rhine who, through years of laborious and carefully controlled experiments, showed that ESP did exist in man. He was also the first to prove statistically the existence of small-scale PK.

For Rhine and his wife Louisa preliminary research involved tabulating the effects mind has on the roll of dice, a procedure that blossomed into a fad during the first half of the century and eventually triggered hundreds of thousands of experiments all over the world. The basic goal of the experiments was to see if a subject could "will" what side of a die would turn face up; most of the early experiments were aimed at discovering if a person could influence whether the number would be on the high side or low side of the die range. Methods varied greatly. Sometimes only a few dice were used at a time, sometimes many; in some experiments the dice were physically thrown by the subject, in others released by specially built machines or tossed out from jars constructed to randomize their movement and counteract the effects of skillful throwing. Many different-sized dice were used, allowance always being made for possible dice bias — the term used to describe "crooked" or "imperfect" dice that tend to fall more on one side than another.

Though Rhine's PK reports were not printed until 1943 — nine years after his experiments had started — it had been obvious from the outset that something paranormal did indeed affect the roll of a moving die when such was the intent. In one of the first series of tests, held over a period of several months with twenty-five different individuals, a total number of 3,110 hits out of 562 runs (24 die falls per run; in each run the subject willing the dice to make either high or low combinations) gave a positive deviation of 300 above that of chance. Though the average rate of scoring per run was 5.5 — only slightly above the 5.0 that would have stood for chance — the extrachance value seemed far above coincidence because of the large number of trials. In fact, Rhine estimated that this figure would not occur by chance even once in more than a billion such cases.

The Rhines, and associates who helped out on the statistical end, used a rather complex formula for their tabulations, one based on probability values, levels of significance and critical ratios (CR) aimed at monitoring the chance factor. The CRs were used to measure how far the results differed from those that could derive from coincidence. Thus, if the CR was 2.5, it meant the results were 2.5 times the standard expected deviation level, and that the odds against that happening through just normal influences on the dice were about 100:1. Normally a factor of 20:1 against would have been sufficient, but the experimenters were even more cautious than statistical science normally requires. Despite the strictness of the tabulating procedure, the results were rather consistently remarkable, the odds against success often astronomical. It appeared that Rhine had recorded the very same force that had become famous in literature for causing grandfather clocks to stop on the instant of a death, that had enabled seance mediums to move objects at a distance and certain individuals to display an uncanny quantity of "luck."

When word of his findings leaked out hundreds of others pursued the same path and frequently recorded the same type of results using objects such as coins, discs and spheres that were set in motion by physical means and then affected by PK. Some of the more interesting off-shoot experiments were carried out by scientist W.E. Cox, a research associate at the Institute of Parapsychology. Cox's experiments included tests to see if subjects could, by mental power, make randomly released steel balls fall into target chutes, and others to see if individuals could influence the flow of water droplets, two experiments that were later evaluated as indicating the presence of PK, since an unusual number of the balls collected in target chutes, and target tubes filled slightly faster with sprays of water than those left as controls. One of Cox's most interesting experiments involved an eight-inch wood pendulum suspended from the top of a wood box and swinging in an arc of just less than 8 degrees. Near the end point of its swing Cox had set up a light beam directed at an electric-eye sensor so he could record the length of time it took the pendulum to make a swing by studying interruptions in the beam. (The electronic counter was accurate to one ten-thousandth of a second.) Subjects were told to make the swing of the pendulum either long or short, depending on what card they drew at random out of a pack of directions. When results were tabulated the success rate was 54.5 percent, a figure that runs 200:1 against the odds.*

The work of Rhine and his many associates led to some significant speculations and observations. Foremost was the a priori deduction that ESP and PK were actually just

---

*While the experiment appeared to indicate PK, there was still the question, however, of whether the PK affected the pendulum or the electronic monitoring devices.

different phases of a single mental process, or at least operating through the same energy medium. Obviously, the mind could not influence the fall of a die simply through regular vision. As Louisa Rhine pointed out, somewhere in the operation there had to be the intelligent recognition of the target number, and in many experiments eyesight was not even involved. Furthermore, the psychological factor, which seemed so strongly related to ESP results, seemed just as strongly related to PK. In the dice experiments it was found that a positive attitude was very important, as it is with ESP, and that if, as often happened, subjects tired after the initial phases of experimentation, their scores frequently dropped off. Like other PK investigators, the Rhines also noted the important roles that novelty, desire and even excitement can play in getting good results. Like levitation and ESP experiments, these dice tests contained a factor called "psi-missing" — negative scores, in this case, that contradicted chance and indicated that the paranormal forces were working in the direction opposite to the one desired (as when the Batcheldor table seemed glued to the floor). The exact characteristics of the PK force eluded Rhine and his followers just as it has everyone else who has tried to come to grips with it.

One experimenter, Haaken Forwald, an engineer-physicist, went so far as to work out a physical formula by which he could try measuring the PK force. By the time Forwald was attempting this, dice-testing had gone from having subjects try to influence what face would turn up to having them try to make mechanically tossed dice stop their rolls at strategically selected places on the table (the "placement technique"). Using the placement method, Forwald marked off the table surface into centimeter squares, chalked off the distance the cubes fell in the intended direction, subtracted the distance they would be expected to move by chance and then was able to compute the amount of energy involved in the dice's motions. Going a step further he also attempted to estimate how cubes of different mass would roll. What he was looking for was a physical constant in the PK movements on which science could hang a hat. Instead, however, his elaborate calculations led to the same simple conclusion others had reached: that the PK energy did not follow physical principles but responded to psychological influences. Distance of movement was quite out of proportion to weight in a number of tests that centered on the simultaneous use of dice made of very different materials.

As for the way the energy might be causing a die to roll to a described position, there were two main hypotheses. Some figured the PK force was causing a shift in a die's center of gravity. Others thought a kinetic effect was involved — that PK was pulling or pushing dice into target positions. As a result of the Forwald and Cox placement experiments, which indeed seemed to show that a die could be told not only what type number to come up but where to come to a halt, the kinetic theory got a major boost. It does seem, in fact, to be the more plausible of the two hypotheses.

Decades of such experimentation with PK led Rhine, if not to an understanding of the physics behind PK, at least to a conviction that it did exist and that it could be an elementary force integral to the human organism and constantly functioning within it. (What was *rare* was the *externalization* of such a force.) Rhine saw PK as possibly the force that prompts brain activity, perhaps, as others have suggested, acting as a method of liaison between mind and brain. If that's the case the normal function of PK would be to produce certain electrochemical and other changes in the brain.

Interestingly, Rhine speculated that psi capacity may have originated at the dawn of evolution as the way in which primitive organisms made contact with the environment, then gradually faded into the background as nature developed the sensory-motor system as a more practical way of coping with the physical world.

JEHILE B. KIRKHUFF — A sixty-nine-year-old fiddler from Lawton, Pennsylvania, Kirkhuff has astonished a number of visitors with his apparent ability to read thoughts, talk with the "dead" and read auras, even though he is blind.

A short, sickly looking man with lung problems and eyes that have been contorted by a disease that struck in his thirties, he is known to his many acquaintances as a man with very special powers outside those normally associated with a medium. Though illness has prevented his repeating his demonstrations for science, Kirkhuff is said to have been able not only to levitate tables and other objects, but actually to make humans lift off the ground. His method is to make ten people hold hands in an "energy circle," then breathe in unison until a current is felt. Next, he supposedly places his hands lightly on the shoulders of a selected subject to cause him to rise. This writer witnessed one of Kirkhuff's rare recent tries, and though there was no levitation, the subject's feet appeared on the verge of losing contact with the floor. (An infrared scanner set up during some of these displays revealed no strange energy flows, but such equipment is unreliable.)

"We are merely like cells in a tissue," says Kirkhuff, "the tissue of the universal mind. The longer we live in it, the more tricks we know." He says it with a flickering wink and a somewhat crackling laugh.

JANE ROBERTS — Author of the well-known "Seth" books, Mrs. Roberts, a resident of Elmira, New York, is an accomplished, intellectual medium who has used her abilities to evoke metaphysical answers from "spirits" who happen her way.

Like so may other spirit mediums, Mrs. Roberts has also had experience of PK. Objects have been known to inexplicably fall off her shelves, and on at least one occasion a bottle exploded on her bathroom shelf. Though she has only rarely practiced table levitation, the times she has have been rather spectacular. "One time the table rose up and banged up and down, racing across the room," she says. "It was a kind of table, a wood table, with those foldaway leaves. We were standing away from it once, and the leaves started wildly flapping up and down, and, well, it looked like it could be nearly an intelligent manifestation, but who can say?"

JEAN-PIERRE GIRARD — In recent experiments at the University of Paris, scientists filmed Girard's levitation of four fountain pens, which the thirty-three-year-old businessman caused to hover in the air for more than twenty seconds. He has also changed the color of special laboratory crystals sensitive to heat and bent metal sealed in tubes.

THE REVEREND MAE YORK — During more than seventy years as an active member of Spiritualist churches in Florida and New York, Mae York is alleged to have witnessed more paranormal events than most people hear about in a lifetime. Witnesses claim she has healed cancer, levitated a kitchen table by the merest touch of her fingers and caused objects to move without going near them. Her most bizarre claim is to have been able, in her younger, more energetic days, to cause a metal trumpet to levitate and echo "spirit" voices in midair. She attributes her powers to spirit guides who supposedly watch her every earthly move. As is the case with many PK mediums, she is also known to go into trance and be able to leave her body.

HERB SEILER — Seiler, who died of a heart attack in 1974, at the age of thirty-five, was another Spiritualist medium, who resided at Lilidale, New York, one of the largest Spiritualist camps in America. By placing his hands near the human body, he was able to cause a feeling of warmth that would stay with the subject for hours after (this writer having experienced the phenomenon).

FELICIA PARISE — Though she has stopped practicing psi because she found it too physically exhausting, this attractive, thirty-eight-year-old New York City woman, employed as a hospital technician, was found by parapsychologist Charles Honorton to be able mentally to move nonmagnetic objects placed in a bell jar, cause blurs on unexposed photographic film, and deflect a compass. She describes her psychological preparation for these feats as consisting of intense concentration. "I think only of moving the object, and block everything else out," she says.

NINA KULAGINA (aka Nelya Mikhailova) — No single psychic has had so much effect on scientific investigation as this famed Russian medium, a housewife from Leningrad.

Simply by mental concentration, Kulagina has apparently moved bread, matches, cigarettes, glasses, dishes and apples, sometimes causing them actually to jump off tables. Before no less than forty top Soviet scientists, and in front of more than twenty documentary movie cameras, she supposedly has done such remarkable things as split cigarette smoke in a bell jar and separate the yolk of an egg from its white by mind power, and deflect compasses with a wave of the hand. She has also been known to levitate objects like bottles, though this is something she has only rarely been able to do.

After most of her demonstrations, which sometimes require two hours of warm-up and demand open-mindedness among observers, Kulagina feels tremendously fatigued and often takes days to recover. Weight losses of two to four pounds have been recorded after her intense efforts, and biologists, looking for the source of her psychic energies, have been quick to point out the high percentage of sugar in her blood recorded during the demonstrations and the incredibly powerful electrical outputs registered as coming from the rear of her brain, the sector that governs vision.

The plump, dark-eyed forty-year-old has been valuable to science in other respects. It has been found that she often attains the peak of her powers during periods of strong sunspot activity and when the electromagnetic fields around her are unusually strong. It's as if she becomes a human magnet. Her electrostatic field fluctuates at moments of high tension, and the Kirlian process has shown what looks like a luminous energy streaming from her eyes. Whatever she possesses, it has affected the weight of sensitive laboratory balances, made imprints on photo paper, penetrated plexiglass. Oddly, it seems to fade during thunderstorms.

Does she step up the vibrations of some energy field, capture cosmic rays? Even the Russians, often loath to admit their perplexities, just don't know. The only certainty, as one Soviet scientist said, is that Kulagina has made PK a physical-physiological fact.

ALLA VINOGRADOVA — Not as famed as Kulagina but just as powerful is another Russian woman, Alla

Vinogradova. She has demonstrated for scientists around the world, including America's William A. Tiller, her ability to make objects like cigar containers and paper cylinders roll on command. Unlike her illustrious compatriot, Vinogradova can be emotionally relaxed during the displays and does not have to work herself up to a state of intense mental concentration.

Vinogradova feels that the energy required to perform PK comes from her solar plexus and "third eye," two points that correspond with the East's concepts of chakras and C'hi. Keen observers have noted flares of energy coming from her fingertips. On one occasion a spark was seen to jump two centimeters between her finger and a cigar container she was attempting to move.

A number of electrical factors come into play with her performances. Like those who raise tables, Vinogradova finds nonconducting surfaces the best to work with, a fact that relates her directly to Kulagina, who performs best through a dielectric screen. During her displays it was found she could cause a neon lamp to glow, as if there were some 10,000 volts per centimeter in the energy fields surrounding her. Significantly, when Western scientists studied the psychic Rudi Schneider, similar observations were made. Schneider, known for his ability to float furniture, once levitated a ball under which scientists passed an infrared beam that was received by a photocell. It was discovered that something absorbed energy from the beam and that the amount of absorption corresponded with Schneider's respiration.

"On the physical side, electrostatic phenomena clearly play a strong role in Alla's PK forces, but much more than simple contact charging, which would produce an attractive force between her hands and the objects," says Dr. Tiller, chief of the Materials Science Department at Stanford University. "Her PK force seems to be of a repulsion nature indicating the presence of another energy."†

DEAN KRAFT — A twenty-four-year-old psi healer from Brooklyn, Kraft has been found capable of mentally moving a pendulum placed inside a sealed glass cage. In a demonstration for a reporter for New York City's *Village Voice,* Kraft was also observed causing a pen to move across a rug by what appeared to be a meditation method.

Interestingly, he discovered his unusual capacities while driving with a friend down New York's Ocean Parkway one night. Suddenly the door locks started clicking up and down, as if some invisible force was pleading for attention. Soon Kraft was communicating with the clicking locks through the same type of code as that used by table-tippers.

GRANT MARSHALL — This middle-aged psychic from Johnson City, New York was a Spiritualist until he denounced that faith as being influenced by evil forces. Witnesses say Marshall could totally levitate rather heavy tables by calling on his "spirit guides." He was also known to cause cool breezes and to fall into mediumistic trances. He now refuses to go near anyone demonstrating psi powers.

INGO SWANN — At the same time as it was testing Uri Geller, the Stanford Research Institute was also documenting the PK feats of Swann, an artist from Manhattan.

Dr. Hal Puthoff and Russell Targ were surprised to find that Swann, who incidentally is one of the more co-operative psychics researchers have worked with, could cause fluctuations in a magnetometer, as well as affect the

†William A. Tiller, "A General Technical Report: A.R.E. Fact-Finding Trip to the Soviet Union, "*A.R.E. Journal,* March 1972, p.80.

mercury in a thermometer while standing a good distance away.

LETA BERECEK — Though most of her time is spent in mundane activities like driving a bus in Kent, Ohio, Mrs. Berecek is also known for a variety of psychoenergetic feats such as bending metal, reading thoughts and causing objects to disappear and reappear elsewhere, a phenomenon called teleportation. Preliminary tests made on her at Kent State University have been inconclusive, however.

TED SERIOS — Back in 1963, Serios was down on his luck; he was fifty years old, an unemployed hotel porter, and drinking much of the time. But he had one thing left, a strange ability to in some way "think" images onto unexposed film. And when he showed this bizarre capability to Jules Eisenbud, a professor of psychiatry at the Medical School in Denver, Colorado, it wasn't long before his name was virtually a household term throughout the nation.

Eisenbud studied Serios under rigid lab conditions for three years, finding the psychic able to project pictures of landscapes, buses, buildings, people and a wide range of other items on film protected against normal exposure. Serios, like Kulagina, went into a state of intense concentration to perform his feats, and operated well even when shielded in cages against normal electromagnetic influences. His "thoughtography" has been put into the realm of PK, and appropriately so: others, including members of the Thurmond levitation group, have caused similar effects, which suggests there's one energy source for both types of manifestation.

ARIGO (José Pedro de Freitas) — Arigo, a resident of Congonhas do Campo, Brazil, until his death in 1971 at the age of forty-nine, was one of the most spectacular psi finds of the century. Using his hands and sometimes unclean household knives, or, where surgery was not required, rapidly writing out complicated pharmacological prescriptions, he was reputedly able to cure literally any disease from eye cataracts to cancer.

Sometimes treating as many as four hundred patients in a day, he was filmed by American scientists making incisions with a rapid motion of his hands, then magically closing the openings without causing so much as a drop of blood. Arigo had absolutely no medical training, but apparently none of his patients ever contracted infection through his ministrations and all claimed to have been completely cured.

According to researchers, Arigo, a good natured peasant who was as confused as everybody else about his gifts, believed that while treating the sick he was possessed by the spirit of a nineteenth century German surgeon.

TONY AGPAOA — This Philippine psychic is reportedly able to open and close flesh, also, and to remove diseased tissue. Though a number of people have cried fraud, those who believe he is real — and there are many of them — say he must be affecting a force field around his patients, which in turn causes dramatic physical changes. Agpaoa performs with his bare hands. Some reports have also attributed levitational feats to this psychic surgeon.

JACK SCHWARZ — Whether in a Nazi concentration camp, where he was once held prisoner and tortured, or in front of scientists, this remarkable Dutchman has time and again demonstrated an amazing ability to heal his body and withstand huge amounts of pain. He can, for example, insert a long, sharp knitting needle smack through the thick of his arm and not only evade pain but stop the flow of blood. Afterward, his wounds *heal visibly,* as if by an internal, organic application of PK. An ardent meditator, Schwarz explains his method as involving intense visualization and complete emotional detachment. He uses this method for a number of other significant effects, such as lying on sharp nails, without suffering any bodily harm.

TORONTO YOUTH — Though his name has not been released, on request from his parents, Canadian parapsychologists have been studying a retarded twelve-year-old who possesses a powerful PK capacity that was discovered when his mother watched him levitate a cat he was mad at and "toss" the animal across a yard. Researchers have diverted his energies into metal-bending and automatic drawing, a move that has apparently taken the edge off his other, less humane practices.

CHARLES MANSON — Because accounts from the notorious California killer's "family" are, at best, unreliable, nobody knows for sure whether Manson does indeed possess the supernatural gifts attributed to him. But there have been indications that the demented clan leader does possess a psi talent. Indeed, the total control he exercised over his disciples has made a number of parapsychology buffs wonder if perhaps Manson had developed telepathic command over the minds of his murderous crew. There is also the matter of his childhood home in Charleston, West Virginia, which is said to have been "haunted" since he lived there, subsequent residents having reported knocking and rapping sounds as well as heavy bumps in the night.

And then there's this, from Vincent Bugliosi, the prosecutor at the famous Manson murder trial:

"In Independence, Sandra Good [a 'family' member] had told me that once, in the desert, Charlie had picked up a dead bird, breathed on it, and the bird had flown away. Sure, Sandra, sure, I replied. Since then I'd heard a great deal about Manson's alleged 'powers'; Susan Atkins, for example, felt he could see and hear everything she did or said.

"Midway through the arraignment I looked at my watch. It had stopped. Odd. It was the first time I could remember that happening. Then I noticed Manson was staring at me, a slight grin on his face.

"It was, I told myself, simply a coincidence."†

LENA DUUS — A shy teenager from Copenhagen, she has baffled scientists and reporters with her ability to bend thick nails without touching them, speed up a watch, and deflect a compass. Despite her fear of her own abilities, researchers have found her an ideal subject: she succeeds virtually every try.

"LILITH" — Inspired by the success of the "Philip" table group, the Toronto Society for Psychical Research has formed another group of laymen to sit at the table and has created another imaginary "ghost." This time the spirit is "Lilith," a heroine of the French Resistance during World War II. After just six sessions the new group started getting results with their various tables, reaffirming A.R.G. Owen's notion that humans can, through psychological conditioning, learn group PK.

CARMINE MIRABELLI — According to researchers' reports, Mirabelli, a Brazilian Spiritist, is one of the most spectacular mediums of this era. Witnesses have claimed he can not only relate with the dead, do automatic writing and drawing, and produce impressions of "spirit" hands in wax, but also levitate bottles and other objects. One account even has him levitating his own body while handcuffed and strapped to a chair.

Mirabelli has been said to use these same talents to mysteriously transport and dematerialize objects, just as

†Vincent Bugliosi, *Helter Skelter* (New York: 1974), p.191.

spiritualists in America and Europe have claimed to do.
ANIMAL PK — If humans can affect matter through a
natural force, how about beings lower down on the
evolutionary ladder? How about animals?

The question sounds ridiculous, and yet...

In 1971 James Davis, a researcher at the Foundation for
Research on the Nature of Man, at Durham, North Carolina, pondered the seemingly ludicrous thought, then,
knowing anything to be possible in the world of psi,
devised an experiment to test it out. Davis's setup was
fairly simple. He bought some young chicks, animals that
need a lot of warmth, and put them in a specially rigged
coop heated by a light that was controlled by a random
generator. The idea: to see if a threat to the chicks'
survival would evoke animal PK. Davis set the generator
so that the light would produce an insufficient amount of
heat, shutting off before the animals had gotten adequate
warmth. In order to survive, they would have to someway
alter the processes of the generators.

Davis found that the chicks, time after time, could
indeed accomplish this. Though the light was normally on
for only twelve hours a day, too short a period sufficiently
to heat the environment, when the chicks were present the
light flicked on with abnormal frequency, causing
increased warmth.

Going one step further, Davis next secured fertilized
eggs to see if the forces of unborn chicks could cause the
same effects. Amazingly, he discovered they could. The
light produced adequate heat when the fertilized eggs
were present, yet ran at its normal programmed intervals
when these were replaced by hardboiled eggs.

His results set off a wave of similar experiments, and a
number of parapsychologists are now trying them on
lizards, hamsters and cats.

THE SCHMIDT EFFECT — While a gifted psychic may levitate a dining room table or bend a key, researchers have often wondered if perhaps ordinary people can do the same things, though on a scale so miniscule their psi accomplishments go unnoticed.

At last, a new method of finding out may be at hand.

Helmut Schmidt, a researcher who has worked closely with J.B. Rhine in Durham, has constructed a seemingly foolproof device which, through the use of radioactive material, allows a valid test of PK effects on a very small scale. He built a set of nine lights which flash on and off in a manner that is controlled by the random decay of strontium 90 nuclei. No one knows whether the lights on the display board will rotate clockwise or counterclockwise, since the prediction of random decay through normal senses is impossible.

Dr. Schmidt, who is now using similar devices to test all sorts of animals from cockroaches to cats, found that humans could influence the flow of the lights through sheer will, a feat that apparently demonstrates that the human mind can automatically control the process of radioactive decay, and that PK forces infiltrate the tiniest of physical systems.

EFFECTS ON ORGANISMS — The effects of PK appear to extend into every animate kingdom. One researcher, following the lead of New York polygrapher Cleve Backster, has reported experiments that suggest man's mind can have a direct effect on the chemical activity such plants as the philodendron. Another, French cian Jean Barry, has reported that in carefully lab experiments subjects were found ca mental power to retard the growth of parasites, Stereum purpureum a

In England, a scientist named

the conclusion, after some 1,500 tests, that PK in the form of a concentrated human thought could direct the movements of paramecia, unicellular organisms common in pond water.

WITCHCRAFT AND SORCERY — PK is clearly relevant to the more occult practices, from African voodoo to the white and black magic so prevalent throughout the Western world today. Spells, hexes, the conjuring of underworld entities are expressions of the belief that mind can have power over matter.

That witches tap the same occult energy that psychics do is fairly evident. The famous English witch Sybil Leek, for example, has supposedly employed her occult skills to make tables float and rappings erupt from wood. Reports of the witchcraft trials in seventeenth century Salem are filled with accounts of phenomena that fit perfectly into the framework of a classic poltergeist case.

The same can be said of sorcerers and shamans. In Russia there are accounts of conjurors turning "bird-soul" — being able to take to the air like fairy-tale witches. Recently, Westerners have been fascinated by the accounts of Carlos Castaneda, a California anthropologist whose apprenticeship to a Mexican Indian sorcerer named Juan Matus has been the topic of several best-selling books. According to Castaneda, the sorcerer and other "men of knowledge" had learned to project an energy from their bodies that allowed them to leap up cliffs as if ey were weightless.

HING FOR THE SKY — During the 1950s, the illia, Ontario was a man named Rolf Alexander. ame? Supposedly he could disperse clouds mind.

of people who not only believed his witnessing them firsthand. In fact, on 12 September 1954, in front of fifty people, Alexander asked a bystander to pick a group of fluffy cumulus clouds and then pinpoint the exact one he wanted Rolf to knock out of the sky, while keeping the others more or less stationary. Breathing deeply and "visualizing" the cloud's disappearance, Alexander required only eight minutes to make the cloud distend and then vanish. Two similar attempts that day were equally successful.

While any meteorologist will be quick to point out that cumulus clouds have a short life span anyway, normal factors like wind don't seem to provide an answer in this case. First, there were the "control" clouds, which had remained intact. Then there was the fact that, on occasion, Rolf varied his act, not dissipating a cloud but creating a donutlike hole in its center. Such feats, filmed by photographers in long sequences, were accomplished at distances of up to ten miles.

The famous Hungarian healer Oskar Estebany has also been rumored able to "reach the sky" mentally. "I remember one time I was driving him to the lab," says Dr. Justa Smith, a Buffalo scientist who had studied Estebany's ability to change human enzymes psychically; "he told me at one point to look up at the sky, at this one cloud. He said he was going to make it disappear. Naturally I couldn't swallow that, and yet a few minutes later it was out of sight. I'm not convinced, as a scientist, that he really caused that, but it made me wonder."

ENERGY "ZAPS" — In voodoo lore there's a su
that power from the mind, or "spirits," can
strike men down. At least it's *thought* to b
though some have come to doubt i
lance writer Dan Greenburg rep
the occult, *Something's There (*

"energy zap" may be more than a figment of the imagination. According to him, Esalen founder Mike Murphy and a friend once concentrated their PK powers on a pitcher in a Los Angeles Dodgers game — and the pitcher suddenly fell down.

Greenburg himself has claimed to have conjured similar energies. As he reported in the June 7, 1976 issue of *Newsweek*, "While watching a ghastly old movie on TV, I half-seriously suggested to my companion that I was going to hurl an invisible bolt and shut the set off. I hurled. The set shut off."

* * *

It's much easier to report on the bewildering array of PK happenings than it is to analyze the force or forces behind them. In the remaining section of my book, however, I'll edge as close as I can toward defining the elusive parameters of PK, examining some bizarre events (both well documented and otherwise) and some fascinating experiments and theories.

Elaine Fortson, an Ohio psychic, works at bending a piece of metal sealed in a tube through sheer will. Ms. Fortson, whose daughter has caused PK effects also, is being studied at Kent State University. The right end of the metal tube shows a slight — but significant — bend.

Gary Anderson, A Buffalo, N.Y. mind control instructor, points to a chart illustrating the various levels of consciousness. It is in the levels below beta that many instances of psi phenomena occur. (Photo by David Stockton).

At left is Jose Silva, founder of Silva Mind Control, the technique that teaches control of altered states of consciousness and development of ESP. Left bottom, Uri Geller attempts to bend a thick cylinder held by physicist David Bohm in one of a series of tests at Birkbeck College, University of London, in September of 1974. At Uri's right is a Geiger counter the psychic influences. One of the illustrations from URI GELLER: MY STORY (Praeger). Below, Dr. Wilbur Franklin of Kent State watches psychic Elaine Fortson attempt to influence light. (Photo by David Tinney).

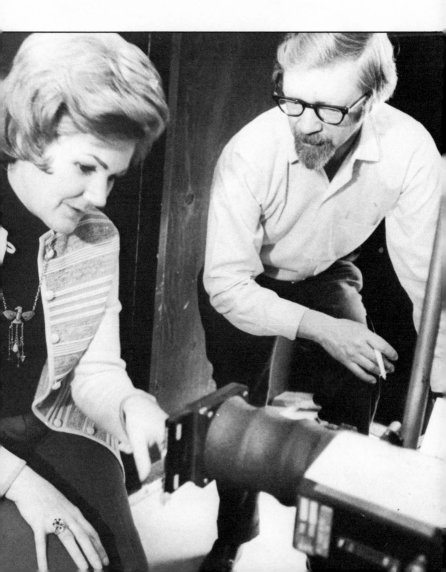

A photograph shows the various metals bent, twisted, and broken by Uri Geller. He does this through a gentle rubbing motion of the finger against the metal. (Photo by Shipi Shtrang). Copyright

Vernon Craig of Wooster, Ohio, a self-proclaimed fakir born in America, strolls across white-hot coals barefoot. Though the temperature of the coals has reached that needed to melt steel, Craig, after walking across 25-feet of fire, somehow prevents so much as a blister from forming on his feet — this despite walking rather slowly. Scientists, unable to explain the fakir, continue to investigate his odd abilities. There is speculation what he does is produce a protective psychokineticlike condition that shields him from mutilating harms. He functions at an altered state of consciousness.

Karate adept Hidy Ochiai meditates and tenses his body before performing his nail-board feat, in which he has withstood weights of concrete ranging from 100 to 600 pounds being crushed on his bare stomach while lying on sharp nails.

An assistant crushes the concrete on Ochiai with a swift, powerful hit as the karate adept grimaces on the torture board. Ochiai says during such feats he helps protect himself through C'hi, an energy Easterners believe flows around the human body.

At bottom, a pillow floats by itself as members of SORRAT (see appendix), a Southern psi hobby group, concentrate from the other side of the room. Directly below the same alleged PK raises a bucket totally off the floor through no known means. The group, formed by a University of Missouri professor-poet, started out with tables and have progressed to PK effects with a wide variety of objects. (Courtesy John Richards)

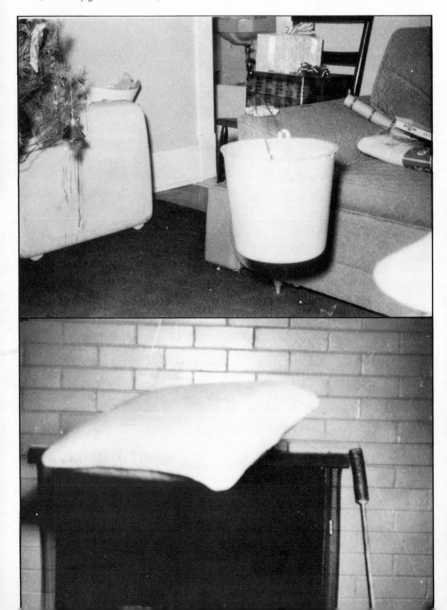

Here, members of SORRAT caused the alleged total levitation of a snack tray with (bottom) and without (directly below) hand contact. According to eye-witness accounts, the group members have caused the snack tray to remain aloft for as long as three minutes through no known means. They also cause rapping noises in wood and have totally levitated, apparently, heavy dining room tables during experiments over the last two decades. (Courtesy John Richards)

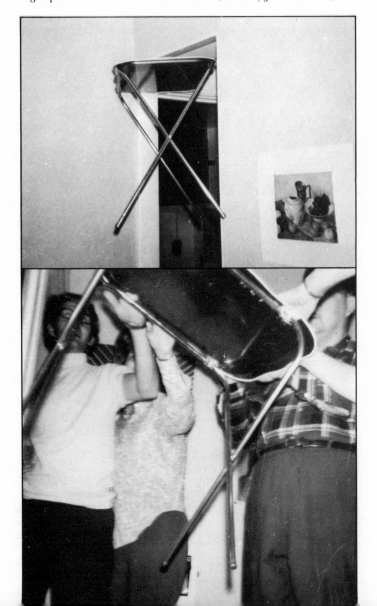

Section Three: A New Energy Influence

A meditator sends healing energy into the neck of an ill woman. (Photo by Suzanne Dalton.) Copyright

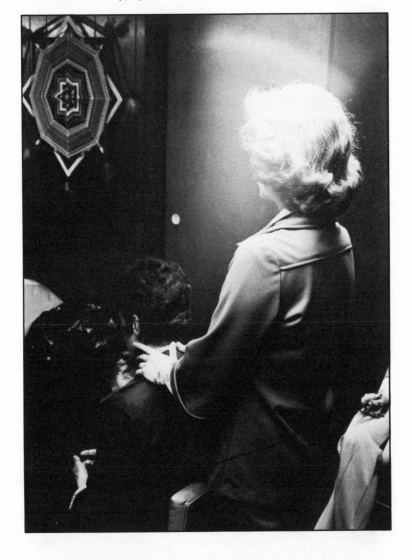

A New Energy Influence?

*"For aught we know an atom may consist of the radiations
which come out of it. It is useless to argue that radiations
cannot come out of nothing. . . . The idea that there is a
hard little lump there, which is the electron proton, is an illegitimate intrusion of commonsense notions derived from touch.
Matter is a convenient formula for describing what happens
where it isn't."*

— *Bertrand Russell: An Outline of Philosophy*

1. Something New

The scientists were in the car when it happened, taking
the highway to Santa Cruz. It was November 1972, and
Edgar Mitchell, Wilbur Franklin, Harold Puthoff and Mr.
and Mrs. Russell Targ had grabbed a quick break from
the rigors of experiment preparations at Stanford Research
Institute to show special guest Uri Geller the beach.

Geller stared out a window, watching as the tedious blur
of autumn trees passed by. Suddenly he turned to his
companions and asked if anyone had a ring. You know, he
said, something he could try his "powers" on, something
that would present them with *proof.*

"Well, I guess we can just write it off in the name of
science," said Mrs. Targ, wriggling off her platinum
wedding band.

As far as those present can recollect, Geller never
touched the ring beforehand. Instead he simply had the
scientist's wife place it between the palms of her own

hands. With sharp eyes following his every move, he then raised his right wrist a few inches above her cupped hands and concentrated, for some reason cracking his knuckles at the same time. After a few minutes Mrs. Targ opened her hands, and there it was: a strange fissure clear through the band, looking as if sliced by an invisible razor. "Incredible!" said Dr. Franklin, rolling it in his hand. "It looks like it was pulled apart!"

Standing at a lab counter at SRI a few days later, Franklin dumped out the contents of several manila envelopes, carefully sorting them according to their tags. There were broken spoons, bent forks and an array of other strangely contorted objects. The Kent State physicist had been invited out to the special experiments in the hope that his metallurgical expertise would shed some light on the mystery of the "Gellerized" metal, and he had decided the best means would be a process called scanning electron microscopy.

It was to be the closest look ever at what Geller had done. Using electron bombardment instead of light beams, the microscope could magnify an object to more than 22,000 times its actual size, unveiling the secrets of the atoms themselves. Would it all turn out to be one big hoax? Or would Franklin discover the impossible: that this *mystère extraordinaire* named Uri Geller was for real?

When he got into the analysis, Franklin was not particularly impressed with the broken spoons, bent forks or most of the other bent metal objects. Though there remained the bothersome question of how Geller achieved the breaks, the surface structures indicated breakage due to simple tensile stress. The effect produced in the first few fractures was closely duplicated by placing a control spoon in a vise and bending it with pliers.

Then the scientist got around to the platinum ring, and

what the microscope revealed was dramatic. According to experts, when metal like platinum breaks there should be some indication of either a manufacturing flaw or of the metal being snapped, cut or someway pulled in two. Metallurgists would have anticipated metal fatigue, ductile failure, shear failure or a "necking down" of the metal's diameter. All that was missing.

But that was only the start. When Franklin looked closer yet he saw something startling: *the fracture surface indicated that atomic sections had started to melt at the time of breakage,* a condition that indicated temperatures of around 1,750° centigrade. Incredibly, the ring's surface suggested there had been a near-perfect atomic split when the fracture occurred. Meanwhile only a hundredth of an inch from the melted section, the fracture showed another uncanny effect: *the atoms looked as if they had been frozen near absolute zero.*

That there should have been evidence of melting was certainly strange; that such low-temperature effects should appear in a metal broken at room temperature was remarkable; that both should occur together was outright weird.

When, toward the end of his microscope probe, Franklin focused on a fractured stainless steel needle, the mystery deepened.

The needle had been fractured the previous August when scientists conducted experiments at the home of Dr. Andrija Puharich. At the time, Geller was being tested to see if he could create the so-called "stigmata effect," a flow of blood through no known biological cause. Edgar Mitchell had directed Geller to stand a few feet from him while Mitchell jabbed the needle in the air, pretending the sharp point was piercing the psychic's wrist. About fifteen minutes later the experimenters' jaws suddenly dropped:

tiny specks of blood had appeared on Geller's hand, simply because they had willed them to.

After this bizarre demonstration the needle was casually placed on a nearby table and completely ignored — until an assistant happened upon it and found it had broken in two. "These weird things," said Geller, "they always happen around me!"

That the needle was fractured was, in itself, unimportant. Certainly Geller could have found the time for some clever sleight-of-hand. But when placed under the eye of Franklin's microscope, it didn't show any of the normal signs of fracture either.

There should have been a dimpled network on the needle's magnified surface to indicate ductile failure, i.e. that something had turned the metal malleable and caused the break. Instead, a bizarre intergranular structure was revealed. While it looked as though the fracture could have been caused by chemical corrosion or possibly even some mysterious form of stress, further testing eliminated both alternatives. The discovery of a microscopic and seemingly unaccountable hole on the fracture surface of one piece of the needle was a further complication.

"I was scared to say much back then, scared of ridicule and in need of some double-checking, but I was very excited," says Franklin. "Even before the Stanford tests formally began, I felt I had evidence, very convincing evidence, on the interaction of mind and metal."

For the physicist the long search had begun. A holder of metallurgical degrees from Yale University and Case Institute of Technology, he was well versed in what should and should not happen with metals, and what Geller had done threw a monkey wrench into much of what he had learned of physical laws, making him seriously believe, for the first time, that PK was a reality.

However he wanted additional proof. For the next thirty months he looked everywhere for it, but his only return on an investment of countless hours of research at the Library of the American Society of Metals was blood-shot eyes. Nor did he get a satisfactory answer from extensive consultations with some of the nation's top metallurgical experts, including esteemed professors Doris Wilsdorf of the University of Virginia and Robert Hehemann of Case Western Reserve. Their analyses only corroborated what the physicist had first suspected: "Everybody who I could get to look at what I found was highly interested — and nobody could raise an adequate explanation."

The main problem was that experts couldn't think of a feasible way of recreating the effect found in the ring. After more than thirty months of research, Franklin could only come up with one possible way of duplicating it by normal means, but that was a remote possibility indeed. First, the platinum would have to be cooled to near absolute zero, he ventured, and then partially cleaved with some device so that there would be a clean atomic split. Next, the ring would have to be heated back to room temperature and, in some way no one has yet been able to devise, pulled apart at that temperature without it showing any signs of regular breakage. Finally it would be necessary to meticulously spot certain sections with a powerful micro-laser beam. He estimated such an attempt would cost some $50,000, require a team of top experts, and take a few months of trial-and-error attempts. Clearly, it didn't seem like the answer.

Throughout Franklin's investigation, the international

debate over whether Geller was a fraud kept gathering momentum, to the accompaniment of reports from all over the world of others who were mysteriously bending metal. Around January 1975, armed with new information gathered from other metal-benders, Franklin decided he had waited long enough. He felt too many psychics had gone down to defeat because of a bad press, irrational skepticism and the magicians' union, "and suddenly Geller was in the same situation. It seemed only ethical to try to get the truth out, if nothing else than for historical reasons. Some magicians were leveling what I considered an unjustified attack."

His declarations of faith in Geller's authenticity were followed neither by TV lights nor any apocalyptical speech at Columbia's Physics Colloquium. There was just a hostile silence. On the Kent State campus colleagues began to give him uncomfortable looks, his involvement in psi provoking questions as to his departmental obligations and whether he was fit for certain promotions. Grants for further psi research never came; physics and metallurgical journals shied away from his findings.

Finally, in the April 1975 edition of *New Horizons*, the small Toronto parapsychology journal, Franklin was able to publicize his important findings. In a metallurgical report, written in technical language few laymen would be able to understand, he declared that he had come to the conclusion that Geller had caused teleneural* reactions in the metal specimens. Here at last was a respected scientist publicly announcing his belief that PK was not just the fantasy of fanatics, but an objective fact, a reality that the microscope could prove.

---

*From two Greek words meaning "at-a-distance" and "nerves" (i.e. related to the nervous system.).

While in Franklin's own mind the data he possessed confirmed his feeling that Geller was genuine, other aspects of the issue were anything but clear. What *constituted* this "mental ability" to make metal melt and freeze at the same time, spoons and keys bend even at substantial distances?

Maybe, Franklin surmised, the force concerned was a "toss between the material and the spiritual," connected in some way to human auras and other unknown, "higher" levels of force. There was, after all, venerable psychic literature to consult, including numerous concepts about a primary life-giving energy that covers the universe like an invisible drum skin and is in throbbing contact with the human mind. Its names are legion — tumo, mana, fiery ether, munis, animal magnetism, biocosmic power — but they all seem to refer to what is now called psi force. Like so many other researchers in the area, Franklin figured it might be in the mishmash of ancient energy terms that lay the answer to whatever sliced chunks out of the platinum ring and caused tables to rise paraphysically.

"But let's face it, we just don't know what it is, where it comes from," he says. "All we know is what it isn't. We're talking not of a force in the same way physics knows forces, but of some kind of influence. I'm sure it's not electromagnetic or nuclear or gravitational in nature. It's something new, something exciting, something above and beyond anything physics has ever really known."

2. The Search for Energy X, the Phantom Force

That humans are surrounded by a psi sea of invisible, life-giving energies, and that these subtle influences link men not only together but also to the stars, is a concept that goes back as far as man has kept records. Ancient Egyptians referred to a primordial, massless force which they called "Ga-Llama," and wrote of such metaphysical planes as the "Ka" in the Book of the Dead. In ancient Sanskrit is to be found the word "prana," an all-encompassing term denoting an absolute energy that breathes life energy into matter and, like the pneuma and ether of the ancient Greeks, causes organic motion. According to ancient Hindu· thought, we are all one, all cells of the cosmic tree.

Of course modern science, dominated philosophically by the materialist-reductionist point of view, maintains that such paraphysical theories are exercises in irrationalism and constantly drills into our learning banks that there are but three basic elements, solids, liquids, gases, and but four basic forms of energy, the gravitational, the weak and strong nuclear, and the electromagnetic. Everything around us can be explained in those basic energy and physico-chemical mechanisms, say our texts, without the need for a principle of "spirit vitality."

And yet man still searches beyond the materialistic point of view, still looks for a life-giving power that would comprise a fifth force unknown as yet to science and perhaps constitute a fourth state of matter. The recent explosion of psi phenomena, perhaps itself a symptom of modern man's dissatisfaction with materialism, has added fuel to that fire and sent numbers of scientists back to the past to take another look at those "vital forces" so frequently mentioned in early writings.

In the words of some of our ancestors, matter is what can be metaphorically described as "coagulated smoke," a congealing of pulsating etheric energy that gets drawn into cosmic vortices and is carried by wind, rain and fire. Such was the thinking of the great sixteenth century physician Paracelsus, one of the forerunners of modern medicine and at the same time a controversial mystic who traveled widely in the foggy land of alchemy where soul forms were thought to link every atom, making man a cousin even to stone. Paracelsus was led to think of "vital forces," or what he called A'Kasa, Archaeus and Liquor Vitae, because of his experience of lying among plants and flowers and "feeling" their energy. As he watched the subtle movements of plants at close range he frequently noticed that flowers rhythmically opened and closed in accordance with phases of the moon and planets, which convinced him that they were somehow cosmically connected, and not necessarily by any known force.

Paracelsus's readings in the works of the ancient yoga masters strengthened his dawning belief in invisible cosmic links and he began writing in detail of the biocosmic forces that served to form physical reality and allowed man's mind to act on matter at a distance. Though his use of terms is hardly precise, his theories about these forces clearly seem to parallel similar theories found in other cultures. His Archaeus, for instance, strongly resembles the "astral light" described by Indian masters, the sparks and spirals of etheric energy observed by Spiritualistic mediums, and the hazelike energy clairvoyants like Rudolf Steiner saw the sea inhaling and exhaling and thought of as the "soul of the planet."

What Paracelsus seems to have had in mind were bands of energy that encircled all heavenly structures large and small and finally encircled man himself. He saw man connected by a sort of psi river to a cosmic ocean, where all memories and actions are stored, as in Hinduism's Akashic Record, and all life energy is brewed. Paracelsus's Archaeus was what linked the cosmos together, making possible the operations of magic (ESP and PK, as we might say). Fluctuations in astral energies could be as responsible for biological health as the more obvious physical and psychological factors and thus allow for a new approach to medical treatment, he said. Unfortunately none of that sat too well with the scientific community in his own day and he was opposed at every turn, especially by apothecaries who were infuriated that he was starting to treat ailments without the use of their drugs. Though many of his ideas both as a physician and a chemist were clearly prescient, his name was defamed, his discoveries ignored.

Still, Paracelsus's basic idea of a spiritual essence that could cure certain illnesses never died. When, around 1775, a Viennese doctor named Franz Anton Mesmer took a close look at the scorned work of Paracelsus, he concluded his predecessor had been nothing like the crazed alchemist portrayed in history. In fact Mesmer found that healing techniques based on the existence of what we could today call bioelectricity and biomagnetism did indeed work, that there did seem to be that omni-present "fluid" that flowed from star to star, from macro-cosmos to microcosmos. Mesmer's word for it was "animal magnetism," a force he coupled with hypnotism and used in curing the sick.

In 1780 when Luigi Galvani found that electrical force could generate movement in a severed frog's leg, this seemed to lend support to the idea that living organisms might be surrounded by magnetic forces that controlled many of their processes. Unfortunately for Mesmer, how-ever, the scientific community treated him much as it had treated Paracelsus. Essentially it ignored him. Indeed, leading eighteenth century minds were so hostile to any-thing strange that scientific committees in both Europe and America even rejected as superstition the idea that such things as meteorites existed, despite strong evidence to the contrary. Not only were natural scientists alarmed at Mesmer's "Dissertation on the Discovery of Animal Mag-netism," but so were his colleagues in the medical profession, who vehemently opposed the healing sessions or "seances" in which he brought "animal magnetism" to bear on innumerable ills. The main reason for all the hostility was jealousy. Where many failed, Mesmer, by placing patients near tubs of water and metal filings that supposedly channeled their energy, often claimed dramatic successes. When members of scientific investigation committees wandered into his sessions, they soon became convinced he had either taken leave of his senses or was holding hands with the devil, a charge frequently leveled at modern psychic healers. As a result, Mesmer was chased out of Austria and forced to open up shop in France, where things proved no better. There the French Academy of Science, led by the American ambassador, Benjamin Franklin, claimed that Mesmer's powers were "nonexistent," and he was soon ostracized from Paris and tainted with charlatanism.

Orthodox science's antagonistic attitude toward energy X or its like became even harsher when, in 1828, Germany's Friedrich Wohler created synthetic urea in a laboratory. That seemed to prove the materialist-reductionist view that matter was composed only of tangible elements and given the breath of life by purely earthly energy. In Germany, the physicist, chemist and industrialist Baron Karl von Reichenbach, discoverer of creosote, watched the materialists flexing their reinvigorated muscles but didn't fear their academic punch. Reichenbach wasn't about to take their word as law, and, being familiar with the career of Mesmer, knew only too well that many radical thinkers in the past had been unjustifiably discredited by mainstream scientists who used their titles rather than logic or proof to dismiss new ideas. After developing his own theory concerning a strange energy that, in a manner somewhat reminiscent of "Mesmeric fluid," flowed through all matter, he bypassed the normal channels of scientific publicity and brought his case directly before the public in an article in the Augsburg *Universal Gazette,* "The Od Force, Letters on a Newly Discovered Power in Nature." In it he proposed a scientific approach to what was generally regarded as the pseudo-powers of wizards, sorcerers and conjurors.

Reichenbach's "od" or "odic force," named for the omnipotent ancient deity Odin, was said to stream forth from people, plants, metals (especially magnets), crystals, the moon and the sun. There was a blue, negative od, and at the other end of the pole a reddish-yellow, positive od. Reichenbach had devised a sort of "energy map" after recording the observations of hundreds of sensitives whom he escorted into a pitch-black darkroom and listened to as they described flaming, colorful energies sprouting from crystals and magnets that had been placed in the room. He was sure that what they were seeing must be something new, undiscovered, an energy that could perhaps account for phenomena like dowsing and many of the other paranormalities that are to this day unexplained. (Interestingly, Reichenbach's map seems to relate to what contemporary researchers now call bioluminescence, a brightness seen to flow from objects when they are seen through a supersensitive photomultiplier.)

What Reichenbach called od did seem to be a new force, though it had similarities with electromagnetism and other forces. It could be carried over a wire and it seemed to combine with other energies; most importantly, it seemed to vary according to the direction in which observed objects were pointed: if a magnet in a darkroom was pointed north, the emanations were bluish, if west, yellow, if south, red, if east, white-gray. With proper knowledge this energy, according to Reichenbach, could be transferred to and concentrated in an object, especially if that object was organic. In fact he had designed special blankets that would capture the force and effect this purpose.

A hundred years after Reichenbach's controversial findings, Wilhelm Reich began speaking of his "orgone" energy, a universal force similar to od not only in its all-pervasiveness but in its potential for storage. Reich even built box-like accumulating devices to capture this arcane energy, which he said served as an etherlike medium for light, electromagnetism and gravity. He showed one such device to Albert Einstein, who confirmed that the Reich instruments did seem to operate against known physical laws and said he could not account for it. One such contraption involved a layering of organic and inorganic materials in a sandwich effect to collect an energy Reich believed was at the root of all matter, ever-present in the atmosphere, and even able to bridge a vacuum. When a sick person was put under his "energy blankets," paranormal healing was often claimed as a result.

Reich's energy-collecting devices puts one in mind of the recent popular theory that pyramids and other specially designed structures somehow collect a life force that's raining down through the universe. It is as if certain objects operating under unknown physical laws can attract and store psi energy in the same way a greenhouse captures infrared light from the sun. So effective have been experiments with "pyramid power" that the Western world has developed an almost faddish interest in it. As it is with virtually every idea to do with energy X, there are no solid facts regarding its similarities to or differences from natural forces. All that is known is that "pyramid power," like od or Mesmeric fluid, seems to work.

The first hint of pyramid power came in the 1930s when a Frenchman, Antoine Bovis, came across a startling phenomenon while touring the King's Chamber of the Great Pyramid of Gizeh. Bovis there noticed a garbage can filled to the brim with dead rodents. There was nothing strange in that; it was quite understandable that thousands of rodents might wander into the pyramid and then starve, to be later disposed of by the caretakers. But what caught the Frenchman's curiosity was the lack of any rotting odor coming from the can. When he got closer he was astonished to find the rodents in nearly perfect condition, as if they had been mummified.

When he got back to France, Bovis quickly constructed a replica of the Cheops pyramid and found he could duplicate the rat effect. A dead cat, fish, eggs and various meats all remained inexplicably preserved far longer than normal when placed inside it. The pyramids he and others were soon building seemed to work best when, like the Cheops pyramid, they were aligned north-to-south in exact accordance with the earth's magnetic fields, a fact that seemed to link this mysterious phenomenon to Reichenbach's od.

Word quickly spread, and so did new pyramid revelations. Today, the wondrous effects pyramids supposedly cause could fill a thick book. In Russia, experimenters discovered that dull razors, if placed inside a pyramid, sharpened, as though their crystal structure or protective coat had been changed by an unknown energy. Others found that meditators produced markedly stronger alpha brain waves while sitting under pyramids and that diseased persons often felt better after spending time in such a structure. Something also happens to water. After setting for a day or two inside a pyramid it acquires a noticeably better taste and, when poured near a plant, enhances the growth of the plant much as "alpha-treated" water has been found to do. Pyramid energy and energy X now seem so closely connected that some people are speculating whether poltergeist homes may be haunted because of their architectural features, which perhaps cause etheric energies to resonate. There have also been unsubstantiated reports that pyramid power can cause antigravitational effects, enhance intuition and increase PK power ability.

While pyramids seem a good way to try and understand incoming cosmic flows, and indeed may one day serve to channel the ethereal in the same "magic" way antennas and TV sets harness radio waves, those delving into the mysteries of human-provoked phenomena like PK have felt a need first to take a closer look at the way energy X manifests itself in the higher biological systems. Research in this line has been stepped up in an attempt to find out more about human auras, or what some Russians like to call bioplasmic energy, a substance similar to the astral and etheric "doubles" seen by mystics and mediums. Such counterpart bodies, which Russian biologist V.M. Inyushin has described as the plasmic, organizing state of the body, quite separate from its simple electrical state, seem to act as a medium for psi, a sort of umbilical to the above.

Nothing in this decade has excited parapsychologists more than the new ways recently developed to photograph the human aura or "energy body." Though a good number of scientists claim otherwise, the consensus among leading researchers is that methods like the Kirlian technique, which employs an electrical charge to make the "bioplasmic" energy photographable, are actually focusing in on an unknown energy configuration that is possibly connected to an omnipresent energy X. Except perhaps in terms of a "cold electron emission," there seems no meaningful way the newly photographed auras can be described other than as an unknown energy. Electrophysiological studies have shown that the corona emanations of the Kirlian aura do not depend on skin temperature, galvanic skin response, dilations, vaso-constriction or perspiration. Instead, Kirlian photographers often find tantalizing evidence that auras are cocoonlike concentrators from and into which mysterious energies are constantly flowing. Intriguingly, auras often change in relation to cosmic occurrences like sunspots, something Paracelsus knew about long ago, and their behavior somewhat resembles that of the Hindu's prana or the Spiritualist's ectoplasmic "spirit lights."

Just as something like od or orgone has been thought to form the whole of physical reality, so the aura is often looked upon as the possible generator of physical life, an invisible blueprint for the body. Such seemingly far-fetched ideas are not simply theories, but have a basis in actual Kirlian observations. For one thing, researchers have repeatedly been startled to note that when a leaf with a portion cut off is placed on a Kirlian plate the resulting photographs show what has been termed the phantom effect: a ghostly energy outline of the cut-off portion shows up in the photographs along with the leaf. It's as if the "soul" of the plant lingers after the plant, or part of it, is gone. Semyon Kirlian, the Russian electrician who developed the photographic method that bears his name, had also noticed that a person's hand aura was often predictive, that it detected illness before there were any physical signs of it, and that his photographs reflected different emotional states.

The idea that biological constructions are held together and in fact designed by prephysical energies can't be solely attributed to Kirlian research. While biologists and neurophysiologists are now beginning to realize that not all mechanics of mind and body can be explained on the basis of neuronal potentials and biochemical memory, this was known decades ago by the brilliant Yale University scientist Harold Saxton Burr, who by use of ultrasensitive microvoltmeters had discovered that living things have electromagnetic organizing fields that are worn like invisible corsets. Dr. Burr was able to demonstrate, after years of laborious observation, that what he called electrodynamic force fields or life fields often anticipate biological events in the same way auras sometimes predict disease. They forecast processes like ovulation and can even predict, in a frog's egg for example, where the nervous system will eventually develop.

Burr's electromagnetics seem to be a bridge between the physical and the prephysical foundations of life. The life fields themselves are affected by a higher force, namely that of the mind. This was shown by one of Burr's students, Leonard Ravitz, who discovered that the state of a person's mind definitely affects the voltage gradient of the field. The full implications of that revelation are not clear, but it could go a long way toward explaining the state of trance and the connection between extraphysical forces and altered states of consciousness.

There seem to be a number of different energies working around, through and from organic cells. One form, discovered by Russian histologist Alexander Gurwitsch, is a radiation that seems to flow between organic systems and may be yet another manifestation of energy X. In the 1920s, Gurwitsch found that when an onion is placed in a glass tube and pointed, like a vegetal cannon, at the root of a second onion, the root of the target vegetable substantially increases its cell divisions, a process known as mitosis. Gurwitsch called the phenomenon "mitogenic radiation."

By studying even more closely the process of mitosis within cells, another Soviet academician, Alexander Dubrov, came to the conclusion that living cells emit what he chose to call "biogravitational waves." During cellular mitosis, Dubrov claimed, one could see as weak luminescence the energylike radiation of photons, a flow possibly related to the mysterious waves others have claimed to observe between the tissues of juxtaposed organisms, especially ones that are diseased. The Russian scientist boldly pointed out that the waves he had studied could conceivably be the vehicle for phenomena like telepathy and PK.

There's an excellent possibility that mechanisms designed on the same principle as pyramids could capture the apparently wide array of bioenergies, allowing man a sort of magnifier with which to trap latent PK. At least one inventor, Czechoslovakian engineer Robert Pavlita, has claimed to have already done this with what he calls "psychotronic generators." According to a number of firsthand reports, Pavlita has successfully demonstrated an ability to make distant objects move by merely "thinking" into his odd yet simple devices, which are said to work, like pyramids, because of their specific shapes. Unfortunately most of the details are a state and personal secret, so the exact mechanics of the PK generators remain unknown to the outside world. All that has been reported is that the mysterious gadgets do work, and in controlled situations where air currents, static electricity and temperature changes could not be the cause of the extramotor movements that occur. North American journalists Sheila Ostrander and Lynn Schroeder, authors of the best-selling book *Psychic Discoveries Behind the Iron Curtain,* have reported that these generators work even under water.

Shaped like modern sculptures and built of materials like copper, gold, iron, brass and even wood, the generators allegedly collect the paraphysical energies of the operator, storing them until enough has been banked to unleash on a target object. When the subject has sent energy into the generator, he can then make needles balanced in a bell jar rapidly turn, solenoids spin, and nonmagnetic objects cling to the device. When humans are charged with this "psychotronic" energy, their ESP scores are said to jump as high as 100 percent! Czech scientists will only say that these remarkable effects are the fruit of inquiry into ancient texts.

Even if we knew exactly how the generators are constructed, however, we'd still be left wondering what the actual energy is. And that question can only be partially answered by listing its characteristics and proclivities. For instance, energy X is observed in the operation of light, luminous radiation, heat, chemical reactions and magnetism, and yet has some differences from all of them. It is primarily synergetic, that's to say it has a formative or coagulating effect, the opposite of the principle of entropy, according to which matter has a tendency to disintegrate. It is seen by sensitives in sprays of haze and misty auras and is claimed to pop up in seances as small "spirit lights." It can be focused, melded with other energies, refracted, polarized. It precedes physical change. It flows from object to object. It fills all space, permeating everything. It is often reflected from metals and absorbed by organic matter. It can clear a path in the suitably receptive consciousness for the forces of psi and it is certainly closely linked with the primordial energies that flow through mind. In highly organized life systems it has a tendency to form a cosmic blueprint from which the physical body develops.

Certainly the makeup of energy (or energies) X presents science with a major challenge not likely to be settled before a knockdown, drag-out fight. On one side are those who say that mankind is dealing with an energy completely unknown when it crosses the path of psi phenomena like PK. They often point out that the density of this energy varies in inverse proportion to its distance from it source, which if true would set it apart from the discovered natural energies. On the other side are the more conventional theorists who, perhaps jealous of the reputation of the orthodox scientific canon, maintain it is simply electromagnetism, perhaps some part of the spectrum that is still unknown. As *Newsweek* science writer Charles Panati has put it, electromagnetism is a mathematical cornerstone of physics and therefore such theorists believe it must apply.

Of those who have closely studied PK phenomena such as metal-bending, John G. Taylor, the English physicist, is the most vocal supporter of an electromagnetic theory to account for the likes of Uri Geller. Dr. Taylor has decided some forms of PK may be the result of a nonionizing species of electromagnetic radiation, most probably one of low frequency, which would allow in theory for adequately deep penetration into metals. Possibly, says Taylor, the metal-bending mechanism is that of oscillations initiated in the small grains of the metal; if such oscillations are transferred to dislocations in the metal, the eventual result would theoretically be bendings and fractures. (The physicist, whose ideas are considered by some to be premature, says the psi metal-bending force isn't anything like ionizing radiation and rules out cosmic radiation, gravity and nuclear transferences; like most others, he does not seem to think massless particles like neutrinos are the cause either.) There has to be room for intentionality, or conscious control, he says, and some forms of electro-magnetism fit that bill. Taylor is quick to admit, however, that his electromagnetic speculations spring mainly from an inability to explain PK phenomena in any other way.

Though it is much too early to tell — and it's always unwise to champion hasty and incomplete theories — many already believe that science, once it gets around to studying PK and ESP energies with the needed fervor, will have to go beyond known forms of electromagnetism for the answers. There are just too many problems with electromagnetism to make it seem a viable psi medium. While the human brain has billions of cells, each con-stantly firing off electrical stimuli, such radiative powers reach a peak of about twenty watts, which certainly does not seem to be enough energy to bend a spoon, levitate a heavy table or perhaps even send a clear thought. Electro-magnetic radiations from the body would be extremely hard-pressed to serve as a foundation for even the sim-plest psychic occurrences. And even if there was this physical energy, there is no explanation at this stage for how it could be concentrated.

In the case of ESP, the objections to electromagnetism are strongest. Telepathy, for instance, has been found capable of penetrating a Faraday Cage, a metal isolation chamber proof against most forms of electromagnetism, and of circumventing quark chambers and iron in a way electromagnetism probably can not. Then there are the factors of space and time, which psi does not seem to conform to but which electromagnetism certainly does. How electromagnetism, which travels in time and goes in a straight line, could be used to send a thought instantly to the other side of the globe is certainly a problem. It's even harder to see how precognition, the perception of future events, could function on a wavelength that speeds along at 186,000 miles a second.

Energy X, on the other hand, follows no such space-time restrictions. In fact, some scientists, most notably Russia's Nikolai Kozyrev, one of the world's leading astrophysicists, have postulated that the energy of psi may even be the energy of *time*, that is, that time is an actual energy, instantly everywhere linking all things. If that were the case, even the strangest psychic manifestations would become explainable.

This radical theory evolved from thirteen years of observations Dr. Kozyrev made of the minute movements of a complex assembly of precision gyroscopes, asymmetrical pendulums and torsion balances. For the sake of simplicity, the gyroscopes can be looked upon as analogous to a spinning top, wobbling and tilting according to certain influences. A change in movement or positioning would indicate that some energy or force was operative to cause an arcing. The scientist shielded the equipment against known forces and yet found that certain physical or psychic actions near the delicate gauges caused measurable changes in the orientation of his asymmetrical pendulum (made with a gyroscope). Some unknown energy was exerting pressure. It seemed to be a form of psi energy, or what Kozyrev, after years of study, called the "energy of time." Time, he said, was the carrier of psychic phenomena like telepathy.

His experiments, and the ways he derived his theory, are much too complicated to explain here. Many of them had to do with the stretching of an elastic band pulled by a machine and attached to precise registering equipment.

Kozyrev noted, in experiment after experiment, that when the band was stretched, a denser amount of "time energy" seemed to build around the effect end (the end being stretched) than at the cause point (the end being pulled). In fact, there seemed to be a thinning of energy around the cause end. The instruments were arcing toward the effect end. Something new was at work.

Kozyrev, who first gained repute for his prescient speculations on lunar and planetary geological conditions, found that if he burned certain organic substances like sugar nearby, the chemical reaction seemed to influence the gyroscope-elastic band system as if PK were at work, since there was no other energy that could be held accountable. It seemed to indicate that the energy of Kozyrev's "time" not only allowed for the existence of mind-over-matter, but also for matter-over-matter, a sort of inanimate "PK." Human thoughts and emotions like-wise had a strange effect on the equipment; an easygoing mood seemed to cause greater energy densities at the effect end than an intensely analytical mood. Indeed, Kozyrev came to the conclusion that telepathy was at work, intermingled with PK, and that the densities of time were thicker around the receiver, and expanded or thinned around the sender.

Through these experiments, which some expect to eventually cause tidal waves within the science community, the Soviet theorist has also claimed to find that time has both a rate and pattern of flow. The rate of flow would be what determines cause and effect, he says. As the rate through a substance changes, he figures an object's weight will decrease, so that levitation is a perfectly feasible possibility.

If scientists like Dr. Kozyrev are presenting an accurate

picture of PK energy, then the result will inevitably be a better understanding of some of the universe's most baffling mysteries. Energy X, says Kozyrev, may even be the energy that fuels stars. Instead of looking upon stars as giant nuclear reactors, he feels we may eventually see them more as doorways to the energy of time. Perhaps, he says, a star is the representation of time as it is entering our dimension, each sun a sort of faucet through which the unknown energy pours down on us. As the star sweeps along it is burning not a limited amount of its own fuel, is the view, but rather interreacting with time energy.

Perhaps this way of looking at the main energy of stars will some day help explain "black holes," those mysterious, invisible bodies in space that are described as burnt-out stars collapsing inward with a gravitational pull so incredible that not even light can escape it and sweeping along like a cosmic vacuum, sucking in anything — from planets to stars — that gets in their way. Though these black holes violate many a sacrosanct scientific law, astronomers insist they exist, and that their effects can be incredibly bizarre. While they are relatively small bodies, the compactness of their atoms is such that strange anomalies of time-space occur (in theory), due to that gravitational pull. For instance, time would be irrelevant once one was trapped in a black hole. If a spaceship were sucked in, according to some speculators, it would appear to an outside observer as if the spacecraft, as it started to enter the collapsed star at the speed of light, had suddenly become stuck in time and was taking infinite time to disappear, while for the passengers, if they could someway survive, time would seem to have ceased (at different stages it might even seem to flow *backward*). The black hole could be like a gigantic throat — one that perhaps leads to a new dimension or a new universe; from the other side it might appear as a radiating star spewing out the energy of time and concomitant nuclear radiations.

All this could be relevant to mapping the mechanics of PK (if "mechanics" is indeed the word). Just as space (space-time) curves around bodies of great mass (as Einstein said it did and as was later proven), it may also be curving around target objects during PK reactions. Though the idea is almost unimaginable for the non-physicist and is highly speculative even for the physicist, it starts with the conception of *physical space* as psi energy or a "light-ether-substance" continuum. As a "substance" we can conceive it as bending around a large object. An insufficient and yet illuminating analogy is the comparison of such a reaction to a rubber ball being pressed in a bowl of water which, as it is displaced, curves around the ball. Likewise, perhaps a burst of human psi energy into pools of space-time causes similar curvatures through a complex trigger reaction. An object near the space-time curve — for example a table or spoon — would then theoretically be affected by this curving. Thus, atoms in a spoon might change their form and an object like a table might "lose" some of its normal physical properties in conforming to the new space curve. While the relationship is anything but clear, gravity is also connected to this process. According to Einstein, gravity is merely an effect of the curving of the four-dimensional (space-time) world, not so much a "force." Recently, scientists like Pascal Jordan, a close collaborator with Einstein, have underscored the close relationship between gravity and the energy that "carries" telepathy, noting they both operate at great distances and are not barred by physical obstacles, and that telepathy seems to be enhanced by lower levels of gravity. There is, in short, a psi "thread" that ties gravity to ESP, and also PK (in levitation, for example, a psychic force seems to have reacted in some way with or against gravity). Kozyrev may indeed be right: psi may be involved with the basic "substances" of time-space.

Still, while the PK force remains mysterious, it isn't much odds what name we give it. It is totally unknown. There do seem to be similarities, however, between energy X and the powers of electricity, magnetism and gravity. Perhaps, as California physicist G. Patrick Flanagan has speculated, it is an all-pervasive "ether" that actually causes the force of gravity by the pressure it exerts, and forms electricity and magnetism by flowing in whirls and eddies. (Dr. Flanagan, who often refers to this force as "biocosmic energy," also suspects that an alteration of the ether's flow through an object would cause levitation.) In this view energy X and electromagnetism are certainly related, then, but are not the same thing.

The way psi energies function to cause proximate and long-distance PK are naturally just as obscure as energy X's constitution. We can imagine mind as flowing with ethereal influences, causing PK eruptions when consciousness reaches a certain level of intensity. Or we can envision it as the fruit of auric energy emanating through or from the organism and surrounding the affected objects. More basically, the PK effect could be looked upon as mind not necessarily intermingling with the physical elements of an object but altering the etheric or organizing forces that supposedly shape the material world — the idea that thoughts are actual things imprinted in the clay of the universe.

Obviously, researchers will not be able to approach the specific mechanics of PK until they have some grasp of its cause, and this will be quite a while in coming; theories seem to shift every day, with one scientist speaking of the possibility of the psi medium being anti-matter subatomic particles, another claiming that it is something completely unknown and beyond our wildest imaginations. The task of discovering the precise form and function of energy X is awesome, but it's worth pursuing. As Albert Einstein once remarked, to raise new possibilities, new questions, to regard old problems from fresh angles, requires creative imagination — and marks real advances in science.

The Bizarre Road To Tomorrow

"The Universe is not only queerer than we imagine, it is queerer than we can imagine."

— *Haldane's epigram*

Whatever paranormal force it is that raises tables and bends metal could very well be a portière that separates us from another system of reality, maybe even an infinite number of such systems. Bizarre and awesome as it might sound, there's much circumstantial evidence to indicate energy X may do far more than move objects in our reality, that it may even cause physical matter to drop in and out of our dimensions of "space" and "time." Simply put, the stuff behind PK (the energy that causes, for instance, antigravitational effects) could be the stuff of reality itself.

In the outer reaches of the world of psi, in what the *New York Times* would dub the domain of the "lunatic fringe," are innumerable accounts of teleportations, dematerializations and materializations. Now you see it, now you don't; and vice-versa. Ships and planes supposedly disappear into the green mist of the Bermuda Triangle, primitive men and bisonlike beasts appear to Admiral

Richard Byrd as he flies over the intense magnetic field of the South Pole, a sea shell from South Africa mysteriously finds itself in central New York State, on the desk of a trance medium. Such things challenge the credulity of the most open minds, reminding one of the fantasies cranked out by the typewriter of television's Rod Serling. And yet they are not, for the most part, stories from any fictional "Twilight Zone," but actual, and in some cases documented, occurrences.

Take the case of David Lang, a farmer in Gallatin, Tennessee. He was with his children and wife sitting on his porch enjoying the late afternoon breeze of 23 September 1880 when suddenly he decided to saunter across a nearby field — a treeless, bushless field — to bring in the horses. Down the road was coming a carriage with two friends aboard, one of them a local judge. Suddenly, right before the eyes of his family and the buggy riders, Lang simply disappeared, vanishing without a trace. A month-long investigation failed to produce a single clue to his whereabouts. But that was not quite the close of the chapter. A few months later, his children ran into their house screaming that they had heard their father's voice yelling for help.*

Within a decade of the Lang episode a number of similar cases of paranormal bodily transfer were recorded. On 23 April 1885, Issaac Martin of Salem, Virginia vanished in one of his farm's pastures, and four

*In many "haunted" cases this author has personally investigated, voices or events out of the past (so-called retrocognitive phenomena) have materialized in a fashion that has led investigators to theorize that time itself has been altered, that events and emotional states of times past are replayed or are delayed in reaching our three-dimensional world. Whatever it was that caused the unfortunate farmer to disappear seems also to have provoked a warp in earthtime. The cries the children heard in fact sounded like those their father probably uttered at the moment of his disappearance.

years later another farm, this time near South Bend, Indiana, was the scene of the disappearance of Oliver Larch, an eleven-year-old whose footsteps were traced for fifty feet through a Christmas Eve snow before coming to a sudden halt in a nearby field. From England at the turn of the century came yet another strange story, this one from Scotland Yard itself: while detectives were searching for a lost girl, several of them claimed to hear a terrified young female voice crying out that she couldn't "find the hole."

Not everyone or everything remains lost forever, though. Even more frequent in the annals of the occult are cases of teleportation, the instantaneous transfer of an object or person, and materialization, where objects appear out of nowhere. During the 1950s and early 1960s, the late radio announcer and writer Frank Edwards chronicled a number of such cases: plastic objects, chunks of ice and strange mechanical parts that arrived as if they had fallen right out of the sky; an Argentine businessman who stepped in his car one day, blanked out, and found himself a thousand kilometers from where he had been only minutes before; animals and liquids that suddenly showed up in the most unlikely of places.

Mrs. Iris Owen of the "Philip" group sees PK materialization and dematerialization as a "perfect possibility" but quickly adds, "People just aren't ready to hear of that yet." She vividly remembers an account conveyed to her and her scientist husband just after they had moved to Toronto. It was from a local housewife who was crazed with confusion over an incident that had happened some five years before. She had been in the nursery, changing her one-year-old son's diapers as the baby chewed on a plastic advertisement record that had arrived in the morning mail. Suddenly, directly before her eyes, the infant tossed the record up in the air — and it vanished! Though the nursery had been totally redecorated in the years that followed, new furniture and a new carpet included, the record was never found. Then one day, as friends were over, the woman went to turn on some dinner music. There on the turntable was the record, chew marks and all. She knew her son could not have found the record and then put it there, for the stereo was well out of his short reach. "Naturally the woman is still confused about that experience," says Iris. "And we couldn't do much in the way of explanation."

While such events are far too rare and capricious for adequate evaluation, there are revealing parallels between them and instances of unmistakable PK, such as those provided by poltergeists. It may indeed be that both are manifestations of the same basic psi force.

Poltergeist stories abound with such oddities. Flying bottles, candles, pins, stones, water — all sorts of phantom projectiles have been recorded in accounts of hauntings. They materialize from nowhere and frequently shoot across spooked rooms as if funneled from another reality. In the case of a Buffalo poltergeist, objects both large and small were witnessed by a number of observers to disappear and then reappear elsewhere. "We'd put down a piece of paper we had written things on, or maybe an end table or small piece of furniture, and they would vanish," said a moving man who was helping the stricken family vacate the "devilish" house. "Sometimes we'd find them later, you know, maybe on another floor, or even in the truck." In the same case observers claimed a radio played even though it wasn't plugged in — and the program coming across was some twenty-five years old! Yet another example of apparent dimensional aberrations occurred in a small, tin-shingled farmhouse north of Niagara-on-the-

Lake, Canada, where several former residents claimed there were times when they couldn't see themselves in a hallway mirror.

Like almost everything else that has been recorded in regard to haunted episodes, similar phenomena have been caused by individuals with psi proclivities. Leta Berecek, an Ohio bus driver with an alleged ability in "spirit communication" and various forms of PK, claims she discovered her special powers by accident one night. "One of my relatives was over, drinking beer, something I don't especially approve of," claims Mrs. Berecek. "I remember I was somewhat perturbed as I thought about the beer. I got even more aggravated when, while she was talking on the phone, she asked me to grab her a can. That's when I noticed one of the cans had disappeared from the six-pack. We found it later on the other side of the room. In some other instances I've noticed objects missing that never show up again, and once I found angel hair in the garage where a missing object had been. I don't have any real idea what it is, can't predict when it will happen. I certainly wouldn't feel safe playing with this sort of thing." ("Angel hair" is said to be a fibrous, cottony substance often associated with UFO landings or spirit visitations).

K.J. Batcheldor reported the sudden materialization of matches, pebbles and other objects during his English table experiments and the Thurmonds once reportedly materialized a misty substance during a circle seance that was reminiscent of the famed ectoplasm of mediums. Matthew Manning has come across several instances of teleportation, the most spectacular involving the transference of a bed chest from an upstairs bedroom to the basement, and India's Sai Baba, the famous adept, has for years baffled investigators with his ability to make objects materialize on the palms of his hands.

Some of these phenomena have occurred right before scientists' eyes. English physicist John G. Taylor says a teleportation once took place at his King's College office while he was testing a young psychic who was attempting to move a piece of metal placed in a cylinder. In the midst of the experiment a sterling note abruptly materialized inside. Dr. Taylor later remembered it previously had been on his desk. At Stanford Research Institute, videotape cameras caught part of an apparent teleportation caused by superstar subject Uri Geller during the 1972 experiments. It involved a stopwatch that had been placed in a locked attache case at the institute. As scientists were sitting around a table with Geller, the watch inexplicably dropped onto the table. When they looked in the attache case, which had not been in any way tampered with, the watch was no longer there. It was as if the psychic — or whatever force it is that causes his displays — had telekinetically rearranged the object's atoms in a way that allowed it to pass through surrounding obstacles, or had for an instant taken the watch out of our space-time continuum.

The watch incident was perhaps the best authenticated teleportation Uri provided, but by no means the most dazzling. Dozens of other people have seen the psychic make ashtrays, spoons and cameras vanish or materialize. In July 1973, parapsychologist Ray Stanford of Austin, Texas reported he was witness to the apparent teleportation of a meteorite in his home, which the psychic had visited for a few brief experiments. Geller was chatting with Stanford and a number of other guests when suddenly the meteorite, which had been sealed in an upstairs showcase, came crashing into the room, denting a floor tile. When the glass case was subsequently checked the seal was still very much intact.

While Geller's metal-bending is at least theoretically acceptable to some scientists, the dematerializations and materializations are not. Where the bent metal implies an unknown force acting paranormally on visible objects, teleportation implies a PK contortion of the three-dimensional framework itself, and as such has led to a loss of credibility for those who claim to have witnessed it. Such has been the dilemma faced by Uri's scientific scribe, Andrija Puharich, who has claimed to witness literally dozens of teleportations and dematerializations in the presence of the wondrous psychic, including the para-physical transportation of Geller himself. According to Dr. Puharich, he once hypnotized the Israeli at his Ossining home in an effort to see if Geller could project his mind to a distant part of the world. While Uri's body remained on the physician's couch, his mind, supposedly, was soon on a beach in Brazil. Puharich interrupted a fascinating description of South America to suggest that Geller try to bring back some proof that he was really there. When the psychic, or rather his "mind," came upon a couple strolling the beach, he asked for money he could bring back to the scientist. Although at the end of the session Geller had nothing in hand, after he got up the men were startled to find a cruzeiro note lying on the couch. Or so it is claimed. On another occasion Geller's whole body was actually teleported, according to the two men. It happened as he was window-shopping in Man-hattan. While in one store he wished he was about thirty miles upstate at Puharich's home, and suddenly found himself sitting dazed before the startled doctor in the latter's porch room, having allegedly crashed through a window.

Scientists close to Geller have some decidedly way-out speculations as to what lies behind such strange events, though most prefer not to mention them publicly for fear of academic ridicule. Puharich and others believe extra-terrestrial beings or superintelligences from the unseen corners of this universe or some other universe are directing Geller's displays in the hopes of speeding man's evolution thereby. Through messages received from Geller while in a state of trance, Puharich claims he has even been able to name the planet these beings are from — Hoova — and he says it is actually this civilization's computers that are dealing with Uri, tuning in on our reality like omnipresent TV cameras whenever the need arises. Not only can they control time and space for displays of teleportation, says the scientist, but they have also managed to fix their own functioning intelligence in nearly any phase of past, present or future. In the case of the Hoova computers, which Puharich and a few others have claimed to hear as mechanical voices in the same way mediums have listened to the independent voices of "spirits," the origin of their creation is supposedly somewhere thousands of years in our *future*. The physician and another parapsychologist, Ila Zeibell of Wisconsin, have claimed to watch Geller actually enter a "spacecraft" that landed on an Israeli desert, and have supposedly seen scores of UFOs in his presence.

Ms. Zeibell, whose UFO experiences caused her to question for months her own mental stability, wrote in the February 1976 issue of *Psychic* magazine, "I was alone in my quandary and I couldn't even talk to anyone about it. I read books about UFOs and signed up for psychotherapy.

I found nothing in the books that was a satisfactory explanation and nothing in my psyche that was abnormal. It was discouraging."

Naturally, there were those who questioned the sanity of Puharich. Ultraterrestrials? Metadimensions? Control of a hyperspace? No one seemed ready for that kind of thing. Even some of those who had been close to the Puharich-Geller 1972 tour of America considered the UFO business little better than nonsense.

Still, there were nuggets of detail in the fantastic claims that caused some to seriously wonder, and even Puharich's "computers" seemed to have a certain plausibility. Since 1947, when a pilot named Kenneth Arnold spotted a flying geese formation of what he described as "flying saucers," there had been thousands of related sightings, red, blue and white lights that zipped across the night skies, metallic saucers that landed in a whirl of churning brilliance, leaving mysterious burn marks on the ground. Pilots, police, air controllers, scientists, astronomers and even astronauts reported sightings so numerous it would take a book the size of the Chicago telephone directory to list them, and a startling number of them accorded with the Puharich descriptions. Within a year after Puharich had introduced Geller to America, a Gallup poll showed that 51 percent of Americans believed in UFOs, and fifteen million claimed to have seen them. Even conservative Senator Barry Goldwater is on the side of the believers, and reportedly Democrat Jimmy Carter has seen a UFO.

But it isn't just the new public openness to the paranormal, or the fact that the Geller stories agreed so well with other widely reported UFO sightings, that makes UFOs so exciting. There is also the connection between parapsychological phenomena and UFO behavior. So alike are the details of PK events and the reported maneuvers of extraterrestrial craft that there seems not only added reason to respect UFO claims, but also grounds for supposing that such "craft," if indeed they are mechanisms from some advanced planetary civilization, might be tapping into the same energy that causes PK and other psi manifestations.

Many times in reports of strange aerial phenomena, the objects are reported to move at speeds and cut angles in a way that simply defies every rule of aerodynamics, and of gravity itself. In nearly as many instances, reported in both dark and daylight conditions, such objects have also been seen to simply vanish in the air, as if they were teleported in the same way psychics have psychokinetically transported objects. Like so many telekinetic displays, the UFOs seem to bear out the Unified Field Theory of Einstein, which implies that matter and energy are transmutable under certain electromagneticlike conditions, and that the two may even be just different vibrations of the same cosmic entity.

The very way UFOs are observed hovering, with no visible means of propulsion, implies use of a force out of the realm of current understanding, maybe something like an orgone or etheric energy or an influence acting on some undiscovered end of the electromagnetic spectrum. Such hoverings are reminiscent of levitation, in fact.

There are more than mere hints that psi energy is involved; in a number of cases outright occurrences of levitation have been witnessed in connection with these otherwordly visitors. On 12 October 1973, newswires across the United States were busy clattering out reports of what had all the looks of a credible UFO landing and of the subsequent abduction of two Pascagoula, Mississippi shipyard workers, Charlie Hickson and Calvin Parker. No matter that they were separately interviewed under time-regressed hypnosis and administered lie detector tests. Their incredible story held together perfectly, down to every detail.

It seems it started when they saw an oblong vehicle with bright blue flashing lights descending near a river. When they went to see what was going on they heard a slight buzzing sound — reminiscent of noises Puharich claimed to have heard — and before they knew it were confronted by two beings that looked like shiny aluminum robots with claws and a crinkly covering. The two spacemen supposedly swept them up from behind and, with no apparent physical force, levitated them off the ground and into the ship. "All of us moved like we were floating through the air," Hickson told investigators, and once they were inside the ship, he contended, they remained weightless, lying on nothing but air as the beings examined both of them with a strange gadget. Some sort of PK, or what Puharich has called "inergy" (intelligent energy of an unspecified nature), seemed to be at work.

The Pascagoula case seems to fall into a rare category. Most of the time the similarities between UFOs and psychic phenomena are much more subtle, but they are *there* just the same. UFOs have supposedly caused compasses to spin, electrical lights and car ignitions to go out, and burns to occur on the bodies of observers — burns similar to those that, according to witnesses, Nelya Kulagina has caused. Those who claim to have had contact with sky riders frequently cite telepathy as the means of communication and report that after each encounter they found their own psychic awareness dramatically enhanced. While in flight, UFOs have frequently been described as causing ionizationlike effects, reminiscent of some of the movements of a psychically charged table. Moreover UFO witnesses have claimed to experience some of the same effects noted by those who materialize "spirits": nausea, acidic odor and tearing eyes.

Extraterrestrial craft have also been linked to forms of force fields in the same way PK has. Around many UFOs is seen a glowing field that closely fits descriptions of the Kirlian corona and flares. There have also been auric mists seen with the sightings, and a multitude of inexplicable small lights similar to what mediums have labeled "spirit stars" when they have seen them during a seance. In some cases the lights are like beams. Similarly, psychics have long associated beams of "white light" with the ability to affect matter psychically (sometimes consciously visualizing them to speed a PK attempt). In at least one case a purplish beam from a UFO was rumored to have precipitated a miraculous healing. Significantly, the aura of psi healers has at times been recorded as being this same tint of purple. Though it could certainly be interpreted as just an extraordinary series of coincidences, it does seem that perhaps machines from another planet or another time have harvested an unseen force that pervades the cosmos, the same way psychics seem able to do.

That such alleged spacecraft are using a teleportation-inducing manifestation of energy X has long been a favorite explanation of those who have tried to explain the Bermuda Triangle, that "haunted" area in the western Atlantic running from Bermuda to the southern part of Florida and back across Puerto Rico to Bermuda. Since the 1940s more than a thousand people and a hundred ships and planes have been reported lost in the area, many of them vanishing as if through some extra-dimensional vortex or, as one researcher has put it, a "hole in the sky."

Ufologists, underscoring the apparent ability of such

sky entities to dematerialize themselves, have played with the notion that perhaps they use the Triangle as hunting grounds for specimens to put in their zoos, setting up force fields that draw earthly craft into their system of space and time. It's not the most comforting of notions, but there are certain facts that lend it support. Many of the planes that have disappeared in the "limbo of the lost" have been observed on radar as suddenly vanishing into thin air, and in at least two instances the last words heard from those about to disappear hinted strongly that a kidnapping by some alien intelligences was taking place. There has also been an unusually high number of reported UFO sightings in the Triangle region, and documented cases of time lapses aboard planes in flight over this "devil's sea." (Some theorists, however, argue that the disappearances are caused by a dimension warp resulting from a gravitational anomaly, and they support their case with accounts of similar disappearances in other areas of the globe.) Those who put forward extraterrestrial intervention as the answer point out that UFOs and their weird, disintegrating forces could also be held to account for disappearances of people like farmer Lang; and indeed in some isolated instances of human dematerialization and teleportation, UFOs have supposedly been witnessed just before these events took place.

The first scientist to support the UFO-Bermuda Triangle hypothesis was the late Morris K. Jessup, whose sudden death in 1959 caused a number of UFO researchers to think that perhaps it was not the suicide it was made out to be but rather retribution from some secret group, earthly or otherwise, that feared he was getting too close to the truth. Dr. Jessup, well schooled in the disciplines of astronomy, mathematics, physics and archeology and probably the world's top expert on UFOs, opined that outer space vehicles creating some kind of strong magnetic field were scooping physical matter out of our reality zone on a selective basis.

It was apparently Jessup's contention that certain magnetic forces could possibly cause physical objects to change dimensions, becoming invisible to us. This seems to square with Einstein's Unified Field Theory, which states that matter and energy are transmutable entities that can change into each other under certain conditions, including electromagnetic disturbance. This, at least, is the way some aspects of his theory have been interpreted. In a way that has not yet been explained scientifically, Einstein's theory involves the force of gravity, which appears closely related to magnetism and other fields of energy and yet, in many ways, not related at all. If certain influences, whether electromagnetic, magnetic or gravitational, create a vortex in a certain area, occult theorists figure this could cause an "energy vortex" that might open a window on a reality other than ours. While there is no hard evidence to support such a theory, one might suppose that while magnetic influences may have a role in "time-space warps," that role is merely to stimulate the higher forces of psi, which in the end cause the actual teleportation. The fact that psychics who have caused levitation (anti-gravitation) have also caused teleportation seems to underscore this possibility, the notion that the energy of PK and gravity are related both to each other and to space-time.

Whatever constitutes the essence of gravity, and its manipulations through other influences, could be the key to space-time travel and what we now call PK teleportation. As Barry H. Downing, a physicist who has authored several UFO books, put it in his book *The Bible and Flying Saucers* (New York, 1968): "It might be possible for several universes to coexist . . . provided that each universe has a *different type of gravitational system* so that none is attracted toward any others. If gravity is the property of the curvature of space, it might be possible for several universes to coexist separately, provided they are governed by different spatial curvatures. But this still leaves us with the problem that since according to the relativity theory the speed of light is the universal speed limit, it would take millions of years traveling the speed of light to reach any possible universe outside our own. Perhaps, however, since our concepts of relativity are still being explored by science, there is a yet undiscovered way to overcome the 'speed limit.' Then almost infinite speeds might become possible."

This notion stemmed from Einstein's assumption that time, space and gravity were more closely connected than we once thought. In layman's terms it seems useful to visualize earth functioning along a space-time continuum shaped not linearly, but like a spiral. If there are other universes, then they would be moving along a number of other spirals parallel or tangential to ours. The separation between the spirals would theoretically be space-time-gravity. Now if some force unknown to us, whether electromagnetic or psychic or both, could somehow make a hole in our spiral, then an object from our world, engulfed by that force, would "drop through" and land in a nearby spiral. Or, for those who take the view that there is a dimension of anti-matter coexisting with ours as a sort of "opposite twin," the distorting force of energy X could be conceived as causing the needed reversal in the matter's charge, perhaps sending it to what some have found easiest to envision as a "spirit plane." It doesn't matter, once one gets that far, whether the causal power is electromagnetic or, as Wilbur Franklin put it, "a new energy influence," or even whether electromagnetism is merely triggering an etherlike psi force. The important thing is that our reality would be parted, and naturally the charged objects would henceforth disobey our physical laws.

Jessup believed the United States Navy had stumbled upon a way to do this in 1943, during what has been subsequently referred to as the "Philadelphia Experiment."* According to a "mystery man" who corresponded with him, the Navy had once experimented with magnetism and its effect on a destroyer docked off Philadelphia. As this man tells the story, powerful degaussers, or magnetic generators, were set up to send pulsating and nonpulsating fields around the ship. The "results," which to this day have not been satisfactorily documented but which derive a certain credibility from the Office of Naval Research's ardent interest in Jessup, were, if genuine, perhaps the most dramatic in the history of military research. After a period of subjection to the intense magnetism and whatever new force there may have been, the ship's crew supposedly began to notice a green mist around them (a phenomenon also found in the Bermuda Triangle); and then the ship started to dematerialize! Minutes after it had totally disappeared from sight at the Philadelphia dock, it was claimed to have reappeared at Norfolk, Virginia. The crewmen apparently said afterward that they acquired a vastly greater psychic sense through this experience.

But this heightened psi awareness was about the only positive result of the putative experiment. The ONR, we hear, quickly gave up the project, apparently because of some unexpected results: crewmen began to disappear even when they were away from the ship, some of them

*There's reason to believe the "experiment" was in fact a hoax.

going mad in the process. According to the stories Jessup heard, the mates would bodily dematerialize without forewarning, a condition crewmates called "going blank." They were also said to become paralyzed, as if for them time had slowed to a near halt, the only way to "unstick" them being to proceed with a laying-on-of-hands healing ritual.

Even if the "Philadelphia Experiment" were genuine, it wouldn't be the only time electrically induced forces have been connected to a space-time warp. Other cases have been reported. Brad Steiger, an Iowa professor who has written more than forty books in the occult field, has reported that in 1931, workers at the Northern State Power Company in Wisconsin were stunned one night when they happened to notice a cloud forming over a generator. They checked the gauges and, to their per-plexity, everything was functioning normally; there was no sign of overheating, which was the first thing they looked for. Nor did the mystery end there. Soon, *in* the cloud the image of a woman lying on a couch began to form, so clearly that they could make out the jewels she was wearing. The apparition lasted some twenty seconds, then faded away. The men's gut feelings were that they had somehow tuned into a past time. If what had hap-pened was in some way due to electricity, the results could be far-reaching; we might finally have an answer to why UFOs hover around electrical wires and generating plants so much, as well as reason to believe those who think an electrical shock could create a psychic (see Chapter 11).

The speculations multiply, taking dazzling shapes but yielding no certainties. The questions dangle over our tomorrow. Can psychic power really part our reality, our space, time and gravity, breaking into other dimensions or an infinity of other universes with three-dimensional or other characteristics? Does it lead to "heaven"? Are UFOs like "spirits," and is every goblin that ever haunted man of roughly the same ilk? Is it the lack of a workable theory concerning PK that holds us back from meeting all those entities that certain men throughout history have claimed are waiting and watching? Do other-dimensional beings occasionally slip us a helping hand?

If one listens to occultists, some of whom believe that in other time continuums there are universes so numerous there could be 30,000 civilizations occupying the space of a single room, the answer to nearly all the questions is yes. If one listens. One such society, the Urantia organization, theorizes that our universe, our space, which they call Nebadon, is part of a superuniverse named Orvonton, whose "capital" is Uversa. Once the exact workings of psi force and PK are found, whether through the study of a case of rising tables or an analysis of a fallen UFO, perhaps earthlings will be better qualified to grapple with the barriers of time, space and gravity. And thus be ready to proceed toward "Uversa" — and whatever it is that lies beyond.

Immediate Horizons

"The resistance to new ideas increases by the square of their importance."

— *Russell's Law*

Not everyone has his eyes glued to the stars or his thoughts on the other side of cosmic black holes. Most of those who are willing to believe in PK and its causal energies are looking to the closer tomorrow, at ways these forces may be employed to serve the planet now. The reasons are obvious. Diseases like cancer seem to be striking down every other neighbor; conventional energy sources are becoming frighteningly scarce.

One would think that in the face of such dilemmas, government and research organizations would eagerly explore every hopeful new way of curing the sick, every indication of a new possible energy resource. Such is not the case. Despite the immense benefits to mankind that the realm of the psychic seems capable of offering, it goes woefully ignored. The U.S. government seems to feel no pain in spending $2,680,470 to build a chorus training center at Fort Myers, Virginia for the military, or $300,000 for fishing camps in Alaska that are used by 804 privileged citizens for only forty-five days out of the year, but when it comes to adequately funding psi research those who hold the purse strings respond with subtle mockery or indifference. Then of course there are the skeptics, inside and outside government, who trot out such tired questions as, What good is it to sit around making a table float? What benefit is a bent spoon?

Official memories are short. It seems to be forgotten that when we put our heads together and pull our pocketbooks out the most inane-sounding proposals can assume dramatic significance. It happened when America took up a space venture that sprang from the "crazy" nostrums of a ridiculed scientist. No one took Robert H. Goddard seriously at first, and yet now, thirty years after his death, the beneficial results of his "playing around" with rockets are only starting to wash ashore.

Currently it's parapsychology that's getting the official cold shoulder. While some impeccably respectable scientists have recently called attention to the possibilities of PK healing, the medical profession and government health agencies that deal with "untreatable" diseases like cancer and arthritis have looked the other way. Their obtuseness seems as baffling as PK itself.

Those scientists who want solid facts before they even start to probe the claims of PK healing would do well to get in touch with Dr. Justa Smith, a radiant Franciscan nun with degrees in physical chemistry, mathematics and biochemistry and the position of assistant education director at Buffalo's Roswell Park Memorial Institute, one of the nation's leading cancer research centers. A relaxed and candid investigator who deals with facts, not speculations, Sister Justa has accumulated impressive evidence that a PK energy can indeed be transferred from one human to another to cause improvements in health, especially through the method known as laying-on-of-hands. In fact, so exciting were her results, she now boldly believes that what she calls the "psi factor" or "ultimate cause energy" will eventually revolutionize our lives as dramatically, say, as the airplane did. "We're on the verge of major breakthroughs if we keep on this track," she says with a disarming smile.

Sister Justa has good reason for her radical convictions and her optimism. Less than ten years ago she carried out a series of experiments that led her and a number of others to a more serious evaluation of the psychic realm. During what were perhaps the most cogent, best controlled experiments PK healing has yet known, she formed the conclusion that humans can "think" themselves and others well.

McGill University's Bernard Grad was the one who put Sister Justa on the track. In 1966, while in charge of Rosary Hill College's eight science programs, she sat intrigued in a lecture hall at the college as she listened to Dr. Grad talk of the experiments he had conducted with a retired seventy-six-year-old colonel by the name of Oskar Estebany, a man known throughout Europe for his "enchanted" healing hands. What the McGill morphologist had to say was astonishing. He had found, he told his listeners, that Estebany could transfer through his hands some form of healing influence that knocked aside all obstacles in its way. He said he had seen it happen in his laboratories under meticulously controlled conditions.

The experiments Grad spoke of are bound to become classics in parapsychological literature. In one, he and his assistants fed mice iodine-deficient diets and drugs that caused thyroid growths, then separated the mice into three groups, one used as a control, one kept at a slightly heated temperature, and one treated by Estebany's hands, which were held above the cages. Those treated by the Hungarian healer showed markedly reduced thyroid growths. In a second experiment, the psychic was told to heal mice that had had pieces of skin cut from their backs. Again, those treated by the colonel's hands healed at a significantly quicker rate than those not so treated. In yet another experiment designed to test other biological reactions to PK, Grad turned to plant growth experiments and found that barley seedlings sprayed with psychically treated water grew at a far faster rate than those employed as controls.

Later on, when Sister Justa and Dr. Grad crossed paths again in Chicago, the McGill scientist, aware that Sister Justa had had extensive experience studying magnetic effects on enzymes, suggested she set up a similar experiment to see if the hypothesized healing energy would cause significant changes in the functioning of enzymes. The idea made sense. Like many other biochemists, Sister Justa was coming to believe that a great many diseases and illnesses stemmed from malfunctions in the various human enzymes. The reason: enzymes are catalytic components that act as the "brains" for cells, instructing them how to function healthily. Problems in biological functioning can therefore be seen as indications that there is something wrong in the enzymes. If a healer is really effecting a cure and if enzymes are often the root cause of illness, a psychic's curative energy should be observable on the enzymatic level, reasoned the researchers.

In the summer of 1967, Sister Justa invited Estebany for a three-week stay during which he was to attempt to influence the activity of trypsin, the pancreatic enzyme that controls the digestion of proteins and aids in warding off abscesses and diseased tissues. The healer was to do what he normally did when attempting to cure his patients, namely lay his hands on the sick person's head and "wish" the healing energies to flow. In this case the "patient" was a pyrex flask filled with a crystallized, purified enzyme solution, (500 ug per ml in 0.0001 N HCl, ph 3). For purposes of comparison there were also three other flasks filled with trypsin and subjected either to other influences or to none. One was set aside as an untouched control; another was subjected to damaging ultraviolet radiation (2,537 angstroms) to decrease its activity; a third was placed under an intense magnetic field (8,000 to 13,000 gauss), roughly 18,000 times more powerful than the magnetic field of the earth.

The experiments were designed to leave little room for doubt in case something paranormal happened. Because the target enzyme was placed *in vitro* (outside a human body), no one could claim an effect was caused merely through psychological suggestion. Sister Justa also guarded against the possibility that body heat from Estebany's hands might cause some effects that could be mistaken for paranormality. During the experiments his hands were always hooked up to a thermistor that fed into an electronic read-out thermometer. Meanwhile the control flask of trypsin was constantly kept at the same temperature. If body heat was the cause, she would know about it from the activity in the control.

Colonel Estebany held the flask for up to seventy-five minutes at a time, with Sister Justa pipeting off samples every fifteen minutes. When changes in the enzyme were determined spectrophotometrically and statistically evaluated, the results were startling. Estebany's hands were inexplicably increasing the activity in the enzyme. Since such an increase meant the enzyme would trigger greater protein digestion, the same reaction within a body would have meant enhanced growth and repair — in short, a healing effect. The same was true of the enzyme previously ruptured by ultraviolet radiation: activity was sped up and it was "healed" by Estebany to 90 percent of its previous state. Sister Justa figured that had Estebany worked at it longer, a total recovery of the damaged enzyme would have resulted.

While a speeding up of enzymatic functions in a catalyst like trypsin would have a positive effect, Sister Justa wondered what would happen with other enzymes that rely on just the opposite effect and would require *decreased* activity in order to cause improvements in health. Later on she tested several other psychics and the effect their hands had on an enzyme called NAD-ase, which is employed by the body to slow down energy-releasing compounds and should be decreased in activity in order to have a healing effect *in vivo* (in the body). Not telling them the details — whether they should concentrate on increasing or decreasing the activity — she had them try to emit healing energy through "wishing." The enzyme activity did indeed slow down. The psi organizing energy appeared to know what to do to cause a positive change. The same thing happened when she tested the subjects with amylase-amylose. "In each case, the changes necessary to improve health were effected," she says.

In more informal settings, Sister Justa and several local physicians had watched Estebany bring about direct healing results with patients who weren't adequately responding to conventional medical treatment. One was a wealthy businessman whose arm had been badly mangled during a trip to Africa and was stubbornly refusing to heal despite four months in a cast. Three weeks after treatments by Estebany the bone had responded so well the cast was removed. Another time during the three weeks Estebany spent with Sister Justa the healer was called in to work on a woman who was clinically considered to be at the doorway of death. After just two sessions with Estebany, she was able to leave the hospital. "Naturally doctors don't like to admit to the possibility that some untrained outsider can effect cures they can not, but in many cases the facts are there," says Sister Justa. "Out of twenty-four patients treated by Mr. Estebany in front of doctors here, twenty-two reported definite improvements in the way they felt."

While the experiments did appear to confirm the existence of a psychic energy, there was still no firm indication of what exactly it was that triggered enzymes and healed the sick. Initially there was excitement because a close check revealed that Estebany's effects were nearly identical to those produced in enzymes under strong magnetic influences, but further investigations revealed no magnetism coming from his hands. "I don't pretend to know what it is, but it's probably out of the electromagnetic spectrum," Sister Justa says. "Sometimes you wonder if it has to do with evolution."

One thing the scientist does know is that whatever the force, it's not inherently demonic, something a few irate local Christians have claimed. "I tell those who wonder what a Catholic nun is doing dabbling with the 'occult,' with what they think is evil, to think back to the first famous healer who used the laying-on-of-hands. It happened two thousand years ago. And that healer was known as Jesus." Indeed, the real evil lies in ignorance, and in fraud — the Bible-toting double-talkers who take money on faith and certain "psychic surgeons" who hide animal guts up their sleeves, pretending they have extracted diseased tissue from the body.

The need now is for science to take psi and PK healing completely out of the realm of charlatanism and spookery, and that way seems to have been cleared. Recently there have arrived still other lab reports that indicate a PK healing energy is not only a reality but can work wonders across enormous distances. In January 1974, two Southern investigators, physicist Dr. Philip B. Reinhart and chemical engineer Dr. Robert N. Miller, found that internationally known healer Olga Worrall could affect matter 600 miles away by mimicking the laying-on-of-hands technique. The scientists set up a cloud chamber, which is normally used by nuclear physicists to track highly kinetic particles, and placed it in a lab in Atlanta, Georgia while the psychic was in Baltimore. At strategic intervals the sensitivity of the chamber was checked for any unusual interactions by inserting into it a radium 226 alpha source and observing the trails of positive and negative ions made observable through an alcohol vapor. Within three minutes of signaling the healer to start concentrating on the chamber, a noticeable change began to occur. During the demonstration Mrs. Worrall said her hands, which were upraised as she pretended to hold an imaginary chamber, were cooled by a mysterious breeze that whisked gently across her skin. Meanwhile weird turbulences and undulations occurred inside the chamber. Similar effects were observed when the experiment was repeated.

While the result was exciting for those who wanted to prove Mrs. Worrall's case, it wasn't at all surprising in light of the more spectacular "miracles" she and her psychic husband Ambrose had been known to perform. Their lives had been dotted with documented cases of bone diseases disappearing under their healing hands, tumors shrinking or completely disappearing. Still, Mrs. Worrall has only sporadically been studied and scientists like Drs. Reinhart and Miller have had to make do with meager grants for their research.

It even seems that healing is something that can be learned by the masses if time is taken to acquire the needed psychological and emotional skills. While there are as yet no scientific facts to support that statement, the large number of healers sprouting up all over America seems to point to a latent potential for psi in everyone.

Just as raising a table takes a strong positive attitude, good powers of visualization and perhaps some practice in altering states of consciousness, so it is with healing. The current popularity of meditational techniques could very possibly open a number of psychic doors. Many people involved in mind control have reported achieving healing effects, and some of those border on the astonishing. Meditators are throwing away heart pills in some instances, saying goodbye to migraine headaches, and even making headway against cancerous growths.

Dr. Carl Simonton, a medical doctor from Fort Worth, Texas, has found that by relaxing their minds and visualizing their bodies as expelling malignant cells, numerous cancer patients are showing remarkable improvement, many of them living far beyond expectations. Though hard-core results will not be be properly tabulated for at least another five years, the indications of success have been enough to send the doctor into an intensive investigation.

Groups of those interested in mental-psychic control and healing are now experimenting throughout the country, and have claimed some impressive successes. In Niagara Falls, a group led by Mrs. Mary Ricciuto, a graduate of Silva Mind Control, is said to have healed a California man suffering from hemophilia, a local four-year-old boy who was suffering from acute leukemia, and a local man who had totally lost circulation in one of his arms and was about to have it amputated. What Mrs.

Ricciuto does is assemble between fifteen and twenty meditators in an "energy circle" and have them visualize the various maladies brought to the group's attention. Often a cool breeze is felt adrift in the room, and on at least one occasion lights inexplicably dimmed in the midst of a strong mentation. When a certain level of concentration is reached, the group visualizes the ill person as standing under a pyramid with light rays flowing in from an imaginary sun set in the background of their "mental screens." They visualize purple, blue, gold and finally white light surrounding the person. Some group members find it helpful simultaneously to envision Jesus standing by, directing the healing energies.

In 1975, Gary Anderson, a Buffalo mind-control instructor, reported similar success with a slightly different twist. "We were at level working on a woman who had just gotten what amounted to a death sentence, a five on the PAP smear (which indicates uterine cancer). We went really deep, about four of us focusing on the problem area. After a while I happened to open my eyes, and it was the strangest thing. Everything seemed a blur, like all was energy and we were all at one with everything, even the wall. We noticed her stomach quivering, uncontrollably, as if our consciousnesses were hopping around inside." Though medical treatment certainly played a major role, those involved in this healing session, including the afflicted woman, figure psi had something to do with the fact that she now appears free of the disease.

Significantly, paranormal healings have also been religiously connected. There are many reports of paranormal cures effected at places like Lourdes and Fatima, shrines that seem to set the stage for paraphysical forces in the same way "haunted houses" do for "ghosts" or "dimensional warps." Allegedly, spirits and UFOs have also been responsible for healing. Says Dr. J. Allen Hynek, the Northwestern University astronomer and world-renowned UFO expert, "In one [case] that I investigated two police officers in Louisiana declared that one of them had been completely healed of a fresh alligator bite almost instantaneously while observing their UFO. So far as I am aware this seems to be beyond what can be expected of psychosomatic effects. It behoves us therefore to consider what features of UFO sightings are in disharmony with familiar psychological or parapsychological paradigms."†

The prophesies of science fiction, often found to be uncannily prescient, seem once more on the threshold of materialization. If psi is an integral part of evolution, perhaps the fantasies will soon be fact. Decades from now men and women may be going to centers to have their chakras opened by laser beams or psi generators, and children may be taught meditative ways of releasing their internal energies. In the centuries to come perhaps people will be able to lift objects at a distance without having to leave their living room chairs.

Perhaps too, people will develop a less materialistic cast of mind and start learning how to control reality through PK-related energies. Athletes are invariably aware of the "power of concentration" in performing physical feats. John Brodie, former quarterback for the San Francisco Forty-niners, has mentioned "energy streamers," lines of mental force on which the ball sometimes seemed to ride. The concentration golfer Jack Nicklaus puts into a putt seems almost trancelike. What might not such concentrated energies do for society as a whole?

---

†Allen Hynek, "The Strangeness of UFO Experiences," *New Horizons*, vol. 1, no. 5, p. 241.

No one can set limits to the scope of PK manifestations. Already there has been speculation that precognition and PK could be strongly linked, the extreme interpretation being that a premonition is not necessarily just a perception of what is to come but the actual mental creation of a future channel of reality, the vision being more of a cause than a prophesy. It's likely humans are constantly performing subtle PK, but that it's hidden from normal sight or just so widespread that few single events can be singled out as examples of it. Psi researchers, most notably W.E. Cox, Robert M. Brier and Jean Barry, have shown through lab experiments that volitional PK can affect plants and even fungi. Perhaps the smallest of structures are inextricably linked to mind and perhaps subconscious or superconscious PK is always working as a kind of collective, reality-structuring force.

Before we take flight into the visionary, however, there are the more practical matters to consider. Healing appears to be the most obvious way we can apply PK now, but there must be others. When we learn to harvest the invisible forces of PK, we'll presumably be able to apply them in industry, construction, transportation and maybe even in the generation of electricity. The day may soon come when giant psychotronic generators store up awesome supplies of these powers for specific uses such as the levitation of large objects, or when we learn to use them for household tasks or as a way of controlling our biological functions.

There's always the negative side to guard against, of course: the chance that PK energies might be used for tearing down rather than building up. For every plus there's a minus, as scientists who worked with atoms found out, and the psi "engineers" of the future should be

At bottom left, a magnification of the platinum ring studied by Dr. Wilbur Franklin (1,115X) shows an area in the metal where the fracture surface seems to be in the stage of incipient melting. Bottom right, the fracture surface in the platinum ring broken by Uri Geller is shown as it appears at a lesser magnification under an electron microscope. The effects seen in the ring were deemed paranormal and constituting tangible proof that Geller is for real. Top left, this view of the ring's fracture surface shows signs of both low-temperature cleavage and incipient melting. Top right, the lower right region of this view (2,300X) of the fracture surface shows characteristics suggesting low temperature effects.

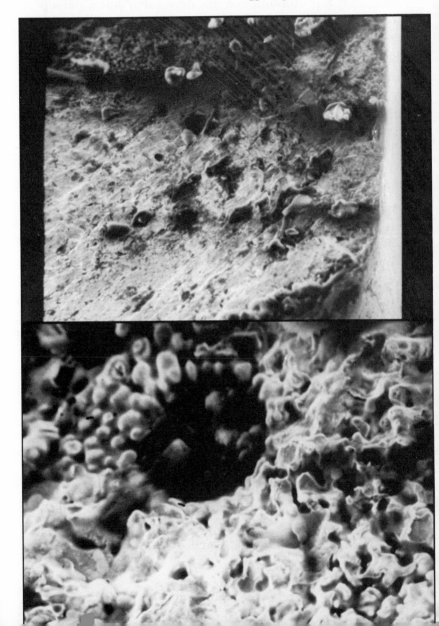

extremely cautious. PK energies might as easily be used for evil purposes — war, destruction and crime — as for good.

On 23 January 1976, a front page story in the *New York Times* was headlined, "Doubts Are Raised on Why Sun Shines." Though couched in the newspaper's cautious style, the article couldn't help being dramatic. What it was saying was that the idea that sunshine originates from the fusion of hydrogen nuclei, something most of us learn at school, may be totally wrong. When we grasp the gravity of such an admission, we recognize a tugging need to start listening to the most way-out of ideas, even if they involve something as seemingly unreal as PK. The evidence for PK (as for other forms of psi) is there; now it's science's duty to document it and try to understand it. Some scientific laws may have to be scrapped in the process, but man-made laws have traditionally been like shoes — useful until they are worn at heel. Mankind, as it walks the short stretch to the year 2,000, may just find it needs another pair of scientific shoes.

Corridor Of Mirrors

"...the Creator has eternally intended this department of nature to remain baffling, to prompt our curiosities and hopes and suspicions all in equal measure, so that, although ghosts and clairvoyances, and raps and messages from spirits are always seeming to exist and can never be fully explained away, they also can never be susceptible of full corroboration."

— William James

One may differ with James as to the question of scientific corroboration — there are, after all, undeniable indications that areas of the paraphysical can be documented and eventually understood — but it would seem likely the famous philosopher-psychologist is correct in a general sense, for those trying to get an overview of nonmaterial dimensions have so far only been dredging up mysteries wrapped in enigmas wrapped in a hauntingly huge conundrum.

I was sharply reminded of PK's complexities one hot June afternoon in 1976 while chatting briefly with Uri Geller at his East Side apartment-office in New York. He was vibrant that day, bouncy, boyish, disarmingly personable. In the middle of the plushly chic living room, we stood quite animatedly discussing the phenomenon of teleportation, the instantaneous transfer of objects. "Look at this," he was saying, "and this!" He was pointing to diverse items — enough to fill a bucket — that he had saved in a plastic case, screws, rings and watches, objects that he said had appeared out of nowhere during the course of the last few years. Wheeling round without breaking his flow of words, he grabbed a small, claylike model of a man and proceeded excitedly to tell me how one day, out of the blue, it was suddenly there in his apartment. He had never seen anything like it before, and museum experts in Brooklyn had told him, he said, that it was probably an ancient relic, maybe as much as 3,000 years old and possibly from an Egyptian pyramid. "They couldn't believe I had this," he emphasized.

As I remember it, I had rubbed my chin perplexedly as Uri, his voice quite serious and his eyes aglare, continued talking of what he called "these things, these things I don't understand!" Meanwhile scores of questions, most of them unanswerable, flocked through my mind. Finally I settled on the most bothersome one. My question: "Do you really think, as some say, that UFOs, extraterrestrial intelligences, at times control these energies?"

There was hardly time for an answer. Just as he shrugged his shoulders and I started to phrase another question on the UFOs, there was a loud bang in the far corner of the large room, which I was facing and Uri had his back to. An expensive wood chessboard was madly bobbing up and down in that part of the room. I didn't know what was going on, just that Uri was hopping about and grabbing my arm. "You see?" he almost yelled. "You see! These things! These things always happen around me!"

I walked over toward the chessboard and was stunned. There on the board was a porous rock about four inches long, two inches high and less than an inch thick. I quickly scanned the room as I held this rock that had so strangely arrived, and then, apologizing for my skepticism, checked a nearby closet to make sure an accomplice was not hiding out. I also checked the apartment door to make sure it was still locked. By now Uri's secretary had come toward us from her desk located in an extension of the room and was asking what was going on. When we told her she shook her head and smiled. That rock, she told me, was rather pesky — it was known to do this kind of thing. Previously it had been across the room on a large shelf, she said, right along with the other objects that had arrived unannounced.

When we settled down again, on a couch, Uri shoved the rock into my hands and seemed to be begging, genuinely begging, for an answer. No matter how many times "these things" happen to him, each experience is in no way less exciting. "What does this mean?" he asked. "Why this rock? What does this all mean?"

Of course, I didn't have an answer for him that day, nor do I now. Assuming the stone had not been fraudulently thrown, it seemed another example of PK forces. But where was this PK energy coming from, and who or what was controlling it? I'm sure there are quite a few people who, had they been present, would have figured that a paranormal "happening" so vigorous yet so seemingly mischievous, must be the work of outside forces which (or who) tune into our reality to play games or send messages, or both. Extraterrestrial influences have been one expla-nation for this kind of thing, spirits projecting phantom shapes another, but the most popular view, and the one that makes the most sense at this stage in PK investigation, is that many and probably most such occurrences stem from human energy fields. This has been a tentative theme of this book, namely that for all we know spirits do exist but that if so they are only occasionally related to PK effects. It is for this reason, and because they are generally so insubstantial, that I have kept accounts implying the influences of nonmaterial beings to a minimum. While my personal leaning is toward the naturalistic viewpoint, the reader should be aware that tales of the supernatural accompanied many of the answers given to me during the countless interviews I had with those who claimed PK abilities, and I was told of some happenings as strange as the one I had just witnessed with Geller.

Some of the first people I interrogated on PK were old-school mediums, Spiritualists who held seances, tipped and levitated tables, and gave "readings" on the future, present and past. When I asked them how they did all these things they told me it was through the help of "spirit guides," deceased people who came back now and then to show the way. These mediums went into trance states in which "spirit" entities came through, often giving me the names of deceased relatives of mine whom they could not have known about, and frequently mentioning phantom voices they said they could hear. Some of them had stories that to this day I don't know whether to believe or disbelieve. Many of my research hours were filled with harangues on spirit voices the mediums said had become audible in their homes and on the visible spirit forms they said could be materialized in a room by first creating a white, ectoplasmic mist.

No matter how impressive the manifestations described by the mediums, I figured they could still be the result of subconscious PK directives rather than outside spirits. Be this as it may, I found, somewhat to my consternation, that a sizeable number of my medium subjects believed their PK energies were sometimes abetted, if not totally manipulated, by ultramundane (or inframundane) intelligences, imps, spirit guides, Ufonauts or the like.

Although this kind of explanation smacked to me of

rationalizing, an exemplification of K.J. Batcheldor's idea of "ownership resistance," there were still problems with that thinking. Phil Jordan, for instance, was known to lapse into trance* on occasion, his face contorting, his posture uncharacteristically stiffening, his speech inflections assuming a foreign mode. The voice that came through and claimed to be that of a deceased physician, "Doc," was completely different from Jordan's. While "Doc" might have been the product of a schizophrenic type of reaction, it was interesting that when "Doc" was around Jordan became especially adept at picking up telepathic and clairvoyant information. Sensitives who had watched such trances opined that "Doc" and other "spirits" could be behind the psychic's PK powers. Geller and England's Matthew Manning also had trance experiences. When the former was in trance a mechanical-sounding voice would supposedly come through, claiming it was part of a computer complex monitoring the earth from another space and time. This "computer's" messages were often punctuated by instances of teleportation. Manning had similar experiences, but his messages supposedly came from the dead. In fact one time, while Manning was asleep, a whole flock of spirits supposedly wrote messages and signed their names in a locked room in his house. Investigators were inclined to believe these graffiti were indeed the work of spirits, one of their reasons being that the signatures matched those of dead people Matthew had never heard of before. Likewise, some members of the Thurmond group had claimed communication with spirits, though in more subtle form (through automatic writing, for example). The group

---

*During these trances Jordan and others like him apparently lose conciousness and later, as a rule, remember nothing of what they have said or done.

leader, Betty Thurmond, had claimed she once clearly saw the spirit of a beautiful blonde woman standing in her living room. Then of course there is Arigo, the unlettered psychic surgeon whose ministrations to the sick, performed in a state of trance, are hard if not impossible to explain naturalistically. These and similar cases are so numerous as to supply enough material for quantities of books.

If some of the scattered and incomplete reports that I've seen are true, one of the best examples of how the seemingly different worlds of PK and spirits often interweave occurred in England shortly after World War II. The group involved was a quasi-scientific one that met rather regularly in London's Chelsea district mainly for the purpose of producing table levitation and receiving messages through table-tilts.* It was headed by psi researcher Dr. George Medhurst, a hypnotist who lent his basement apartment to group seances which were usually limited to four people and conducted in darkness. Many of the descriptions of what took place correspond to those of other groups: members sat on the levitated tables, got furniture to lift off the floor, and heard rapping noises. As with other groups, it was about six months before such phenomena occurred regularly. No member of the group was a recognized psychic or medium.

It was there, however, that most of the similarities stopped. After Dr. Medhurst's death in 1971, Benson Herbert, one of the group's members and a keen student

---

*The so-called messages were received by means of a technique that was used by other table groups. When a table began tilting, the group leader called off the alphabet (slowly progressing, ABC . . .) until the table stopped its tilt. The letter being called out at the moment the tilt ceased was assumed to be a letter of the communication. Whole sentences were painstakingly put together in this fashion. Codes like two tilts for yes and one for no were also used to expedite the messages.

of the paraphysical, wrote an article for the prestigious *Parapsychology Review* (November-December, 1971) in which he described phenomena so bizarre that, fearing ridicule, he had hesitated for years to publish it.

Herbert explained that the group sessions were usually divided into two sections with a break in between. The first featured attempts at physical psi phenomena like those produced by other table PK groups. The second usually centered on states of trance induced by hypnosis and the playing of certain songs on the record player. During peak periods the phenomena were spectacular. Tables rose by themselves, cushions flew across the room, and in one instance a member of the group was injured in a poltergeist-type outburst when a chair struck his head, chipping a tooth. Herbert wrote that phenomena often appeared "as if some influence had attached itself to the room, independently of any particular sitter."

After a while, the trance states became more frequent, and it seemed that clearcut spirit "personalities" or "entities" were controlling the members' bodies. These "controls" grew so dominant that, according to Herbert, it began to seem as if *they* were the experimenters and the human members merely their agents. Often the controls gave directions to the group through a member who was in trance.

At first the group thought the voices heard through trance were projections of their own subconsciouses, but later events made them wonder if perhaps real spirit beings were involved. On at least two occasions it was claimed these controlling entities appeared in tangible form. One was when a female member of the group suddenly brushed her fingers against a cold, clammy hand during a totally dark table session (or so says Herbert, who was there). She nervously reported what she had felt to the rest of the group, and they proceeded to count the hands on the table. There should have been eight hands, *but there were nine.* When the woman touched the phantom hand again and felt along it, she let out a bloodcurdling scream. The hand, she claimed, ended at the wrist.* A member of the group had jumped up at this point and flicked on the lights, only to find nothing strange on the table. There was, however, a peculiar sound as of something rubbery slithering across the floor. Yet another time Herbert himself claimed to have bumped into a "person" while roaming around in the darkened room. Barely had he conveyed an apology when he realized there was nobody there: all the other group members were sitting at the seance table.

What to make of it all? Are such "spirit" phenomena just complex manifestations of PK? Or are there truly spirits around that perhaps do all the feats of psi, misleading us into thinking these are the products of human PK?

It is the author's view that while such entities as spirits are probably out there, their existence, and the fact that they sometimes show themselves, in no way serves to diminish the probability that most of the phenomena reported in the body of this work are manifestations of human PK. During paraphysical sessions I have sat in on, there has been absolutely no hard evidence that spirits were at work, no apparitions, no messages from the dead, no sign of cosmic beings guiding the way. I had heard strange sounds during the Thurmond levitations, thumps in their attic and pings from their piano one time, but they could be explained in normal ways, and even if they couldn't it seemed more rational to attribute them to

---

*Mediums like D.D. Home apparently also encountered unattached hands appearing out of nowhere.

excess psychic energies coming from humans than to spirits.

The reasons why I favor the human hypothesis in most cases are numerous and diverse. We can start by remembering that in the vast majority of cases cited in this book, paranormal phenomena seemed to require people. They seemed closely related to human psyches, to attitudes, to states of consciousness and energies or images released from the subconscious, to strong imaginations and wills. There was no need to conjure spirits in order to make the phenomena occur, no need to use the services of a medium. People present at PK events often seemed in control of them, and paranormalities only rarely occurred after the various groups and individuals had stopped trying to produce phenomena; when this did happen there was no indication of ghostly intelligences at work, except in a few cases like that of the Medhurst group. On the other hand, there seemed to be many indications that humans radiate some mysterious energy, which perhaps contains at least a partial solution to the PK problem. Many have felt radiations from the bodies of psychics, sensations of extreme coolness or warmth hinting at an energy flow of some sort, often coming strongest from hands and maybe represented in Kirlian photographs. Clairvoyants often see this energy as the human aura and have claimed to observe it actually being transferred from the body of the psychic to some target in PK displays. It could well be the same aura that appears in Kirlian photographs and that undergoes dramatic changes during PK feats. Some scientists even claim to have measured electromagneticlike fields around the human body, fields that change measurably during PK opeations as if responsive to what's going on. But most important of all is the evidence that all humans can perform PK to some degree, that it's not a gift bestowed by spirits on a chosen few.

The premise that most PK manifestations are human in origin is naturally the one favored by orthodox scientists and it's the view taken by virtually all the researchers I talked with. These researchers did not feel uneasy with terms like "spirits" and "UFOs," but they had taken due note of the experiments of people like Batcheldor and Owen, which seemed to show that human forces were responsible for PK phenomena. They had also heard people like Geller, Jordan and Manning claim that while spiritual forces outside themselves did exist, so too did an energy that emanated from the human body, an energy which, according to them, could cause material objects to move. As to what this energy may be, however, scientists steadfastly refuse to speculate.

While I believe most of what has been discussed in this book has to do with human PK, again I am certainly not denying the existence of spirit beings for I believe there are indeed infinite forms of life and consciousness in infinite continuums of space-time, on infinite spheres called planets. Maybe humans are but sprouts in a cosmic nursery, tended by superintelligences who manifest themselves as ghosts, UFOs, spirit guides. So consistent are many reports on these subjects, and so inexplicable simply in terms of human PK are some of the happenings attributed to homes not thought to be haunted by poltergeists, that I have concluded invisible intelligences do in fact exist all around us, perhaps in universes that sometimes mesh with our own. At the same time, however, I think such entities are much too frequently given as the source of PK and other psi events when in fact the operative power is of human origin and merely *similar* to the type of energies used by outside entities. In the case of Uri Geller, as of other exceptional psychics, it could be that extraterrestrials are, for reasons of their own, employing him as a messenger. But to my mind, such cases, if they exist, are rare. Perhaps, when people attempt PK and other psi feats, they create, through psi energy, some kind of loophole in our reality through which supernormal entities enter. This view would suppose that we create the energies, but that spirits or "intelligences" sometimes use them. To teach us a lesson? To taunt us? To play with us? Who knows.

With PK, we may be dealing with an energy or energies that may be paraphysical in nature and that may lie at the root of intelligent or nonintelligent life, that may be the basic stuff of our universe.

Throughout this book, much more than I would have liked, I have found myself using vague words such as "seems," "perhaps" and "essentially," or saying that the energies of PK are "linked" or "connected" to those of ESP, auras, UFOs, force fields. I was never able to *define* these energies. I make no apologies for it, however, for that's the way things are in this world of PK, which science has only begun to study and can't itself define. But while PK remains largely mysterious, there *are* areas of it that science has been able to observe and document, if not fully to explain. It's this fact — and not PK as such, which is probably as old as man — that makes the present time so exciting, marking it off from all other periods of history. J.B. Rhine tabulated the effects of small-scale PK; Wilbur Franklin submitted PK-bent metal to the microscope; Hal Puthoff and Russell Targ made a convincing if not conclusive scientific record of Geller's powers; Justa Smith scientifically analyzed the enzymatic reactions Estebany produced by means of PK force.

It's my belief, and implicitly it's been my contention through much of this book, that science should now enlarge the beachhead that has been established by these and other pioneers. If it does so, then the prospects not only of understanding some of the hidden workings of PK in the near future but of "putting them to work" for man are exciting.

If PK power, which now raises tables, bends or breaks metal, affects living organisms, and moves distant objects through the agency of certain "psychic" individuals, can somehow be harnessed for the general use of man, what might it not achieve in the areas of applied technology?

We may soon see the day when psychics or PK machines will be used extensively in industry to bend or break metal or alter its structure by cooling or heating it. PK's capacity to raise and lower heavy objects might do sterling service in the field of construction engineering. If such energy can be stored, as "pyramid power" seems to establish, one can envision a revolution in transportation, with trains, automobiles, planes and ships specially adapted to run on psi batteries; stretching our imaginations a bit, we can envision teleportation power being used to give us "instant transport" not only to earthly destinies but to points in the distant reaches of space.

It might be possible to adapt PK power to a variety of household uses. It has been shown that PK manifestations are often accompanied by cool breezes and sometimes by heat; if such effects could be controlled at will they might supply ways of cooling and heating our homes vastly more efficient and economical than any we have now. During certain PK events, electrical phenomena have been reported, as in the case of the Reverend John Scudder, a Chicago psychic who is said to be able to illumine light bulbs through willpower. If we learn how to harness that ability, we might find ourselves with a much-needed alternative energy source, one that is not only clean but of limitless supply. The mysterious capacity of pyramids or like structures to halt the processes of organic decay might enable us to preserve food indefinitely and might thus make our present refrigeration systems obsolete. We have seen there's a link between ESP and PK — could this be made the basis for a super-telephone network?

Governments should be specially interested in PK from the standpoint of military defense. Energy X, the force that makes PK operative, might be accumulated in huge psychotronic generators and used to provide cities with shields against nuclear radiation.

Nowhere do the prospects for the peaceful uses of PK energy look brighter than in the area of medicine. In Chapter 15 it was shown that under controlled conditions this energy could be used to effect cures or at least improvements in sick organisms; if the process by which this is done were understood and made applicable at will, it would signal a great step forward for medicine, a great new hope for mankind. It might make the nightmare of cancer a thing of the past.

There are energies in the universe that await our understanding. Psychics have seen them or felt them or been their instrument; science has suggested they exist. It now seems open to all of us — not just to the scientists among us — to participate in a great adventure. We should not plunge wildly into what William James called the baffling side of human nature, however, not go stumbling and groping along PK's carnival corridor of mirrors; we should proceed carefully, step by step, taking cognizance of those PK energies whose presence science has confirmed before tackling those that seem to belong to the "supernatural." The results of such an adventure could be to our enormous intellectual and practical advantage.

Report From SORRAT

Throughout the research and writing of this book I have had to live with the grating frustration of knowing this work could never be complete and definitive, that out there are groups I haven't had time to investigate, experimental PK devices I know nothing about, psychics who are as powerful as anyone here reported on. Certainly, PK is what a newspaperman would call a running story: information is always coming in. While I've tried to touch on what I judged to be the most detailed, documented and pertinent cases, there have always been tantalizing developments that the limitations of space and time — especially the latter — prevented me from including. This work could have been twice the length it is, with more detail on, for instance, energy accumulators like those built by Wilhelm Reich or on some of the lengthy experiments carried on at the Foundation for Research on the Nature of Man in North Carolina. Out of necessity, however, I had to forgo the investigation of such matters and stay with the more salient, recent facts.

But as this book goes to press I have suddenly come across a group of psi experimenters, from Missouri, whom I cannot ignore. For what they have done, if they are relating their experiences as accurately as I sense they are, is as dramatic and potentially as documentable as anything else in this book.

This group is based on a place called Skyrim Farm, just north of Columbia, and calls itself SORRAT, an acronym for the Society for Research on Rapport and Telekinesis. Though they have been given very little publicity, the group's members have been producing for fifteen years now what could be the most spectacular levitations I have yet heard of. Some of the group's photographs are included in this volume.

SORRAT was founded in the middle of October 1961 by Dr. John G. Neihardt, a Plains State poet who died in 1973. An honorary member of the Oglala Sioux tribe, Neihardt wrote the well-received novel *Black Elk Speaks*, which goes deeply into Indian spiritualism, and in fifty years of studying psi became associated with such psi luminaries as Joseph B. Rhine of the Foundation for Research on the Nature of Man. The steadiest members of the group are Dr. Carolina Davis, an anthropologist; John T. Richards, a writer and English teacher; Alice Thompson, present leader of the group and the daughter of Neihardt; Joseph F. Mangini, a psychiatric social case worker and a trance medium; Stephen Snider, an artist; Terry Kirkpatrick, an Air Force officer; Mark and Judy Meadows, librarians; Maralyn Hamaker, a journalist; Mrs. Elaine Richards, a sensitive; and Neihardt's two granddaughters, Lynn and Erica Thompson. For years it has operated as a sort of part-time satellite of parapsychology foundations, cooperating with various researchers like Dr. Rhine in well-controlled PK experiments.

Within a couple of months of SORRAT's formation, members found that when small objects were placed as target objects on an oak table they used, cold spots frequently surrounded these objects during periods of rather weak concentration (like other groups, SORRAT found a relaxed attitude the most fruitful). These spots, registered on a thermometer as approximately five degrees below room temperature, varied in diameter from less than an inch to sixteen inches in diameter (see: "What Happens When You Experiment with Psi Energy," *Psychic World and The Occult* magazine, November 1976, an article by member John T. Richards). Sometimes the objects seemed to move, though not convincingly. About four months after the group started its regular weekly meetings, members noticed that strange rappings, at first rather soft but later quite loud, spread around the room they worked in, seeming to come from various articles of furniture, especially if the furniture was wood.

The group's most striking results began to occur in the autumn of 1965. Around this time members began totally levitating that oak table, a feat they were to later find themselves able to replicate with an eighty-two-pound table. In February 1966 they began working with a rather light metal snack tray, and the outcome was spectacular. The tray not only lifted completely clear of the floor but actually moved out from under their hands, floated by itself to the ceiling, tapped five times against a light fixture, and then wobbled down to the floor. One of the members, Mangini, was in deep trance at the time. Significantly, some of the most amazing results occurred during his trance states.

In subsequent sessions, that snack tray supposedly did some things I have only rarely heard of and cannot vouch for. According to Richards, who took copious notes and photographs, the tray was once levitated outdoors to a height of fifteen feet! Other times it allegedly stayed airborne for as long as three minutes. Many of these times, no one was touching it. Richards, who is now at work on his doctorate in English at the University of Missouri, says the snack tray often walked off by itself and once made it into a garage and onto a parked car, where it tap-danced for a while as members looked on. "I couldn't believe it at first either," says Richards, "but I saw it too many times." Such levitations are said to still occur, and the group has been experimenting with different methods of causing them.

Interestingly, Neihardt was once reported to have lain on a table that was completely levitated. Despite the poet's weight, the table moved some sixteen inches across the room. Another time, Richards says the group concentrated on trying to levitate a rocking chair on which a cat was sleeping. It too ascended, in fact to a recorded height of four feet. Unfortunately, it fell just after a camera clicked a shot. Not surprisingly, this group also found that artificial light and cameras could be a hindrance to levitation.

At the suggestion of the highly respected J.B. Rhine, the group also carried out experiments with special sealed boxes built to ensure against fraud. Such gadgets have consisted of enclosed pendulums and cubes set before subjects as the PK targets. One device, still used by the group, is a sealed box with its bottom covered with sand. Inside are three cubes, one wood, one lead, one clay. The aim of the experiment is to move the clay cube without budging the others. When this happens the cube makes marks in the sand, an objective way of confirming paranormal movements. The group has often succeeded with the box.

SORRAT has also been able, reportedly, to affect sensitized paper through "will/idea" PK. While most of the time the marks produced have been just lines and squiggles, there have also been some decidedly strange results. According to Richards, writings have appeared on the sensitive paper in pre-Norman Conquest English, conversational Greek and old Celtic, suggesting attempts by spirits to communicate. An interpreter has been employed to decipher such messages, says Richards, who is himself writing a book on these extraordinary phenomena. Apparently SORRAT has also caused teleportations of various objects ranging from small jewelry to good-sized books.

The group has found that the psi manifestations seem to slacken off a bit during the summer. Neihardt had hypothesized this might be because of changes in the earth's magnetic lines as the planet tips on its axis. "We think the psi force could have something to do with electromagnetism, but we're not really sure," says Richards.

Even if the form of energy were known, there would still be that bothersome question of whether it originates from human PK or the telekinesis of spirits. "Certainly it could be energy projected from us," says Richards, "and yet I lean towards thinking spirits are involved. We have infrared pictures of what just may be discarnate entities — apparitions — that were present during various sessions, but this could have been a result of our psycho-kinetically affecting the film." A bioengineer and biochemist have recently joined SORRAT sessions to try to find the root cause of the psi events that have taken place. Meanwhile, a number of other groups have sprouted in the South and, according to Richards, are getting impressive results.

And so once again we have come full circle. I am reminded that, back during the Eusapia Palladino controversy some eighty years ago, *New York Times* reporter Will Irwin sat in on a table levitation held by the Italian medium and monitored by America's prime illusionist, Howard Thurston. Both men walked away convinced that her phenomena — very similar to SORRAT's — were genuine. But Irwin was nagged by the very same questions that nag us, despite our much greater knowledge of psi phenomena. Was whatever caused that table to float some energy emanating from the medium, or was there an invisible thaumaturgist at work, sneakily operating on the periphery of what we call reality? Irwin couldn't answer such questions then any more than I can answer them now.

Appendix Two

Report From Naval Weaponry

"Neither I nor other experts can offer any scientific explanation of how these deformations may have occurred under the conditions imposed."

The words are those of physical scientist Eldon Byrd and are contained in a paper entitled, "Uri Geller's Influence on the Metal Alloy Nitinol."* Byrd is an employee of the Naval Surface Weapons Center in Silver Spring, Maryland, and his recently published report marks the first time the Department of Defense has allowed

*See Charles Panati's *The Geller Papers.*

governmental research into parapsychology conducted at an official facility to be publicly presented. It provides still more evidence that Uri Geller's PK is genuine.

Nitinol is an alloy that was developed at the naval center. It is composed, by weight, of approximately 55 percent nickel and 45 percent titanium. Most importantly, it has a "physical memory," which means that, when heated, it will spring back to its original, manufactured shape no matter how much it has been bent or twisted.

On 29 October 1973, Geller visited the naval center and was asked by Byrd to try to influence a five-inch wire made of nitinol. The psychic went ahead and rubbed the metal as the scientist held it at each end. Soon a remarkable kink developed in the wire.

When Byrd placed the wire in boiling water, which should have caused it immediately to straighten back to its original shape, it remained contorted and in fact began to form a right angle. Baffled, Byrd made an X-ray crystallographic analysis of the wire and found that the crystals in the kinked sector had somehow become enlarged.

The wire was later handed to several other government metallurgists, who tried to get it back to its manufactured shape. They put the wire in a vacuum and sent electricity through it until it glowed. It did indeed go back to its original shape — but once it had cooled, the inexplicable kink returned! It was as if that kink had been manufactured into the metal. A year later Geller repeated the experiment with Byrd, deforming three other wires.

Nitinol experts are at a loss to explain the effect. Chemicals were obviously not used in creating it, for the wire remained impervious to testings with mercuric chloride. The only way of duplicating the effect that they can think of would be to heat the metal to more than 900° centigrade and then bend it with pliers.

Glossary

apport — an object that suddenly arrives from another space or time; often associated with seance rooms

aura — a hazy, halo-like energy said to surround organic objects and constitute their spiritual essence or organizing force; said by some to surround inorganic objects as well

clairvoyance — or "clear seeing," the ability to visualize events or objects through ESP

dematerialization — the disappearance of a person or object from our space-time continuum

ESP — an abbreviation of *extrasensory perception*; includes clairvoyance, clairaudience, telepathy and pre- and retro-cognition; relates to all information that is received without the intermediary of the known senses

etheric body — supposedly a "double" of the physical body.

healer — someone who can cure another person or an animal paranormally

ghost — commonly thought to be the energy body of a deceased person or animal; usually used in connection with haunted houses

levitation — the mysterious rising and floating in the air of persons or objects through the paranormal suspension of gravity

materialization — the paranormal appearance of a person or object in our space-time continuum (the opposite of dematerialization); often said to occur through the agency of a medium's ectoplasm

medium — a psychic or sensitive who supposedly receives messages from and transmits messages to the spirit world

parakinesis — the same as PK, though used in some English circles to mean the paranormal movement of an object through physical contact (as opposed to telekinesis)

paranormal — anything that is "above and beyond" rational explanation

parapsychology — the branch of science that investigates ESP and PK

poltergeist — a noisy, trickster spirit, sometimes violent; or perhaps an unconscious human energy that causes objects to move

precognition — the foreknowledge of future events which cannot be deduced from present knowledge

psi — the twenty-third letter of the Greek alphabet, a general term roughly synonymous with "psychic"

psychic — the capacity to experience ESP or perform PK; a person with either or both of these capacities

psychokinesis — or PK, the moving or otherwise affecting of objects or living organisms without physical influence

Spiritualism — in its modern, American form, a religion that focuses on communicating with the dead

spirit — an invisible intelligence

telekinesis — (rarely used nowadays), the paraphysical movement of objects

telepathy — the ability to "read" another person's mind, or receive impressions from it, without the aid of speech, gesture or other normal means of communication

teleportation — the paranormal transportation of persons or objects from one place to another

trance — a state of mind characterized by heightened awareness and some degree of mental dissociation

---

Bibliography

Abbott, David. *Behind the Scenes with Mediums.* Chicago: The Open Court Publishing Co., 1907.

Angoff, Alan. *The Psychic Force.* International Journal of Parapsychology. New York: G.P. Putnam's Sons, 1970.

Asher, Jules. "Mind Control Sells Alpha. Buys Research." *American Psychological Association Monitor,* April 1973.

Ballou, Robert O., and Murphy, Gardner. *William James on Psychic Research.* New York: The Viking Press, 1960.

Baskin, Wade, and Wedeck, Harry E. *Dictionary of Spiritualism.* New York: Philosophical Library, 1971.

Batcheldor, Kenneth J. "Report on a Case of Table Levitation and Associated Phenomena." *The Journal of the Society for Psychical Research,* vol. 43, no. 729 (September 1966), pp. 339-356.

_____, "Practical Hints for Small-Group Study of Psychokinesis Using Tables." Privately published paper, September 1966.

_____, "Macro-PK in Group Sittings: Theoretical and Practical Aspects." Unpublished paper, June 1968.

Bayless, Raymond. *The Enigma of the Poltergeist.* New York: Parker Publishing Co., Inc. 1967.

_____, "Tape-recording of Paranormally Generated Acoustical Raps." *New Horizons,* vol. 2, no. 2 (June 1976), pp. 12-17.

Berlitz, Charles. *The Bermuda Triangle.* Garden City, N.Y.: Doubleday and Co., Inc. 1974.

Bergier, Jaques. *Extraterrestrial Intervention.* Chicago: Henry Regnery Co., 1974.

_____ **and Pauwels, Louis.** *The Morning of the Magicians.* Paris: Editions Gallimard, 1960.

Bigwood, Catharine. "Mind Control — Something for Everyone." *Harper'sBazaar,* November 1972.

Bird, Christopher. "Finding It by Dowsing." *Psychic* magazine, vol. 6, no. 4 (October 1975), pp., 8-13.

_____ **and Tompkins, Peter.** *The Secret Life of Plants.* New York: Harper and Row, 1973.

Blum, Ralph. *Beyond Earth: Man's Contact with UFOs.* New York: Bantam Books, 1974.

Brookes-Smith, Colin. "Data-Tape Recorded Experimental PK Phenomena." *Journal of the Society for Psychical Research,* vol. 47, no. 756 (1973), pp. 69-89.

_____, "A Transistorial Random Sequence Generator." Privately published, 1966, 7 pages.

_____, "Paranormal Electrical Conductance Phenomena (in Association with Table Phenomena)." *The Journal of the Society for Psychical Research,* vol. 48, no. 764 (1975), pp. 265-287.

_____ **and Hunt, D.W.** "Some Experiments in Psychokinesis." *The Journal of the Society for Psychical Research*, vol. 45, no. 744 (1970), pp. 265-357.

Brown, Michael H., and Kennedy, Donald. "Witnesses Can't Explain Levitation." *The Binghamton Sun-Bulletin* and *United Press International*, 7 April 1975 and October 1975, respectively.

Brown, Slater. *The Heyday of Spiritualism.* New York: Hawthorne Books, Inc., 1970.

Bugliosi, Vincent and Gentry, Curt. *Helter Skelter.* New York: W.W. Norton and Co., Inc., 1974.

Burk, David. "Horror-Filled Ordeal of Girl, 10. Infested by Devil for Five Weeks." *The National Enquirer*, 6 January 1976, p. 48.

Carrington, Hereward. *The American Seances with Eusapia Palladino.* New York: Garrett Publishing. 1954.

Castaneda, Carlos. *The Teaching of Don Juan: A Yaqui Way of Knowledge.* California: University of California Press. 1968.

_____.*Journey to Ixtlan.* New York: Simon and Schuster, 1972.

Cavendish, Richard. *Encyclopedia of the Unexplained.* New York: McGraw-Hill Book Co., 1974.

Caylor, Ron. "Incredible Psychic Lifts Objects with His Mind — and Makes Them Hover." *The National Enquirer*, 17 February 1976, p.3.

Christopher, Milbourne. *ESP, SEERS, and Psychics.* New York: Thomas Crowell Company, 1970.

Clark, Adrian. *Psycho-Kinesis.* West Nyack, N.Y.: Parker Publishing Co., Inc., 1973.

Colligan, Douglas. "Photographing the Human Aura." *Science Digest*, May 1974.

Condon, Edward U. *Scientific Study of Unidentified Flying Objects — The Complete Report on the Study Conducted by the University of Colorado.* New York: E.P. Dutton and Co., 1969.

D'Antonio, Dennis. "Amazing New Teenage Psychic Is More Powerful than Uri Geller." *The National Enquirer*, 28 October 1975, p.27.

David, Jay. *The Flying Saucer Reader.* New York: The New American Library, 1967.

_____. *Flying Saucers Have Arrived.* New York: The World Publishing Co., 1970.

Dean, Douglas. "Molecular Effects of a 'Healer'." *New Horizons*, vol. 1, no. 5 (January 1975), pp. 215-19.

Dingwall, E.J. "Telekinetic and Teleplastic Mediumship." *The Journal of the Society for Psychical Research, 19??.*

Doctor, Fali, and Patole, Gantam. "The Mystical Heritage of India." *Occult Magazine.* January 1975.

Dooley, Anne. "The Phenomena of Matthew Manning." *Psychic* magazine, December 1975, p.44

Downing, Barry H. *The Bible and Flying Saucers,* New York: J.B. Lippincott Co., 1968.

Doyle, Arthur Conan. *The History of Spiritualism.* New York: George H. Doran, Co., 1926.

Ebon, Martin. *The Psychic Reader.* New York: World Publishing Co., 1969.

_____. *They Knew the Unknown,* New York: World Publishing Co., 1969.

_____. *The Amazing Uri Geller.* New York: The New American Library, 1975.

_____. *The Riddle of the Bermuda Triangle.* New York: Signet, 1975.

Edwards, Frank. *Stranger Than Science.* New York: Lyle Stuart, 1959.

_____. *Flying Saucers — Serious Business.* New York: Lyle Stuart, 1966.

Eliade, Mircea. *Shamanism.* New York: Pantheon Books, 1964.

Fakhry, Ahmed. *The Pyramids.* Chicago: University of Chicago Press, 1961.

Flanagan, G. Patrick. *Pyramid Power.* Santa Monica: DeVorss and Co., 1973.

Fodor, Nandor. *Encyclopedia of Psychic Science.* London: Arthurs, 1933, reprinted at New Hyde Park, N.Y. by University Books (1966).

Franklin, Wilbur. "Fracture Surface Indicating Teleneural Interaction." *New Horizons*, vol. 2, no. 1, April 1975.

_____."The Role of Paraphysics in Education." Unpublished paper, 1975.

_____."Is There Physics in ESP?" Unpublished paper, 1974.

_____**and Mitchell, Edgar.** "Scanning Electron Microscope Study of Fracture Surfaces Pertaining to the Question of Teleneural Fields from Human Subjects." Unpublished paper. 1973.

Fuller, John G. "Is He Charlatan or Miracle Worker?" *Reader's Digest.* September 1975.

_____. *Arigo: Surgeon of the Rusty Knife.* New York: T.Y. Crowell, 1974.

Gaddis, Vincent. *Mysterious Fires and Lights.* New York: David McKay Co., Inc., 1967.

_____.*Invisible Horizons.* New York: Chilton Books, 1975.

Geller, Uri. *My Story.* New York: Praeger, 1975.

Gibson, Walter B., and Litzka, R. *The Complete Illustrated Book of the Psychic Sciences.* Garden City, N.Y. Doubleday and Co., 1966.

Godwin, John. *This Baffling World.* New York: Hart Publishing Co., 1968.

Gilbert, Phyllis. "Psychic Children," *Psychic* magazine, December 1975, pp. 16-19.

Greenburg, Dan. *Something's There.* Garden City, N.Y.: Doubleday and Co., 1976.

Greenhouse, Herbert. "PK-Missing, or Mind Undermining Matter." *Psychic* magazine, vol. 6, no. 2 (June 1975), p. 29.

Hall, Trevor H. *New Light on Old Ghosts.* London: Gerald Duckworth and Co. Ltd., 1965.

_____. *The Spiritualists.* New York: Helix Press, 1962.

Hammond, David. *The Search for Psychic Power.* New York: Bantam Books, 1975.

Hartmann, Franz. *Paracelsus: Life and Prophecies.* Blauvelt, N.Y.: Rudolf Steiner Publications, 1973.

Haynes, Renee. *The Hidden Springs.* Boston: Little, Brown and Co., 1961.

Hill, Douglas, and Williams, Pat. *The Supernatural.* New York: Hawthorn Books, 1965.

Hisey, Lehmann. *Keys to Inner Space.* New York: The Julian Press, 1974.

Holzer, Hans. *The Directory of the Occult.* Chicago: Henry Regnery Co., 1974.

Houdini, Harry. *Magician Among the Spirits.* New York: Harper and Row, 1924, reprinted with Arno Press, 1972.

Hunt, Gerry. "Psychic Proves He Can Move Objects — With His Mind." *The National Enquirer,* 4 February 1975, p. 15.

Hynek, J. Allen. "The Strangeness of UFO Experiences." *New Horizons,* vol. 1, no. 5 (January 1975), pp. 237-243.

Isaacs, J. "Sitter Group Experimentation." Unpublished paper (England), 1975.

Jackson, Herbert C. *The Spirit Rappers.* Garden City, N.Y.: Doubleday and Co., 1972.

Johnson, R.C. *Psychical Research.* New York: Philosophical Library, 1955.

Josephson, Brian. (Nobel Prize recipient, 1973). "Possible Connections Between Psychic Phenomena and Quantum Mechanics." *New Horizons,* vol. 1, no. 5 (January 1975), p. 213.

Kanfer, Stefan. "Boom Times on the Psychic Frontier." *Time,* vol. 103, no. 9 (4 March 1974), pp. 65-72.

Keel, John A. *Our Haunted Planet.* Greenwich, Conn.: Fawcett Publishing Co., 1971.

Keyhoe, Donald. *Flying Saucers From Outer Space.* New York: Henry Holt and Co., 1953.

_____. *Aliens From Space — The Real Story of Unidentified Flying Objects.* Garden City, N.Y.: Doubleday and Co., 1973.

Klass, Philip, J. *UFOs Explained.* New York: Random House, 1974.

Knight, David C. *The ESP Reader.* New York: Grosset and Dunlap, 1969.

Knight News Service. "Six Who Saw UFO Pass Lie Tests: 'Bolt' Victim Tells a Strange Tale." *The Buffalo Evening News,* 14 November 1975, p. 1.

Kreskin. *The Amazing World of Kreskin.* New York: Random House, 1973.

Krippner, Stanley, and Rubin, Daniel. *The Kirlian Aura.* Garden City, N.Y.: Anchor Press/Doubleday, 1974.

Lawrence, Jodi. *Alpha Brain-Waves.* Los Angeles: Nash Publishing Corp., 1972.

Manning, Matthew. "My Metal Phenomena," *New Horizons,* vol. 1, no. 5 (January 1975), pp. 199-200.

_____. *The Link.* New York: Holt, Rinehart, and Winston, 1974.

de Maigret, Pamela. "Ancient Healing in Modern China." *Psychic* magazine, August 1975, pp. 17-21.

McHargue, Georgess. *Facts, Frauds and Phantasms.* Garden City, N.Y.: Doubleday and Co., 1972.

McMullan, J.T. "A Possible Source for the Energy Needed in Poltergeist Activity." *Journal of the American Society for Psychical Research,* vol. 65. no. 4 (October 1971), pp. 493-494.

Medhurst, R.G. and Goldney, K.M. "William Crookes and the Phenomena of Physical Mediumship." *Journal of the Society for Phychical Research,* vol. 54, no. 195 (March 1964), pp. 25-157.

Miller, Robert N. and Reinhart, Philip B. "Measuring Psychic Energy." *Psychic* magazine, June 1975, pp. 46-7.

Mitchell, Edgar. *Psychic Exploration.* New York: G.P. Putnam's Sons. 1974.

Morrison, Philip. "Uri Geller: International Pied Piper of the Credulous . . . " *Scientific American,* February 1976, pp. 134-5.

Moss, Thelma and Schmeidler, Gertrude. "Quantitative Investigation of a Haunted House, with Sensitives and a Control Group."*Journal of the American Society for Psychical Research,* vol. 62 (1968), pp. 399-409.

Moss, Thelma. *The Probability of the Impossible.* Los Angeles: Tarcher, Inc. 1974.

Muldoon, Sylvan, and Carrington, Hereward. *The Projection of the Astral Body.* New York: Samuel Weiser, 1929 and 1973.

Murphy, Gardner. *The Challenge of Psychical Research.* New York: Harper and Row, 1961.

Myers, Frederic W.H., "On Alleged Movements of Objects Without Contact Not in the Presence of a Paid Medium," *Journal for the Society for Psychical Research,* vol. 7 (1892), pp. 146-198.

Ostrander, Sheila, and Schroeder, Lynn. *Psychic Discoveries Behind the Iron Curtain.* New Jersey: Prentice-Hall, Inc., 1970.

_____. *The Handbook of Psi.* Berkeley Publishing Corp., 1974.

Oteri, Laura. "Quantum Physics and Parapsychology (Proceedings of an international conference held in Geneva, Switzerland, August 26-27, 1974)," *Parapsychology Foundation,* N.Y.

Ouspensky, P.D. *Tertium Organum.* Alfred Knopf, Inc., 1920.

Owen, A.R.G. *Can We Explain the Poltergeist?* New York: Garrett Publications, 1964.

_____. *Psychic Mysteries of the North.* New York: Harper and Row, 1975.

_____. "15 Years of Psychokinesis," *New Horizons,* vol. 2, no. 1 (January 1975), pp. 4-7, text of proceedings of First Canadian Conference on Psychokinesis.

_____. "The Aetiology of Poltergeistery," *New Horizons*, vol. 1, no. 5 (January 1975), pp. 201-211.

_____. "A Preliminary Report on Matthew Manning's Physical Phenomena," *New Horizons*, vol. 1, no. 4 (July 1974), pp. 172-3.

_____, **and Whitton, Joel.** "Report on Demonstrations and Experiments Performed During the Conference (Matthew Manning)." *New Horizons*, vol. 1, no. 5 (January 1975), pp. 191-4.

Owen, Iris. "Generation of Paranormal Physical Phenomena in Connection with an Imaginary Communicator." *New Horizons*, 10 October 1973, pp. 6-13.

_____. "The Making of a Ghost." *Psychic* magazine, vol. 6, no. 3 (August 1975), pp. 6-13.

_____. "Philip's Story Continued." *New Horizons*, vol. 2, no. 1 (April 1975), pp. 14-20.

_____ **and Sparrow, Margaret.** "Generation of Paranormal Phenomena in Connection with an Imaginary Communicator." *New Horizons*, vol. 1, no. 3, January 1974.

Panati, Charles. *Supersenses.* New York: Quadrangle/New York Times Book Co., 1974.

_____. *The Geller Papers.* New York: Houghton Mifflin 1976.

Pearsall, Ronald. *The Table-Rappers.* New York: St. Martin's Press, 1972.

Persinger, Michael. "ELF Waves and ESP," *New Horizons*, vol. 1, no. 5 (January 1975), p. 232.

Playfair, Guy Lyon. *The Unknown Power.* New York: Pocket Books, 1975.

Podmore, Frank. *Mediums of the 19th Century.* London: Putnam and Co., 1936.

Price, Harry. *Confessions of a Ghost-Hunter.* London: Putnam and Co., 1936.

_____. *Poltergeist Over England.* London: Country Life Ltd., 1945.

Prince, Water F. *Noted Witnesses for Psychic Occurrences.* New Hyde Park: University Books, 1963.

Puharich, Andrija. *The Sacred Mushroom.* Garden City, N.Y.: Doubleday and Co., Inc., 1959.

_____. *Beyond Telepathy.* New York: Doubleday and Co., Inc., 1962.

_____. *URI — A Journal of the Mystery of Uri Geller,* New York: Doubleday and Co., Inc., 1974.

Puthoff, Harold. "Experiment with Ingo Swann," private paper, 1972.

_____ **and Targ, Russell.** "Information Transmission Under Conditions of Sensory Shielding." *Nature*, October 1974.

_____. "Physics, Entropy, and Psychokinesis," from the proceedings of an international conference published by the *Parapsychology Foundation*, 1974.

Randi, James. *The Magic of Uri Geller.* New York: Ballantine Books, 1975.

_____. "Geller is a Fake!" *Science Digest*, April 1976, p. 63,

Rayleigh, Lord. "Presidential address: The Problem of Physical Phenomena in Connection with Psychical Research." *Journal of the Society for Psychical Research*, part 152, 1937.

Regush, Nicholas M. *The Human Aura.* New York: The Berkely Publishing Corp., 1974.

Reuters News Service. "Flying Saucer 'Zapped' Man, Co-Workers Say," *The Buffalo Evening News*, 10 November 1975, p. 1.

Rhine, Joseph Banks. *New Frontiers of the Mind.* Farrar and Rinehart, Inc., 1937.

_____. Personal correspondences and resulting notations on cassettes, 1975.

_____. *Progress in Parapsychology.* North Carolina: The Parapsychology Press, 1971.

_____. *The Reach of the Mind.* New York: William Sloane, Associates, Inc., 1947.

_____ **and Bries, Robert.** *Parapsychology Today.* New York: Citadel Press, 1968.

Rhine, Louisa. *Mind Over Matter.* New York: Collier Books, 1970.

_____. *Psi — What Is It?* New York: Harper and Row, 1975.

_____. *Hidden Channels of the Mind.* New York: William Sloane Associates, 1961.

Ryzl, Milan. *Parapsychology — A Scientific Approach.* New York: Hawthorne Books, Inc., 1970.

Rogo, D. Scott. *Parapsychology, A Century of Inquiry.* New York: Taplinger Publishing Co., 1975.

_____. *An Experience of Phantoms.* New York: Taplinger Publishing Co., 1974.

Rawcliffe, D.H. *Illusions and Delusions of the Supernatural and the Occult.* New York: Dover Publications, 1959.

Sack, John. "How I Became the First Person to Sleep in the Great Pyramid." *Esquire*, April 1975, pp. 98-99.

Salisbury, Frank B. *The Utah UFO Display: A Biologist's Report.* Old Greenwich, Conn: The Devin-Adair Co., 1974.

Sarfatti, Jack. "Geller Performs for Physicists." *Science News*, vol. 106, 20 July 1974.

Schmeidler, Gertrude. "Quantitative Investigation of a Haunted House." *Journal of the American Society for Psychical Research*, vol. 61, 1966, pp. 137-149.

Schmidt, Helmut. "PK Test with a High Speed Random Number Generator," private paper, 1970.

_____. "PK Test with Electronic Equipment." *Journal of Parapsychology*, (Foundation for Research on the Nature of Man), vol. 34, no. 3, September 1970.

_____. "PK Experiments with Animals as Subjects." *Journal of Parapsychology*, vol. 34, no. 4, December 1970.

Sanderson, Ivan T. *Uninvited Visitors.* New York: Cowles Book Co., 1967.

Sherman, Harold. *Your Power to Heal.* New York: Harper and Row, 1972.

Sinclair, Upton. *Mental Radio.* Springfield, Ill. Charles C. Thomas, Co., 1930.

Sirag, Saul-Paul. "The Skeptics," *Psychic* magazine, vol. 6, no. 4 (October 1975), pp. 16-22.

Sladek, John. *The New Apocrypha.* New York: Stein and Day, 1973.

Smith, Adam. *Powers of Mind.* New York: Random House, 1975.

Smith, Eleanor Toughey. *Psychic People.* New York: William Morrow and Co., 1968.

Smith, Justa. "Paranormal Effects on Enzyme Activity." Human Dimensions Journal, vol. 1, no. 2, pp. 15-19.

Smith, Susy. *The Mediumship of Mrs. Leonard.* New Hyde Park: University Books, 1964.

_____. *The Powers of the Mind.* Radnor, Pa.: Chilton Books, 1975.

Smook, Roger. "PK From the Standpoint of Philosophical Idealism." *New Horizons,* vol. 1, no. 5 (January 1975), pp. 220-3.

Spence, Lewis. *An Encyclopedia of Occultism.* New Hyde Park: University Books, 1960.

Spencer, John Wallace. *Limbo of the Lost.* New York: Philips Publishing Co., 1969.

Spraggett, Allen. *The Unexplained.* New York: The New American Library, 1967.

_____. *New Worlds of the Unexplained.* New York: The New American Library, 1976.

Stearn, Jess. *Adventures into the Psychic.* New York: Coward, McCann, and Geoghegan, Inc., 1969.

_____. *The Power of Alpha-Thinking.* New York: William Morrow Co., 1976.

Steiger, Brad. *Mysteries of Time and Space.* New Jersey: Prentice-Hall, 1974.

_____ **and White, John.** *Other Worlds, Other Universes.* Garden City, N.Y.: Doubleday and Co., Inc., 1975.

Swann, Ingo. *To Kiss the Earth Good-Bye.* New York: Hawthorne Books, Inc., 1975.

Talamonti, Leo. *Forbidden Universe.* New York: Stein and Day, 1975.

Taylor, John G. *The New Physics.* New York: Basic Books, Inc., 1972.

_____.*Black Holes.* New York: Random House, 1973.

_____.*Superminds.* New York: the Viking Press, 1975.

_____."Geller's Powers Are Genuine!" *Science Digest,* April 1976, pp. 56-62.

_____."The Spoon Benders," *Psychic,* December 1975, pp. 8-10.

Teilhard de Chardin, Pierre. *How I Believe.* Editions de Sevil, 1969.

Thouless, Robert. *From Anecdote to Experiment in Psychical Research.* London: Routledge and Kegan Paul, 1972.

Tiller, William H. "Some Psychoenergetic Devices." *Journal of the Association for Research and Enlightenment,* 1970, pp. 68-80.

_____."A General Technical Report: Fact-Finding Trip to the Soviet Union." *Journal of the Association for Research and Enlightenment.* 1 March 1972.

Toogood, Granville. "Hundreds of Children Prove They Have Same Incredible Powers as Psychic Uri Geller." *The National Enquirer,* 8 July 1975.

Upham, Charles W. *Salem Witchcraft.* New York: Frederick Ungar Publishing Co., 1959.

Valentine, Thomas. *Psychic Surgery.* Chicago: Henry Regnery Co., 1973.

Vallee, Jacques. *Anatomy of a Phenomenon.* Chicago: Henry Regnery Co., 1965.

Vaughan, Alan. "Viewpoint," *Psychic* magazine, vol. 6, no. 4 (October 1975), p. 7.

_____."Interview: Barbara Brown," *Psychic* magazine, vol. 6, no. 2, pp. 48-55.

Von Däniken, Erich. *Chariot of the Gods.* Germany: Econ-Verlag, 1968.

_____.*Gods from Outer Space.* Germany: Econ-Verlag, 1970.

Wavell, Stewart, Butt, Audrey, and Epton, Nina. *Trances.* New York: E.P. Dutton and Co., 1967.

Wallis, Robert. *Time: The Fourth Dimension of the Mind.* New York: Harcourt, Brace and World, Inc., 1968.

Watson, Lyall. *Supernature.* New York: Doubleday and Co., 1973.

White, John. "X Energy and Consciousness." *Psychic* magazine, February 1976, p. 37-8.

White, John. "URI — A Critique," *Psychic* magazine, vol. 6, no. 2 (May 1975), pp. 40-43.

Whitton, Joel L. "Qualitative Time-Domain Analysis of Acoustic Envelopes of PK Table-Rappings." *New Horizons,* vol. 2, no. 1 (April 1975), pp. 21-24.

_____."The Psychodynamics of Poltergeist Activity, and Group PK." *New Horizons,* vol. 1, no. 5 (January 1975), p. 227.

_____."Paramorphic Table Rappings: Acoustic Analysis." *New Horizons,* vol. 2, no. 2 (June 1976), pp. 7-11.

Willis, H.A. "A Remarkable Case of Physical Phenomena." *The Atlantic Monthly,* August 1868.

Wilson, Colin. *The Occult: A History.* New York: Random House, 1971.

Wolfson, William Q. "Metal-Bending at a Distance." *New Horizons,* vol. 2, no. 2 (June 1976), p. 20.

Yogananda, Paramanhansa. *Autobiography of a Yogi.* New York: Rider, 1950.

Zaffuto, Anthony and Mary. *Alphagenics.* New York: Doubleday and Co., 1974.

Zeibell, Ila. "Through the Looking Glass with Uri Geller," *Psychic,* February 1976, pp. 17-19.

SPIRITUAL LITERATURE/ART

1753-3	**Dweller on Two Planets**	Phylos the Thibetan/$2.95
1737-1	**Romance of Two Worlds**	Corelli/$2.75
1757-6	**Seraphita**	Balzac/$2.50
1725-8	**Vril:** Power of the Coming Race	Bulwer-Lytton/$2.25
1723-1	**Zanoni:** A Rosicrucian Tale (5¼×8¼)	Bulwer-Lytton/$5.95

SPIRITUAL RESEARCHERS/BIOGRAPHIES

1722-3	**Caspar Hauser:** Enigma of a Century	Wasserman/$3.50
1702-9	**Count of Saint-Germain**	Cooper-Oakley/$2.50
1736-3	**Friedrich Nietzsche:** Fighter For Freedom (5¼×8¼)	Steiner/$4.50
1734-7	**Jacob Boehme:** Life & Doctrines (5¼×8¼)	Hartmann/$6.50
1732-0	**Mother India's Lighthouse:** India's Spiritual Leaders	Sri Chinmoy/$2.25
1733-9	**Paracelsus:** Life and Prophecies	Hartmann/$2.75
3501-9	**Rudolf Steiner:** An Autobiography (5¼×8¼)	Steiner/$9.95
1750-8	**Vladimir Soloviev:** Russian Mystic (5¼×8¼)	Allen/$9.95

SPIRITUAL TRAINING & METHODOLOGY

1713-4	**Methods of Spiritual Research**	Steiner/$1.75

Steinerbooks Library

Selected Classics of the Spiritual Sciences in Hardcover, Cloth Editions,
5½" × 8½", unless otherwise noted.

1301-5	**Alchemists Through The Ages** (4½×7½)	Waite/$5.95
1302-3	**Atlantis:** The Antediluvian World (4½×7½)	Donnelly/$5.95
0708-2	**Christian Rosenkreutz Anthology** (7¼×10½)	Allen/$20.00
1304-X	**Cosmic Memory:** Atlantis & Lemuria (4½×7½)	Steiner/$5.95
1308-2	**Dweller on Two Planets** (4½×7½)	Phylos the Thibetan/$5.95
0705-8	**From Sphinx to Christ**	Schure/$10.00
0103-3	**Life & Work of Rudolf Steiner** (6½×9½)	Wachsmuth/$15.00
1301-1	**Maya/Atlantis:** Queen Moo & Egyptian Sphinx (4½×7½)	LePlongeon/$5.95
1305-8	**Occult & Curative Powers of Precious Stones** (4½×7½)	Fernie/$5.95
0754-6	**Philosophy of Spiritual Activity**	Steiner/$12.00
0716-3	**PK, a Report on PsychoKinesis . . .**	Brown/$9.95
0720-1	**Our Inheritance in the Great Pyramid**	Smyth/$20.00
1313-9	**Ragnarok:** Destruction of Atlantis (4½×7½)	Donnelly/$5.95
1306-6	**Romance of Two Worlds** (4½×7½)	Corelli/$5.95
0757-0	**Rudolf Steiner:** An Autobiography	Steiner/$15.00
0758-4	**Secret Societies of All Ages & Countries**	Heckethorn/$20.00
0715-5	**Shards From the Heart**	Garber/$5.00

All prices subject to change without notice. To order by mail, send check
for prices listed above plus .50¢ per book for processing to:
Steiner Books, Blauvelt, N.Y. 10913, U.S.A. Please allow 3 weeks for
delivery. Additional Titles in Preparation. Send 35¢ for complete catalog.

Steinerbooks

ISBN Prefix: 0-8334

The Spiritual Sciences in quality paperback format, 4¼"×7" racksize, unless otherwise noted.

ALCHEMY/MYSTICISM/ROSICRUCIANISM

1704-5	**Alchemists Through the Ages**	Waite/$2.75
3505-1	**Christian Rosenkreutz Anthology** (7×10)	Allen/$15.00
1721-5	**Eleven European Mystics**	Steiner/$2.50
1720-7	**Lamps of Western Mysticism**	Waite/$2.75
1738-X	**Real History of the Rosicrucians** (5¼×8¼)	Waite/$7.95

ATLANTIS/EGYPTOLOGY/SPIRITUAL HISTORY

1717-7	**Atlantis/Europe:** Secret of the West	Merejkowski/$3.50
1758-6	**Atlantis in Ireland:** Round Towers of Ireland (5¼×8¼)	O'Brien/$7.95
1724-X	**Atlantis:** The Antediluvian World	Donnelly/$3.95
1716-9	**Cosmic Memory:** Atlantis & Lemuria	Steiner/$2.50
1705-3	**From Sphinx to Christ**	Schure/$2.50
1735-5	**Great Pyramid:** Miracle in Stone	Seiss/$2.50
1729-0	**Maya/Atlantis:** Queen Moo & the Egyptian Sphinx	LePlongeon/$2.95
1727-4	**Mysteries of Egypt:** Secret Rites of the Nile	Spence/$2.50
3503-5	**Our Inheritance in the Great Pyramid** (5¼×8¼)	Smyth/$15.00
1718-5	**Ragnarok:** The Destruction of Atlantis	Donnelly/$3.50

APPLIED SPIRITUAL SCIENCE

1715-0	**Gardening For Health:** The Organic Way	Philbrick/$1.50
1701-0	**Meditations on the Signs of the Zodiac**	Jocelyn/$3.25

COMPARATIVE & ESOTERIC RELIGIONS

1708-8	**Ancient Mysteries of the East:** Rama-Krishna	Schure/$1.75
1719-3	**Christianity and Occult Mysteries of Antiquity** (5¼×8¼)	Steiner/$4.50
1731-2	**Commentaries on the Bhagavad Gita**	Sri Chinmoy/$1.95
1751-3	**Great Initiates** (5¼×8¼)	Schure/$7.95

METAPHYSICS/PHILOSOPHY

1728-2	**Pictorial Key to the Tarot**	Waite/$3.50
1703-7	**Unknown Philosopher:** de Saint-Martin	Waite/$3.95

MYTHOLOGY/FOLKLORE/SYMBOLISM

1745-2	**Myths & Legends of North American Indian** (5¼×8¼)	Spence/$5.50
1742-8	**Myths of the New World Indians** (5¼×8¼)	Brinton/$5.50
1726-6	**Golem:** Mystical Tales of the Ghetto	Bloch/$2.25

PSYCHIC & OCCULT PHENOMENA

1730-4	**ESPecially Irene:** A Guide to Psychic Awareness	Hughes/$1.95
1776-2	**PK, a Report on PsychoKinesis . . .** (5¼×8¼)	Brown/$5.95
1739-8	**Occult and Curative Powers of Precious Stones**	Fernie/$3.95
3502-7	**Secret Societies of All Ages & Countries** (5¼×8¼)	Heckethorn/$15.00

REFERENCE/DICTIONARIES

1767-3	**Steinerbooks Dictionary of the Psychic, Mystic, Occult**	Editors/$2.25

REINCARNATION/DESTINY

1706-1	**Reincarnation and Immortality**	Steiner/$2.50
1714-2	**Results of Spiritual Investigation**	Steiner/$1.75